# Learning Mathematics

## Third Edition

Related Titles:

*Teaching Number Sense* – Julia Anghileri
*Teaching Maths using ICT: Second Edition* – Adrian Oldknow
*Teaching and Learning Mathematics: Second Edition* – Marilyn Nickson
*Inclusive Mathematics 5–11* – Brian Robbins
*Inclusive Mathematics 11–18* – Anne Watson and Mike Ollerton
*Pattern in the Teaching and Learning of Mathematics* – Anthony Orton

# Learning
# Mathematics

Issues, theory and classroom practice

Third Edition

**Anthony Orton**

**continuum**
LONDON • NEW YORK

**Continuum**

The Tower Building        80 Maiden Lane
11 York Road              Suite 704
London SE1 7NX            New York, NY 10038

*www.continuumbooks.com*

First published 1987. Second edition 1992. Third edition 2004.
Reprinted 2006

**British Library Cataloguing-in-Publication Data**
A catalogue record for this book is available from the British Library.

ISBN: 0 8264 7113 7 (hardback)
      0 8264 7114 5 (paperback)

Library of Congress Cataloguing-in-Publication Data
A catalogue record for this book is available from the Library of Congress.

Typeset by RefineCatch Limited, Bungay, Suffolk
Printed and bound in Great Britain by MPG Books Ltd, Bodmin, Cornwall

# Contents

**Preface to the Third Edition**                                                ix

Chapter 1   Do Teachers of Mathematics Need Theories?                            1
            The importance of theories                                           1
            The origins of theories                                             6

Chapter 2   What Cognitive Demands Are Made in Learning Mathematics?            13
            The problem of classification                                      13
            Retention and recall                                               13
            Using algorithms                                                   18
            Learning concepts                                                  20
            Problem-solving                                                    24

Chapter 3   Could We Enhance Learning Through Optimum Sequencing?               27
            Behaviourism                                                       27
            Objectives                                                         30
            Programmed learning                                                34
            Learning hierarchies                                               40

Chapter 4   Must We Wait Until Pupils Are Ready?                                48
            Alternative views                                                  48
            Piaget and readiness                                               49
            Accelerating learning                                              55
            Curriculum implementation                                          60
            Critical evaluation                                                63
            Cross-cultural issues                                              68

Chapter 5   Can Pupils Discover Mathematics for Themselves?                     71
            Learning by discovery                                              71
            Gestalt psychology                                                 77
            Structural apparatus                                               79
            Problems and investigations                                        84

|  |  |  |
|---|---|---|
|  | Obstacles and difficulties in problem-solving | 93 |
|  | Logo | 97 |

| **Chapter 6** | Is an Appreciation of Pattern Important in Learning Mathematics? | 99 |
|---|---|---|
|  | Pattern in mathematics | 99 |
|  | Early concepts of pattern | 100 |
|  | Number patterns | 104 |
|  | The approach to algebra | 106 |
|  | Pattern and proof | 112 |
|  | Pattern in relation to shape | 114 |

| **Chapter 7** | Does What We Learn Depend on Where We Are? | 119 |
|---|---|---|
|  | Applying mathematics | 119 |
|  | Everyday mathematics | 121 |
|  | Work mathematics | 123 |
|  | Transfer of learning and situated cognition | 126 |
|  | Ethnomathematics | 129 |
|  | The significance of the situation | 132 |

| **Chapter 8** | Why Do Some Pupils Achieve More Than Others? | 136 |
|---|---|---|
|  | Individual differences | 136 |
|  | Convergent and divergent thinking | 139 |
|  | Mathematical ability | 142 |
|  | Spatial ability | 147 |
|  | Gender-related differences | 150 |
|  | Preferences and attitudes | 154 |

| **Chapter 9** | Does Language Interfere with Learning Mathematics? | 156 |
|---|---|---|
|  | Issues of language | 156 |
|  | The mathematics register | 157 |
|  | Reading mathematics | 160 |
|  | Mathematical symbols | 163 |
|  | Communicating meaning | 164 |
|  | Language, culture and mathematics | 168 |
|  | Word problems | 171 |

| **Chapter 10** | Is There a Theory of Mathematics Learning? | 175 |
|---|---|---|
|  | Mathematics and theories of learning | 175 |
|  | The Dienes theory of mathematics-learning | 176 |
|  | The van Hiele theory of learning geometry | 181 |
|  | Ausubel's theory of meaningful learning | 184 |
|  | Meaningful learning | 184 |
|  | Superordinate and subordinate learning | 187 |
|  | Conflicts and failures in learning | 189 |
|  | A brief note on information processing | 192 |

**Chapter 11**    Can Pupils Construct Mathematical Knowledge for
                  Themselves?                                            194
                       Constructivism                                    194
                       Versions of constructivism                       197
                       Some constructivist teaching experiments         200
                       Constructivism in our classrooms                 203
                       Cognitive obstacles                              209

                  **References**                                        213
                  **Author index**                                     225
                  **Subject index**                                    227

# Preface to the Third Edition

This new edition constitutes a major and fundamental revision of the original text. Nearly twenty years have passed since the manuscript was first drafted, and much has been written on issues of learning mathematics in those intervening years. As one would hope and expect, newly published research continues to provide additional enlightenment. There are also new areas of concern which have come to the fore in recent years and which therefore demanded a place, and this has led to the introduction of three new chapters. Two of these chapters are absolutely new, one relating to issues of situated cognition and transfer of learning, and the other being concerned with the place of pattern in mathematics. The third new chapter is an expansion and reorganization of material which existed in a much more abbreviated form in previous editions and concerns the issue of constructivism.

It had originally been hoped to include chapters on the impact of calculators and computers on learning, and on the issue of advanced mathematical thinking, but unfortunately constraints of space did not allow either of these to be included. Indeed, in order to make room for the three new chapters and for the revision and extension of existing chapters, two of the original ones have been greatly reduced, with what has been retained from them being dispersed to relevant chapters in this new edition. The criterion for discarding any material was solely that it is now better dealt with in other texts. All of the remaining eight chapters have been revised, some have been extended, and many have been largely rewritten.

Although the book is written from a British perspective, issues of learning are global, so the book is still relevant on an international basis, and all of the references to and from other countries which were introduced in the second edition have been retained. The book is not tied to any particular curriculum, though the requirements and constraints of the National Curricula of Britain are fully acknowledged.

The major difficulty in revising the book has been what it has always been, namely that there are so many relevant references relating to the issues of the book, more than could ever be acknowledged without the text taking on some of the characteristics of a catalogue. Once again, I can only apologize to those whose work I have not been able to use.

As a result of this revision, I believe that the text is now an even better resource for teachers of mathematics, students of mathematics education, educational researchers, parents and anyone else interested in how mathematics is learned.

Tony Orton
Leeds 2004

To Jean
who helped.

Chapter 1

# Do Teachers of Mathematics Need Theories?

.

## The importance of theories

Educational issues are rarely clear cut. An individual teacher may hold very firm views on a particular issue in mathematical education, but must at the same time accept that very different, even completely contrary, views may be held by a colleague in the same school. Examples are not hard to find. Some years ago, the introduction of pocket calculators sparked off discussion and controversy about how and when they should be used. If young children are allowed to use them would multiplication tables ever be learned? Could sensible use of calculators enhance understanding? A variety of different kinds of structural apparatus exists for helping children to acquire the concepts of elementary number. Is such apparatus essential? If so, which is the best? Some teachers believe that mathematics should be a silent activity with each of the children always producing their 'own work', but other teachers allow cooperation and discussion between pupils. Is discussion important for all or do some pupils opt out and so learn nothing? The debate about the place of calculus continued throughout the twentieth century and we cannot assume it is settled even now. Is there a place for calculus before the sixth form or is it conceptually too difficult for all but a very few? Although curriculum decisions are only possible within national guidelines, these examples nevertheless illustrate some of the many issues which would be likely to lead to varied opinions and to disagreement amongst teachers.

In accepting a particular viewpoint, or in taking sides on a particular issue, it could be said that a teacher has accepted a theoretical position. Throughout any day in school we adopt particular ploys and use particular methods because we believe they work. Such limited theories are based on experience, intuition and perhaps even on wishful thinking. They may be helpful, but on the other hand they may be dangerous. For example, is it dangerous to teach the division of fractions in the primary school? It might be if, in not understanding, children become confused, frustrated and anxious and come to reject mathematics, seeing it as a meaningless and worthless activity. It appears that the job of teaching cannot be done without accepting theoretical views, however limited and small-scale. In this sense it appears that we do need theories as a basis even for day-to-day decision-making in the classroom.

However, although teachers do need to adopt and practise theories in their daily work it is not unusual to find many who are sceptical or even disparaging about the value of what might be called general theories. Such larger-scale theories, which might enlighten the teaching-learning process, are sometimes dismissed as irrelevant, even without them being given serious consideration. For example, it might not be appreciated by those of us who use and value structural and other apparatus that the invention of the equipment could have been prompted by acceptance of a particular learning theory. One of the earlier kits was devised by Catherine Stern (see Stern with Stern, 1953) because her belief in Gestalt theory (see Chapter 5) demanded that such apparatus should be made available to children. And then of course, it is also possible that some of us reject theories because accepting them might necessitate adopting a radically different teaching style!

A theory of learning should be compatible with children's behaviour in learning situations. Thus, it may initially be based on classroom observation, but it should also ultimately enable us to both understand what we witness and even to take appropriate action. In this sense our theory explains, and could even predict, phenomena. Hopefully, with sufficient data on which to construct hypotheses, our theory might present a systematic view of phenomena whilst at the same time remaining relatively simple to grasp. The general theories which are sometimes rejected without serious consideration have usually been based on a systematic view extrapolated from a much wider range of events and situations than any one individual is likely to have experienced and contemplated. The view which underlies this book is that education is too important for us to be able to dismiss as irrelevant theories of learning which attempt to do what has just been described. Child (1986) explained it by saying, '. . . innovation and speculation in learning . . . are more likely to succeed when they are informed by sound theoretical frameworks'. Larkin (1989) provides eight reasons for explicit theories, and supports the view that, '. . . more concern for theory could be beneficial to the field of mathematics education'. Her reasons include the claim that attempting to formulate even partial theories exposes defects and gaps which could otherwise go unaddressed. Also, trying to unify our data clarifies relationships which might have gone unnoticed. She concludes by saying that:

> formulating theories that clearly and succinctly relate data is challenging, creative work. It makes us think hard about what we know and pushes our curiosity to enquire further about what we do not know. (p. 275)

One major problem is that there can appear to be a large number of conflicting or contradictory general theories in existence. Historically, one might say that two major kinds of theory have been developed, referred to here as 'behaviourist' and 'cognitive', and these two certainly do conflict, though there have been some attempts at reconciliation. Within these apparently very different schools of thought there have been variations and amendments over the years. The most important distinction between the two can be illustrated by referring to a situation in primary mathematics. It is very important that all pupils come to a working understanding of place value. At a certain stage in the education of young children it would be reasonable to ask them to write 'four hundred and twenty-seven' as a number. Some children would write

$$40027,$$
$$\text{others} \quad 4027,$$
$$\text{or even} \quad 400207,$$

and these would not be the only answers offered from within the class. Most children, it is hoped, would correctly write

$$427,$$

but the incorrect responses, however few, would require remediation. How should remedial action be taken? Indeed, how should the children have been taught the concepts in the first place?

If our theoretical view is that children learn through practising to produce the correct response to a given stimulus, then we should give them more practice. Such an approach might incorporate the use of apparatus, but the fundamental objective is based on the belief that practice makes perfect. In this approach there might well be the underlying assumption that we are there to feed information and knowledge into the mind of the child. In an extreme form the approach might be referred to as rote learning. If, on the other hand, we believe that children learn through making sense of the world themselves, we would wish them to learn for themselves the essential relationships through interaction with an appropriate environment. Thus we might well base the learning experiences on structural or other apparatus and devise suitable activities, allowing exploration of the structure of the situation. It would, of course, be necessary to ensure that the notation emerges as being logical and efficient, so some teacher intervention is inevitable. In this way we would expect understanding to grow from within, as it were. Any attempt to hasten the child by using rote methods might not only be unsuccessful, it might persuade the child that mathematics is meaningless.

It should be stressed that these two contrasting approaches are not intended to explain fully the difference between particular behaviourist and cognitive beliefs, they are merely intended to illustrate how possible interpretations might manifest themselves in mathematics lessons. It would be wrong to tie rote learning too closely to the behaviourist approach and by implication suggest that it has no place within any other approach. There is, after all, the eclectic view, that children do need to develop their own understanding from within, but that there might be a very firm place for practice, and even perhaps for some element of rote learning. In relation to place value, used here as an example, it has long been known as an early concept which presents young children with a real intellectual challenge. The difficulties and misconceptions associated with it have been documented over the years by many mathematics educators, and Branford (1921) offered a very early discussion of the issues.

It is unfortunate if conflicting theories and variations on a common theme lead some teachers to reject them all. Some conflict is, after all, only to be expected within a discipline with a very short history. It is sometimes forgotten that the so-called 'pure' sciences of physics, chemistry and biology have been the subject of many battles throughout hundreds of years and that, even now, disagreements can still exist. Scientific theories are continually being modified, elaborated and clarified and, from time to time, radically new ideas are produced. In the world at large decisions have to be made, and they are made on the basis of existing theoretical views. Not all such decisions ultimately turn out to have been correct. Particular theories of learning might also be wrong, or might subsequently need qualification or amendment. But the formulation of a theory and the observation of it in action are both part of the process through which we improve our understanding (see Davis, 1984, pp. 22–6, for further discussion on this issue). We can learn more about the learning process if we are prepared to encourage the formulation of theories and then test out those which appear most likely to help.

Learning is a mental activity. We might therefore understand more about learning if we knew more about the functioning of the brain as a processor of information. The brain receives information, interprets it, stores it, transforms it, associates it with other information to create new information and allows information to be recalled. The brain also only develops and retains the faculties which it is called upon to use (Winston, 2003). In recent years considerable attention has been accorded to information processing as an approach to learning theories, and this has led to greater interest in what goes on inside the brain. It has been known for many years that different learning activities take place in different parts of the brain, though that very simple statement glosses over complexities which are certainly beyond our scope for the present. What is clear, however, is that there is a relationship between the chemistry of the brain, the nerve impulses which are generated, and learning. Chemical imbalances, unusual electrical activity and inadequate or inappropriate diet can therefore all affect mental processing. Thus it should be clear that we might understand much more about learning, as an aspect of psychology, when we understand more about the workings of the brain as an aspect of physiology.

One of the traditional justifications for teaching mathematics is that it teaches logical thinking. Unfortunately, the logic of mathematics is not necessarily the same as the logic of any other sphere of human intellectual activity. The argument therefore stands or falls on the theory that the ability to think logically in mathematics is a transferable skill and can be put into practice outside mathematics. This assumption has been known in the past as 'transfer of training'. Shulman (1970, p. 55) said: 'Transfer of training is the most important single concept in any educationally relevant theory of learning'. There is no doubt that the former view that studying geometry or Latin made one a better logical thinker is now discredited. Nevertheless, some lateral transfer must be possible, lateral implying the transference of skill in one domain to the achievement of a parallel skill in another domain (though 'parallel' is not easy to define in this context), for, without it, learning would be extremely slow and would be limited to what had actually been encountered in the course of instruction.

There is no general agreement about the extent to which lateral transfer can take place in mathematics. There have been psychologists and learning theorists who have expressed the view that broad transfer can take place, that ideas and strategies can be transferred within a discipline and perhaps even outside. Thus it might be believed that mastery of the idea of balance, as a physical property using weigh-scales and weights, can be transferred and applied to the solution of linear equations, and might even be transferable to studies of balance in nature and in economics. It might also be believed that learning how to prove results in Euclidean or any other sort of geometry would be transferable to proof in other branches of mathematics, to proof in other disciplines such as science and even to proof in a court of law. Other psychologists have believed that transfer only occurs to a very limited extent, perhaps only to the extent that identical elements occur. This latter view probably carries more conviction than the former at the present time. Some transfer must be possible, but it will probably be limited and might depend on the conditions under which learning takes place. It is certainly not wise to assume that transfer will just happen, when teaching mathematics, because it frequently does not.

The learning difficulties which one observes as a teacher of mathematics raise many other questions for which one might seek an answer from theories. For example, although reflection on our own experience should suggest to us that learning cannot be achieved in a hurry, some children appear to learn incredibly slowly. Other children make rapid progress, a few even making astounding progress when given the opportunity to learn at their rate rather than the class rate. What determines rate of learning? Is it possible to accelerate the learning of mathematics for more pupils or even for the majority of pupils and, if so, how? At the moment it seems that for some children it is not a matter of whether they can learn mathematics more quickly; rather it is a question of why they appear to take in hardly anything at all. So might it even be that mathematical ability is a peculiar aptitude not possessed by all?

Individual differences are very significant in many spheres of human activity. Some of us are barred from particular occupations because of physical characteristics, like being too small, too overweight, or having poor eyesight. Many of us who have become teachers of mathematics because of an apparent aptitude and a liking for the subject would not have been able to become teachers of other subjects, like English, history or art. Amongst international athletes some are good only at running, others at jumping events and yet others at throwing events. Individual differences might be important even within mathematics. Hadamard (1945), in discussing mathematicians, drew attention to great differences in the kind of mathematical aptitude which individuals have displayed. In the classroom it might be that different learning environments and different teaching styles are needed for different pupils. This would present very great teaching problems, taking into account that any individual teacher also presumably has aptitudes and preferences which are in accord with only a proportion of the pupils. Any acceptable theory which enables us to understand individual differences would be very valuable.

One interpretation of the evidence of what children appear to learn and appear to find difficult is that there are serious obstacles or stumbling blocks in the logical structure of mathematics, and some of these will be looked at in more detail in the next section of this chapter and later in the book. With many young children, the ideas of place value appear to present hurdles which cause frequent falls. With slightly older children the introduction of algebraic notions causes problems for which some pupils never forgive us. There are mathematical ideas, like ratio and rate, which frequently cause difficulty for many adults, even though the notions are important and relevant to daily life. It is possible to survive in life without understanding the implications of a fall in the rate of inflation, but it is still regrettable that so many adults have little understanding of key mathematical ideas. So what is it about particular aspects of mathematics, such as place value, algebra and rate of change, which makes them so difficult? When we analyse the structure of mathematics in order to devise the optimum teaching sequence, how do we allow for the fact that the logical order of topics might not be appropriate for psychological reasons?

A major complexity in learning any subject is the relationship with language learning. At a surface level the effects may be observed when a child cannot master the mathematics because the particular language used is not understood. There are many examples of peculiar language and of familiar words used in different or very specific ways in mathematics. At a deeper level, to understand the language is to understand the concept which a particular word symbolizes. More fundamental still is the relationship between language and learning. Does language merely enable one to communicate learning that has already taken place? Is language the vehicle which enables us to formulate our ideas and manipulate them to create new meanings? Is it that language development is inextricably tied to overall cognitive development and cannot be thought of as a separate entity?

It has been suggested earlier that the environment might be an important factor affecting both what mathematics is learned and how understanding of mathematics develops. It might, therefore, be postulated that the richer the environment the more efficient the learning, but to some extent that begs the question. What constitutes a supportive learning environment in a subject which is basically a creation of the human mind and in which the aim is to enable abstract argument to take place through the mental manipulation of symbols? The belief that young children must be allowed and encouraged to interact in a very active manner with physical or concrete materials is a theoretical stance suggested through experience of teaching young children. If we accept this and provide an environment rich in equipment and learning materials for young children, how soon can we wean them away from it? Do we need to do anything for older children in, for example, coming to terms with algebra? Or should we not be attempting algebra until the pupils can manage without concrete apparatus? When can learners begin to learn only from exposition and from books?

These are some of the many aspects of mathematics learning for which we might seek answers, and many of the theoretical viewpoints expressed in subsequent parts of this book do attempt to address questions raised above. It has already been suggested that teachers need theories, hence major theories of all kinds and from many sources are included within the discussion of particular questions. They are introduced, chapter by chapter, in an approximate chronological order. First, however, some comments on the investigation of children's understanding are pertinent. Before we can consider what any theory might suggest in relation to learning mathematics, we ought to be fully aware of the extent of the problems experienced by pupils.

## The origins of theories

As teachers, we may be involved in writing and interpreting syllabuses and preparing detailed schemes of work. Many of us are guided, or more likely constrained, in such tasks by a national curriculum. In this planning, and indeed in the preparation of a national curriculum itself, it would seem to be important to take into account the evidence of what children appear to be able to learn, and in what sequence. There is no point in defining unreasonable objectives, though a major objective is always to challenge the pupils and extend their knowledge and understanding. We may also need to take note of any substantive evidence that pupils in countries other than our own are achieving more than our own pupils are. After all, we currently live within a political climate of constantly trying to prove that standards, however they may be defined, are going up. But in seeking the right road for our pupils we may choose a middle route and so get it wrong for many. On the one hand, evidence of children failing to learn because of unreasonable aims might be ignored, as we try to impart as much of our own mathematical knowledge as we can in as short a time as possible. On the other hand, we might believe that some groups of pupils are not being sufficiently extended.

At most stages in the education of the majority we find an extensive and arguably frequently overloaded mathematics curriculum, with pupils hastened along through material which, at best, is only half-learned by a considerable proportion of the children. Naturally, it must be admitted that it is difficult for anyone to achieve complete mastery of anything, in the sense that there might always seem to be further extensions, just as climbing one mountain peak invariably reveals a view of even higher ones. The point at issue is whether the pupils achieve adequate mastery to enable them to proceed with what we have decided comes next. The available evidence suggests that many pupils frequently fail to match up to our expectations in this respect. Indeed we, the teachers, can be very easily misled. Young children can often learn to recite numbers long before they fully comprehend what the numbers represent and how they are related, and we can easily assume they know more than they do. Pupils can appear to be attaining correct answers to set tasks, but they might be slavishly following the routine we have suggested and might not grasp why the method works.

Place value has already been used as an example of a topic which creates difficulties for many pupils. It has been discussed in greater detail elsewhere, in for example Brown (1981b) and Dickson *et al.* (1984). The Cockcroft Report (1982), drawing on Brown's research, referred to a 'seven-year difference' in respect to the age at which pupils might be expected to provide a correct answer to the sum

$$6399 + 1,$$

in the context of counting spectators through a turnstile. The conclusion was that the task is in general mastered by the 'average' child at around age eleven years, but that some seven-year-old children would be able to cope and some fourteen-year-old children would not. It is not that such learning difficulties experienced by pupils have only recently been detected, for awareness of the problems encountered by many pupils has been growing over a long period of time – see, for example, Branford (1921) and Renwick (1935). However, it might be that not enough people have been aware of the extent of such learning problems in the past, as Fogelman (1970, p. 72) has suggested:

> It is only in the last few years that we have adjusted ourselves to the idea that seemingly simple concepts . . . are acquired only gradually during the period of primary schooling. It is not yet appreciated that a sizeable minority of children cannot handle these concepts even after they are in secondary school.

Place value is a key concept in the early stages of learning mathematics, and it cannot be avoided. Thus, we need to be fully aware of the difficulties faced by some children, and we need to search for ways to help individual children to grasp this fundamental idea.

In contrast, it is doubtful whether any mathematics teacher would wish to argue that long division is a key concept. In recent years, there seems to have been disagreement between educators and others in society about the importance of this topic in the primary curriculum. Where there is a similarity with place value, however, it is in the fact that children, seemingly down the ages, have struggled to master long division. Indeed, teachers have always found it hard to explain the method and why it works. In this context, it is important to stress that there is a very big difference between the concept of division, as manifested perhaps in short division tasks, and the complexity of many traditional long division questions. Renwick (1935) reported American research that the optimum mental age for beginning to learn long division was twelve years seven months. Her Majesty's Inspectorate (HMI) (1985, p. 12) have suggested that, '. . . some standard written methods of calculation, such as a long division, which many pupils find difficult and few really understand, should no longer be generally taught'. Yet it could be said that it is the widespread availability of cheap calculators which has prompted this statement, not the difficulty of long division. We certainly cannot claim that we did not know that long division was difficult, and we should not turn a blind eye to the evidence whatever our curriculum dictates. However, although we might now regard long division as less vital than it once was, and too difficult anyway, it still seems that this conclusion has not yet been accepted by our political masters and by the wider community.

Learning is rarely easy, of course, but there are many topics in our primary school mathematics curriculum which pupils find particularly difficult. The primary school curriculum convincingly illustrates how our enthusiasm to introduce pupils to all the interesting mathematics we can think of can blind us to the magnitude of what faces the average child. Naturally, we are obliged to try to extend all of our pupils, and we need to provide just as fully for the most able as for the weakest. But the new freedom from the old restrictions of the 11+ selection examinations, obtained in the second half of the last century, immediately led to a considerable broadening into extra topics without a corresponding reduction of existing ones. Why, for example, does work with fractions still constitute such a substantial part of the primary curriculum? Nearly all of what we teach of fractions in the primary school is re-taught, often every year, to pupils in the secondary school, because many pupils never seem to achieve adequate mastery. Although we may pride ourselves that we can explain to our own satisfaction why the method of division of fractions works, very few pupils grasp our explanation. We can often mislead ourselves that, because our explanation has been lucid, clear and logical, the message has been received, but one cannot deliver a curriculum! Is it really necessary that children should be able to add, subtract, multiply and divide a wide range of sometimes awkward pairs of fractions? Essential ideas illustrated by very simple cases might make much more sense, particularly at primary school level. It was Skemp (1964) who, in devising his own curriculum and textbooks, emphasized the view that fractions provide the obvious example of a mathematical idea previously assumed to be elementary which analysis of concepts reveals as very far from simple. This message itself was not new and had already been comprehensively discussed in Renwick (1935), but we clearly need to keep reminding ourselves of such facts.

Fractions are not irrelevant to the curriculum, however, even if we may be over-ambitious in what we hope to achieve with many of our pupils. Fractions are rational numbers, and ratio is without question a fundamental concept in the development of mathematical understanding. One reason for the importance of teaching ratio (and proportion) is that it provides a useful problem-solving technique, either by direct manipulation or by the method variously known as 'the unitary method', or 'the method of practice'. A simple example of this would be: 'given that seven pencils cost 63 pence, find the cost of three pencils'. Beyond such elementary problem-solving, other mathematical concepts build on the basic concept of ratio. Geometrical theorems and results based on similarity and on parallel lines and intercepts require a grasp of proportionality. The idea of gradient, which is fundamental to the algebra of graphs and to calculus, also depends on ratio and proportion. Simple trigonometry, likewise, has its beginnings in the study of equal ratios. Rational numbers are studied throughout most years of a child's school life, progressing through operations on fractions, decimals and percentages, and perhaps culminating in a more formal study of the number system. Ratio also underlies pie charts, scale factor and the slide rule (now superseded by calculators). Ratio and proportion not only pervade much of the mathematics curriculum, they also support topics within other school subjects. The development of scientific understanding relies on the ability to handle ratios, for example in the definitions of density, velocity and acceleration; in calculating chemical equivalents; in applications of the ideal gas laws and in using many laws of physics. Other school subjects make use of proportionality through simple calculations such as the pencil problem, through percentages, through scale drawing and through graphical representation.

Although ratio and proportion are important in so many subject areas, pupils often struggle and find it difficult to handle situations involving the notions. A considerable quantity of evidence from children's responses in proportionality situations has now been assembled. A typical basic proportion task was devised and used by Karplus and Peterson (1970), in one of the early large-scale research projects on understanding proportion. This particular task has subsequently been used in many countries around the world, because it encapsulates the concept of proportionality so concisely, and in what is such an elementary situation (to a mathematician). The task is based on the heights of two pin men, known as Mr Short and Mr Tall. A diagram is provided (see Figure 1.1), and two different measuring techniques are described, using objects such as paper clips and buttons. Thus, Mr Short is first found to measure four paper clips, and then Mr Tall is found to measure six paper clips. Finally, Mr Short is measured

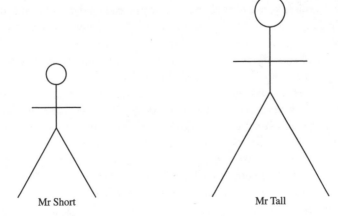

Mr Short          Mr Tall

Figure 1.1

with the buttons and is found to measure six buttons in height. The question is how many buttons will be required to measure Mr Tall? In any secondary school year group the percentage of correct responses from a sample of pupils across the ability range can be surprisingly small. More able pupils naturally have a higher success rate than other pupils, but the success rate only grows slowly with increasing age.

Since 1970, ratio has been extensively researched, and it has become abundantly clear that, like place value, it presents real problems, but this time to many secondary school pupils. The understanding of proportionality develops late in the school life of many pupils, if it develops at all. The difficulties which ratio and proportion present to pupils have been known about for a long time. Renwick (1935) suggested that the concept was far beyond the intellectual range of intelligent pupils of eleven years of age. For intellectually weaker children it seems to be beyond their range at fourteen, and for some it seems doubtful that it will ever be within their range. We must take this not as an indication that proportionality should be avoided at all costs, for it is so fundamental to mathematics, and therefore must be included in the curriculum. We should rather continue to seek a better understanding of the difficulties in order to inform our teaching. More detailed information about ratio, including attempts to achieve greater understanding, are to be found in, for example, Hart (1981) and Hart (1984).

Indeed, there are many other serious learning problems in secondary school mathematics, algebra being another obvious example. Sometimes textbooks with a high algebraic content and intended only for very able pupils have been used with weaker pupils as well. Cockcroft (1982) was very critical on this point, suggesting that the majority of secondary school pupils were following syllabuses which were of a difficulty and extent appropriate only to about a quarter of pupils. The current curriculum of the General Certificate of Secondary Education (GCSE), and the specifications for the various National Curricula of the United Kingdom, together suggest that the inherent difficulties of algebra have now been to some extent acknowledged. Overall, however, it seems that we, as teachers of mathematics, have a very mixed record when it comes to taking into account evidence of what children can learn. We still frequently have a tendency to want to teach mathematics which we know countless previous generations have been delighted to reject as both unintelligible and worthless as soon as they leave school.

However, it has to be admitted that it is not easy to be sure of what children can learn. We may feel that we have imperfect, even conflicting, evidence on which to base our decisions. In the first place we do not know precisely what children can learn, only what they appear to have learned on the evidence obtained on the day of a test or more informally in a class lesson. We are forced to use measuring instruments which may be far from perfect. Certainly the evidence gained even from typical school tests and written examinations may be very flawed. Probably the best vehicle for investigating what has really been learned and what misunderstandings and misconceptions still remain is the individual interview, widely used by Jean Piaget and by countless other researchers as they discovered its value. In this method the teacher, or researcher, asks the child questions, records the responses, and subsequently analyses the interview data obtained. That sounds very straightforward, though it may only occasionally be possible in a normal classroom situation. There is, however, usually rather more to the collection of reliable data than this simplistic outline suggests. Questions or tasks need to be carefully structured, sequenced and standardized, so that there will be validity to data collected from a large number of interviews with many different children. It is often necessary to have a range of alternative standardized questions, and to be ready with appropriate supplementary standardized questions to be used according to the initial response or reaction of the child. It is not always easy to train oneself to become a researcher of this kind. It is very easy to fall back into the role of the teacher and make suggestions, or coax, or just simply talk too much instead of listening. It is very hard to allow free rein to the child whilst still being systematic in the collection of evidence. Piaget (1973, p. 20) summed up the problem as follows: 'The good experimenter . . . must know how to observe . . . [but] must constantly be alert for something definitive, at every moment he must have some working hypothesis, some theory, true or false, which he is seeking to check'. In the context of this book, it is interesting to note the reference to theory in Piaget's statement. Naturally, we do not need to collect data and then leave the children in ignorance of their weaknesses. We can subsequently set about trying to remedy any deficiencies in understanding all the better for having an accurate picture of what the problems are.

Even if one is able to collect useful research data there can be other complications, for example apparent inconsistencies. Sometimes it seems that children can answer a question on one day but not on the next. Sometimes it seems that children can answer one question but cannot answer another which seems to us to be exactly alike. Sometimes our evidence might suggest that task A is harder than task B, and sometimes the reverse might appear to be true. Sometimes the accessibility of appropriate language might not be adequate for the children to convey adequately what they really do understand, but how do we know? Sometimes the variety of responses, the complexity of the data collected, almost defies analysis. Often, children are learning from our questions. Such are the difficulties, but all research must present comparable difficulties. Despite these problems, and possibly many others, the evidence strongly suggests that there are widespread misconceptions, that there are limits in terms of levels of understanding which are achievable by individual children at particular moments in time.

We must also take into account that we all have a greater capacity for learning when we really want to learn. We cannot ignore the effect on quality of learning of motivation, interest, determination and the desire to succeed. We know that pupils' self-confidence can affect their success in mathematics (Askew and Wiliam, 1995). We know that a novel approach can assist in lodging new notions firmly in the mind (Winston, 2003). The search to find ways of making school mathematics more appealing and exciting, more relevant and more obviously useful, must never end, because we know that children learn much better under such circumstances. High levels of motivation and interest in individual children who do not shine in school mathematics can make them experts in very diverse areas of knowledge from pop records to computer games, from football to British butterflies. At the opposite extreme is the problem of demotivation through anxiety. This might be created through unsuitable subject matter, unsympathetic teaching and a whole variety of environmental factors. Also, some children do appear to panic quite badly, and this is clearly not helpful in fostering learning (see Buxton, 1981). We do not know what such anxious children might achieve under different circumstances if we could find a way to dissipate the anxiety. It is not possible to completely separate out the cognitive factors from the affective (where *cognitive* may be thought of as pertaining to the recall or recognition of knowledge and the development of intellectual abilities and skills, and *affective* as pertaining to interest, attitudes, values and appreciations – see Bloom *et al.*, 1956 and Krathwohl *et al.*, 1964).

The topics of place value, long division, ratio and algebra have been used in this section to justify the claim that many pupils experience real difficulties in trying to grasp the ideas and concepts of mathematics. Experienced teachers of mathematics will already be aware of such difficulties. The major issues which any theories of learning need to address include both a consideration of why it is that learning is not straightforward, and why it is that there are notable stumbling blocks in the mathematics curriculum. We should also hope that a by-product of any theory would be at least some hint of what might be done to ease learning and thus improve the lot of the children and of their mathematics teachers. Thus, the origins of theories must lie with the struggles experienced by the pupils, and with the well known difficulties caused by critically important topics. The data on which any theories are based must originate with the children and largely in their classrooms, and must be collected in a reliable and objective way. More immediately, and in the next chapter, we shall consider more deeply the nature of what it is that we are expecting our pupils to learn. What kinds of knowledge and understanding does mathematics incorporate?

## Suggestions for further reading

Branford, B. (1921) *A Study of Mathematical Education*. Oxford: Clarendon Press.
Ginsburg, H. (1977) *Children's Arithmetic: The Learning Process*. New York: Van Nostrand.
Holt, J. (1964) *How Children Fail*. Harmondsworth: Penguin Books.
Renwick, E. M. (1935) *The Case Against Arithmetic*. London: Simpkin Marshall.

## Questions for discussion

1.  What do you believe are the most effective teaching methods for promoting the learning of mathematics? (These beliefs might change as a result of reading this book!)
2.  To what extent should the teaching of mathematics be intuitive and pragmatic and to what extent should teachers be deliberately trying to put theories into practice?
3.  What issues concerning mathematics learning and their implications for teaching are debated or discussed in your school? What should be discussed?
4.  What mathematical topics or ideas appear to be particularly inappropriate because pupils experience learning difficulties? What is it about these topics, do you think, which makes them so difficult?

# Chapter 2

# What Cognitive Demands Are Made in Learning Mathematics?

## The problem of classification

There have been various attempts to classify the mental constructs involved in learning. Gagné (1985) listed and described eight types of learning. Bloom *et al.* (1956) provided a detailed analysis of the objectives of education in the cognitive domain. Skemp (1971) discussed the processes which need to be adopted in doing mathematics. Polya (1957) attempted to analyse the process of solving mathematical problems, a theme subsequently taken up by Wickelgren (1974). Brown (1978) suggested that there were four types of mathematical learning, namely simple recall, algorithmic learning, conceptual learning and problem-solving. Her Majesty's Inspectorate (1985) listed five main categories of objectives for mathematics learning, and these were facts, skills, conceptual structures, general strategies and personal qualities. The four cognitive categories here bear a close resemblance to those of Brown, and basically provide a suitable structure for further discussion, although in reality all four are inextricably linked in the learning process.

## Retention and recall

Children are expected to be able to recall from memory a variety of different facts or qualities in mathematics, for example:

- words (e.g. length, metre, triangle)
- symbols (e.g. $+$, $-$, $\times$, $\div$, $/$)
- numerical facts (e.g. addition 'bonds', multiplication tables)
- formulas (e.g. $A = lb$, $C = 2\pi r$).

Memory has been the focus for considerable research effort by psychologists over many years. At one time it was believed that our powers of memory could be improved by exercising them, in other words by being made to learn *anything* – relevant and useful or otherwise. Such an extreme view is not now acceptable, though the value of exercise in the form of meaningful practice still has a place in education. The modern view of memory is that it is a feature of overall intellectual capacity, and that different people might even have differing capacities regarding what kinds of knowledge or understanding can most readily be remembered. As with the processing powers of the brain, human capabilities in terms of memory have been studied from physiological perspectives. There is no doubt that the chemistry and physics of the brain might provide the ultimate answers to problems studied in educational psychology but we do not have complete answers yet. Such physiological studies are therefore not considered to be within the scope of this book.

It should be pointed out that psychologists have expressed the view that we possess both short-term and long-term memory. What we certainly wish to achieve is accurate long-term storage together with ready recall, and the problem is how to achieve these. Retention of knowledge has often been associated in the past with rote learning; drill (repetitive practice) was thought to be the answer to the problem of fixing knowledge in the memory, though subsequent difficulties of recall suggest that drill alone does not necessarily achieve long-term retention. The recent history of curriculum development in mathematics, however, reveals a clear, new view from innovators that the emphasis should be taken off memory work so, for example, formula lists or booklets are now provided for candidates in certain examinations. There is considerable doubt whether this movement has carried all mathematics teachers along with it, but it has happened. There is an obvious efficiency factor in having knowledge readily to hand, and nothing is more 'to hand' than the forefront of our own mind, so there is much to be said in favour of being able to remember mathematical facts and results. The view from psychology is that committing knowledge to memory is important in terms of efficient processing but at the same time rote learning without meaning is relatively unhelpful. Cockcroft (1982) did include practice of skills and routines in the list of features of good mathematics teaching, but there was much more besides. Rehearsal is certainly a necessary part of learning, but it is unlikely to be sufficient, as we all prefer to have an underlying meaning to the knowledge we are expected to acquire. In other words, retention and recall are easier if what is learned is meaningful in terms of the network of knowledge held in the mind of the learner. At the same time, however, repetition of a kind is often what establishes the link to the appropriate networks (Winston, 2003).

One difficulty in accepting the view that repetition is inadequate on its own immediately emerges. What must we do for learners at the very beginnings of mathematics when there is virtually no network of mathematical knowledge in the mind of the learner? How, for example, is the child to learn the symbols 0 to 9 and the corresponding words? There is clearly meaning to be learned in the ideas of 'oneness', and 'twoness' and so on, but the symbols and words are essentially arbitrary and therefore have to be learned by rote. Even as a child progresses through mathematics some element of rote learning must remain, in particular in relation to many words and symbols. Some words may be remembered more easily because they are used in everyday life, for example, 'length'. Other words like 'litre' and 'centilitre' are not often used in everyday speech and need to be practised in order to be remembered. Meaning is also involved, however, in the relationship between the capacities which these two words represent and the connection with the prefix 'centi'. The word 'triangle' would seem to be very meaningful in its bringing together of the two ideas of three-ness and angle, but there must be considerable doubt as to whether this is helpful when the teacher first talks about triangles because the concept of angle is still likely to be relatively unformed. Symbols must frequently involve rote learning. Some require very careful discrimination, for example + and ×, and also − and ÷. In learning mathematics, and particularly in the early years, it seems inevitable that learning by rote or by simple association will be involved to some extent.

There is a variety of ways in which retention can be fostered. Novelty of presentation is effective, but is difficult to achieve regularly in most classroom lessons. Generally, we have to settle for more ordinary attempts at variation, such as in the layout within text and exercise books. Different type styles, different colours, the placing of certain key elements in boxes and summary notes are all helpful. Repetition, or rehearsal, has a part to play, both spoken and written. Constant 'sung' repetition of multiplication tables was once commonplace in mathematics lessons. Such learning techniques cannot be considered bad if they achieve their objective, but of course they often did not, and in any case there are patterns, relationships and properties within tables which give a conceptual component to them which suggests that repetition is not likely to be the only way of promoting the learning of tables. Rehearsal, however, must not be rejected out of hand as a way of assisting in the fostering of retention of facts. Periodic revision, likewise, is also important.

Retention can also be promoted by using deliberate contrivances such as mnemonics. The use of a variety of such devices has always been common in learning the basic three trigonometrical ratios, for example, '<u>o</u>ranges <u>h</u>ave <u>s</u>egments (<u>s</u>ectors), <u>a</u>pples <u>h</u>ave <u>c</u>ores', for:

$$\text{sine} = \frac{\text{opposite}}{\text{hypotenuse}}$$

and

$$\text{cosine} = \frac{\text{adjacent}}{\text{hypotenuse}}$$

or the more lengthy statement, '<u>s</u>ome <u>o</u>fficers <u>h</u>ave <u>c</u>urly <u>a</u>uburn <u>h</u>air <u>t</u>o <u>o</u>ffer <u>a</u>ttraction', which includes cues for the tangent ratio as well. It is interesting that mnemonics have not been used widely outside trigonometry. It may be that opportunities for using other mnemonics in the rest of mathematics are very limited, but they do work, and we must acknowledge that and use them as appropriate.

Even if retention is achieved we cannot test it without recall, and recall can be a serious problem. Sitting and thinking, hoping the elements will come back, 'racking one's brains', is frustrating and tiring. Often, however, presenting the learner with an appropriate cue 'jogs the memory', but it is how to arrange for the right cue which is the difficulty. Memory is, to some extent, context specific, which is why our memory is sometimes jogged by reconstructing the situation in which the original experience occurred. Teachers are willing to provide children with appropriate cues, but there comes a time when pupils might have to manage without external help. In the case of mnemonics, the 'rhyme' provides the cue. Structure built into the retention greatly assists recall and figuring out. Learning which has been achieved simply by rote and without a link into a network of knowledge does not facilitate recall. Askew and Wiliam (1995, p. 8) comment that: ' "Knowing by heart" and "figuring out" support

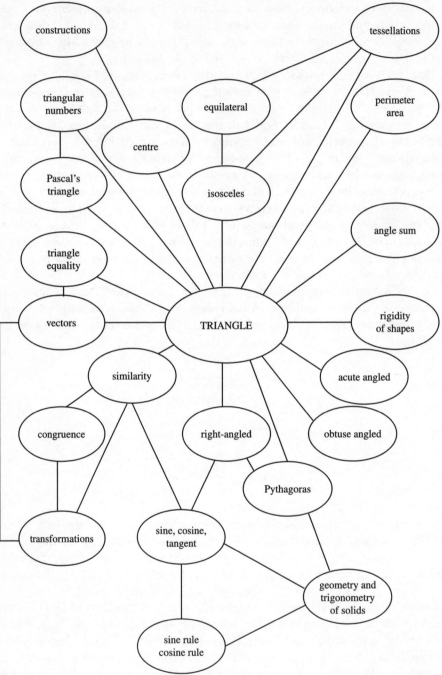

**Figure 2.1**

each other in pupils' progression in number'. A concept map fixed in the mind might also help. It may enable the child to follow the network to the required element, or might release a complete structure of elements once a few key ideas are remembered. Considerable attention has been given to the idea of concept maps since their first introduction. A concept map is simply a linked network of related elements

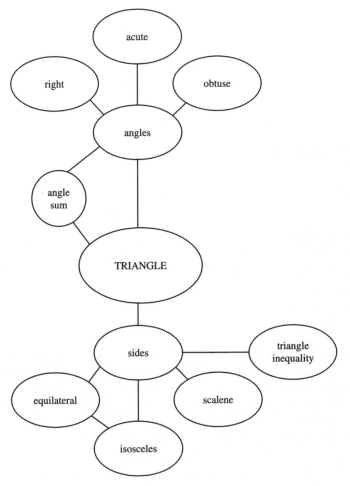

**Figure 2.2**

of learning material. It can be used in a variety of ways. It can be used by teachers in course planning, it can be given to pupils as a model for revision, and it can be used by a learner in a deliberate way in the learning process. An example is given in Figure 2.1 which is a map of mathematics associated with triangles and triangularity. This map, as with most such maps, is not exhaustive. At the same time, it may be too difficult for most children to appreciate that there are so many related mathematical ideas, so more limited maps might be more useful in assisting remembering, for example the diagram in Figure 2.2, which was created by a middle years pupil.

In connection with using concept maps there are provisos which need to be mentioned. First, there is much more to be learned, for example, about triangles, than can be memorized without understanding, so that in introducing concept maps within this section we have certainly gone beyond the basic ideas of retention and recall. Secondly, and unfortunately, the effect of concept maps presented by the teacher, in helping to foster retention, is also likely to be limited. The basic problem here is that, when learning, we each put our own structure on the material that we absorb into our minds. Modern constructivist views suggest that learners do not remember material exactly as it was taught, that meaning is not absorbed but is constructed, and that retention involves an active process of construction (see Chapter 11). There is, therefore, the suggestion that many of the learning difficulties recorded in the previous chapter are not caused by failure to absorb all that was taught but rather that they are failures of reconstruction. Retention and recall are clearly not simple processes.

## Using algorithms

Learning mathematics is very much concerned with learning algorithms, for example, the following:

- long multiplication
- long division
- adding and subtracting fractions
- multiplying fractions
- dividing fractions
- multiplying matrices.

Clearly, memory is also important here, but in using algorithms the pupils have to remember a step-by-step procedure rather than isolated facts. A worrying feature about algorithms in mathematics is that many which we expect children to remember and use with confidence lack meaning for the pupils, in terms of worthwhile knowledge, and sometimes appear completely irrelevant. The distinction between *instrumental understanding* and *relational understanding* (Skemp, 1976) is helpful in appreciating this point, and this is illustrated below.

One of the less obvious school algorithms is for converting denary (decimal) numbers to binary. Assuming that 13 is our denary number, we divide it by 2 and record the quotient (6) and the remainder (1). Next we divide 6 by 2 and record the quotient (3) and the remainder (0). We continue until the quotient is 0, as shown here.

$$
\begin{array}{c|c|c}
2 & 13 & 1 \\
2 & 6 & 0 \\
2 & 3 & 1 \\
2 & 1 & 1 \\
& 0 &
\end{array}
$$

Then the required binary number is 1101, formed from the remainders – but in reverse order! It may be possible for pupils to learn this as a procedure, but it is doubtful if many would appreciate why it works, let alone why they need to know it. Thus, they might understand what to do to get the answer, in which case they have achieved instrumental understanding, but they have not necessarily achieved relational understanding, when the procedure makes total sense. There is something of a parallel between this distinction and that between memorizing by rote and memorizing through establishing connections in the mind.

Another example is the addition of two fractions, as follows:

$$\frac{a}{b} + \frac{c}{d}$$

$$= \frac{ad + bc}{bd}$$

However, this algorithm is sensible for some fractions, such as $\frac{2}{3} + \frac{1}{4}$

but is not sensible for $\frac{1}{2} + \frac{1}{4}$

nor for $\frac{1}{6} + \frac{2}{9}$

because these sums may be obtained more simply. Furthermore, the subtle variations in method which are sensible for the latter two examples can only be appreciated through relational understanding, incorporating the idea of lowest common multiple. Recently, this algorithm has been linked with the idea of equivalent fractions. Since the equivalence of fractions depends on the equality of ratios (proportion) it is open to question whether such use of equivalence leads to any greater understanding (see Chapter 1). In any case, why should we wish young children to be using a routine process to add fractions in the first place?

The worst scenario concerning fractions involves division, for example,

$$\frac{3}{5} \div \frac{7}{10}$$

The equivalent fractions approach suggests using $\frac{6}{10}$ and $\frac{7}{10}$, but how do we then justify the rest of the procedure which leads to the answer? To find the answer instrumentally, one 'inverts the second fraction and replaces the $\div$ by $\times$. This seemingly arbitrary set of instructions often leads pupils to confusion. Which fraction is the one to invert? Or is it both? Relationally, of course, we wish to know how many $\frac{7}{10}$ there are in $\frac{3}{5}$, and this may be attempted through a progression of examples starting with very simple ones. However, it might not be possible to progress as far as this rather more difficult example, in which case – is the instrumental approach justifiable? Is it necessary? If it is necessary, at what age is it appropriate to aim for relational understanding? In reality, relational understanding of the division of all possible pairs of fractions does not appear to be achievable by most pupils within the compulsory years of schooling.

A major problem with algorithms is that we often appear to introduce them before the pupils see a need for them. For example, we teach pupils how to solve linear equations in a kind of algorithmic way by applying a set of rules when the equation can, and often will, be solved by inspection, or by trial and improvement. At the time of introduction to the procedure the equation

$$2x + 3 \quad = \quad 11$$

will not be willingly solved by the method:

$$\therefore \quad 2x + 3 - 3 = 11 - 3$$
$$\therefore \quad 2x \qquad = 8$$
$$\therefore \quad x \qquad = \frac{8}{2}$$
$$\therefore \quad x \qquad = 4$$

This reluctance to accept the taught routine is because anyone can see almost at a glance (or by trialling) that $x = 4$! Hart (1981, p. 212) stated:

> We appear to teach algorithms too soon, illustrate their use with simple examples (which the child knows he can do another way) and assume once taught they are remembered. We have ample proof that they are not remembered or [are] sometimes remembered in a form that was never taught, e.g. to add two fractions, add the tops and add the bottoms.

One of the difficulties we must contend with, however, is that we cannot be sure that relational understanding must precede the use of an algorithm, or is indeed necessary at all. There is some evidence that relational understanding can be developed by thoughtful use of an algorithm over a period of time, in other words that instrumental application might help to promote relational understanding. Learning is so complex, and we all learn in so many different ways, that it seems like another chicken and egg situation. Which comes first? Nevertheless, there seems to be no doubt that too much instrumental learning is accepted in mathematics with pupils for whom relational understanding seemingly will never come, and that too much dependence on instrumental understanding in learning mathematics can be rather like building a tower on insecure foundations. Such a tower will eventually crumble, and perhaps from somewhere quite near the bottom. As with so many aspects of learning, it is not easy to find the right compromise. This compromise might, after all, be different for different pupils! If we decide that a particular algorithm has some value is it justifiable to teach it, even knowing that relational understanding is impossible to achieve? Are there any essential algorithms anyway? If so, which are they?

## Learning concepts

There are problems in remembering facts in mathematics, and there are difficulties in learning algorithms meaningfully, but the conceptual structure or basis of mathematics is likely to be even more demanding. Learning mathematics consists very largely of building the understanding of new concepts onto and into previously understood concepts. Examples of concepts are so widespread that it is almost unnecessary to quote any, but for comparison with simple recall and algorithmic learning here are a few:

- triangularity
- percentage
- relation
- similarity
- limit.

Strangely, however, it is not easy to explain what a concept is. A dictionary might tell us that a concept is an 'abstract idea'. The definition by Novak (1977, p. 18) is rather more helpful, namely: 'Concepts describe some regularity or relationship within a group of facts and are designated by some sign or symbol'. Novak went further and also defined a 'theory' as being like a higher order concept, 'in that [it] may suggest order or relationships between less inclusive concepts'. However, it is probably easier to understand any definition of concept retrospectively, as it were, after thinking about particular concepts and what is involved in using them.

Skemp (1971) discussed exactly this point in a very helpful illustration of how concepts are learned. Considering the hypothetical situation of an adult born blind but given sight by an operation Skemp suggested that there is no way we can help the adult to understand the concept of 'redness' by means of a definition. It is only by pointing to a variety of objects which are red that the adult might be able to abstract the idea of redness, as one particular property which is common to all of the objects. Clearly, one would also assume that counter-examples, involving objects which were not red, would also help to clarify what was meant by 'redness'. Skemp was claiming that the learning of mathematical concepts is comparable. We must not expect that children will learn through definitions. We need to use examples and counter-examples. Thus, in exactly the same way, we can run into difficulty in trying to define what we mean by a concept in mathematics unless we have many examples in mind.

The clear implication is that we learn about triangularity through examples of triangles and the contrast with other shapes. The concept of 'triangle' is probably relatively easy to grasp in this way, but we must not take it for granted. After all, children are sometimes very reluctant to admit that the shape in Figure 2.3 is a square, and often wish to call it a 'diamond', and indeed sometimes vehemently deny that it is a square. It would seem likely that our examples of squares, from which abstraction of the concept takes place, have not included a sufficient number for which one side is not parallel to the bottom of the page, chalkboard or whiteboard. This is a point made by Dienes (1960) in connection with his theory of mathematics learning (see Chapter 10). Other concepts, such as 'similarity' and 'relation', are certainly much more difficult to learn (see Orton, 1971). The idea of a 'function' in the language of modern mathematics was always very difficult to introduce, and probably irrelevant to most children anyway. Using functions without trying to define the idea abstractly may be the best starting point, and a more abstract definition of function can then be

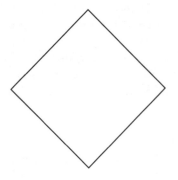

Figure 2.3

provided much later only to those for whom it is appropriate. We need to be very careful when trying to introduce abstract mathematical ideas. Some ideas may be more abstract and therefore more difficult than we imagine. Skemp (1964), in drawing attention to the surprises we may get through concept analysis, cited not only fractions as being very much harder than we had previously thought but also sets as being very much easier.

The precise mathematical definition of a concept, based on many years of handling examples, is something the mathematics teacher needs to have, but even that might cause problems. We all know exactly what a triangle is, but do we know what a natural number is? To many professional mathematicians the natural numbers are 0,1,2,3,4,5 . . . but to others they are 1,2,3,4,5 . . . . The definition of prime numbers at one time included unity, and may still do so for some people, but nowadays most definitions of prime numbers exclude unity. Some books might define rectangular numbers to include the square numbers, and others might not. Some books might define both 'rectangular' and 'oblong' numbers in order that rectangular numbers should include square numbers, with oblong numbers being those rectangular numbers which are not square, but other books might not accept 'oblong' as a useful idea. Yet it is possible to learn mathematics without having a completely 'watertight' definition of certain concepts. Certainly, our concepts grow and develop over the years. We introduce children to 'numbers', meaning only the numbers we count with. Subsequently, and over many years, other kinds of numbers are introduced, namely fractions (rational numbers), integers, irrational numbers and real numbers. Thus our original numbers have had to be redefined as natural numbers. Despite the apparent complexities of concept redefinition which are implied, learning can still take place. There are other problems too. As we have seen, Skemp (1964) expressed the view that sets were relatively simple to understand, but how should we introduce the notion of the empty set? The emptiness of particular intersections of sets or of particular defined sets is an easy idea but not so the uniqueness of the empty set, nor the fact that the empty set is a subset of every set (contemporary school curricula are not likely to include this complication). Yet learning about sets can still take place successfully, and can still enlighten certain mathematical ideas, whether the topic of sets is included in the statutory curriculum or not.

Boundary disputes might be less likely in mathematics than in other areas of knowledge, but they do exist, for example whether a square is a rectangle. Distinguishing between blue and green around the boundary between two colours might lead to disagreement, but is unlikely to hold up learning or cause argument. We do not fully know what the boundary problems are for children in learning mathematics, and how much they interfere with learning. The definition of concept by Child (1986, p. 72) acknowledges that there is a boundary problem:

> With most concepts there are wide margins of attribute acceptability. . . . In some cases, the boundaries which distinguish concepts are hazy and ill-defined. But generally speaking, there is a large measure of agreement in the definition of most class concepts within a given culture.

The suggestion by Skemp that we do not learn concepts from definitions is not the only major strand of recommendations. In Nuffield (1967, frontispiece) we find the simple proverb:

I hear, and I forget;
I see, and I remember;
I do, and I understand.

Here is a strong activity message, also found in the Schools Council Report (1965) and in many other documents including Cockcroft (1982). The assumption in all of these references is that children, particularly young children, learn best by proceeding from the concrete to the abstract. Perhaps, to a large extent, we all learn through concrete examples, though thinking purely in abstractions does become more possible, though not certain, in adulthood. Cockcroft, in many paragraphs, emphasized this kind of message, and suggested that it is important that we do not assume that practical approaches should be limited only to young children, or to children whose attainment is low. Cockcroft also stressed the slowness of the progression from concrete materials to abstract thinking. The Schools Council Report (p. 9) emphasized the same in: 'Children learn mathematical concepts more slowly than we realized. They learn by their own activities'.

Such views as those recorded above, and many other related views, are common to most publications which set out to make recommendations to teachers about how to help children to learn mathematical concepts. The theories of learning which are discussed in some subsequent chapters of this book all face up to the crucial issue of how to promote concept learning. In fact, many of the above references show clear evidence of close association with such theories of learning anyway. It is interesting to note that one theorist, Gagné (1985), was at pains to claim that some concepts can be defined. He suggested that there are two kinds of concepts, *concrete concepts* and *defined concepts* and, whilst admitting that many concepts require a concrete approach, since they are fundamentally classes of objects, events and qualities (for example, 'angle', 'triangle' and 'regularity'), he pointed to other concepts such as 'pivot', 'uncle' and 'sell' which cannot be learned from examples. This issue will be raised in the next chapter. Suffice to say at this stage that Gagné's view is open to debate, and if a distinction exists between concrete and defined concepts it is not a clear distinction, at least in terms of learning mathematics. What neither Gagné nor any other major theorist has denied is that, in the case of young children learning mathematics, attempts to define concepts are unlikely to be successful. Concrete approaches are often very necessary, though no approach will ever guarantee that relational understanding will be achieved.

Skemp and others have drawn attention to the implications for concept learning of what is perhaps best described as the hierarchical nature of mathematics. In some subject disciplines there might be very considerable freedom in terms of the order in which topics may be taught. In mathematics it is usually much more important that we find a right sequence for the learner. Often the very examples which we use to promote concept learning are themselves other concepts, and we must be sure that these other concepts have already been adequately understood. A mature understanding of what we mean by 'number' as a generalization may depend on an understanding of natural numbers, rational numbers, irrational numbers, integers and real numbers, together with, perhaps, an appreciation that this might not be a completely exhaustive list of different number sets. Various authors have tried to elaborate the hierarchy of concepts, or topics, through which learners must pass. Two such attempts are in Nuffield (1970) and Skemp (1971). It does not seem likely, however, that such hierarchies can ever completely solve our problems in the sequencing of learning in mathematics, though they should help. One other feature of concept learning is that we continue to refine and extend our understanding of concepts throughout life. A thorough and complete understanding of a concept is sometimes not only unnecessary to enable a learner to move on to the next concept, it might even be unattainable. It might be that it is the study of parallel or even more advanced concepts which leads to enhancement of the understanding of previously encountered concepts. Another feature of learning mathematics is that some flexibility within the hierarchy of topics is possible, even though we have to be more careful with our sequence than in some other knowledge areas. Learners are not identical in their needs, after all, and do not all achieve identical levels of understanding of particular topics in a hierarchy. Hence the good sense of the well known statement by Ausubel (1968, frontispiece):

> If I had to reduce all of educational psychology to just one principle, I would say this: The most important single factor influencing learning is what the learner already knows. Ascertain this and teach him accordingly.

It is not completely clear how to promote concept formation most effectively. Obviously, examples and counter-examples must play a large part in helping pupils to extrapolate essential characteristics and classify according to features, properties and differences. The examples, however, must be presented in as many variations as possible, for example, of position and orientation, and in as many environments as possible. This is so that, for example, pupils do not reject as squares those which look like 'diamonds'. Askew and Wiliam (1995, p. 15) state that: '. . . teachers should use a mixture of examples and non-examples and should choose the examples so as to "rule in" as much as possible, and should choose the non-examples to "rule out" as much as possible'. They also point out that there is research evidence that a sequence of examples followed by a sequence of non-examples is more effective than random sequencing, and that the ideal examples to use are 'only just' examples, whilst the ideal non-examples are 'very nearly' examples. Howard (1987) suggests many techniques, such as matched and unmatched pairs and the idea of coordinate concepts, though his examples come from across the whole curriculum and not just from mathematics.

## Problem-solving

Considerable attention has been accorded in recent years to the place of problem-solving in mathematics and to how to help children to become better problem-solvers. It is first necessary to declare exactly what is meant by 'problem-solving' in this context. In fact, it is perhaps better to clarify what we do not mean. At the end of a section of a mathematics textbook there is often a set of routine exercises, which may even be referred to in the text as problems, but these are unlikely to involve 'problem-solving' in the sense intended here. The routine practice provided by such exercises may be important, and can be thought of in terms of rehearsal as a way of fostering retention in the memory. Some such exercises might require the learners to apply their mathematics to situations which arise in the real world and, as such, could be termed applications. Some such applications may also involve a degree of novelty.

Problem-solving is now normally intended to imply a process in which the learner combines previously learned elements of knowledge, rules, techniques, skills and concepts to provide a solution to a situation not encountered before. It is now generally accepted that mathematics is both product and process; it is both an organized body of knowledge and a creative activity in which the learner participates. It might, in fact, be claimed that the real purpose of learning rules, techniques and content generally is to enable the learner to do mathematics, indeed to solve problems, though Ausubel (1963) would appear to be one respected educationist who has expounded a contrary view. Thus, in a sense, problem-solving could be considered to be the real essence of mathematics. Gagné (1985) has expressed the view that problem-solving is the highest form of learning. Having solved a problem, one has learned something new and possibly vital. One might only have learned to solve that problem, but it is more likely that one has learned the essence of how to solve a variety of similar problems and perhaps even a variety of problems simply possessing some similar characteristics. Descartes expressed the view that each problem that is solved becomes a rule which serves afterwards to solve other problems. One might therefore be tempted to enquire what is the difference between problem-solving and discovery? Both require 'thinking', leading to the re-creation of some knowledge or capability which the learner did not have before. Another term which is currently in frequent use in current mathematics curricula is 'investigation'. An investigation might be closed, in the sense that the intention is to lead to an established mathematical result, or it might be open, in the sense that the result is not known in advance, or there might not even be a clear result which can be stated simply. Investigations could clearly lead to problem-solving. Investigations also, hopefully, lead to discovery. In short, whatever we mean by the separate terms, 'discovery', 'investigation' and 'problem-solving', there are clear connections between the processes involved. For this reason, a more detailed consideration of problem-solving is contained within Chapter 5, which is about discovery.

Thus by definition problem-solving is not routine, each problem being to a greater or lesser degree a novelty to the learner. Successful solutions of problems are dependent on the learner not only having the knowledge and skills required but also being able to tap into the relevant networks and structures in the mind. Sometimes a flash of insight seems to occur when solving a novel problem. Although this is a phenomenon which is not fully understood, it seems it may involve the realization of some previously unacknowledged relationship or connection within the knowledge structure. It therefore depends on having the richest possible knowledge base from which to draw, this base including awareness of possible strategies. Askew and Wiliam (1995, p. 24) sum all this up in: 'Success in problem-solving requires both specific content knowledge and general skills'. It is also known that problem-solving is assisted by turning over the problem in the mind thoroughly, trying out avenues of approach, and thus bringing to the forefront of the mind a whole range of techniques and methods which might be appropriate. Further, it is known that the solution will often not come immediately, but might come subsequently, after a period of time away from the problem, as if the subconscious mind, freed from the constraints of conscious attempts to solve the problem, continues to experiment with combinations of elements from the knowledge base.

There is considerable interest at the moment in aiming to improve the problem-solving skills of pupils in school. Polya (1957, 1962) has led the way in the consideration of how to establish a routine for problem-solving and, therefore, in how to train people to become better problem-solvers, though his problems are more relevant to older students. Wickelgren (1974) too, basing his work on Polya but elaborating and extending this, claims to have evidence that his methods do produce more competent problem-solvers. It is interesting to speculate, however, that, although such training in problem-solving strategies might have considerable pay-off, any form of training might be moving us towards a more algorithmic approach, with all the inherent weaknesses of algorithmic learning. In fact, in contrast to Polya and Wickelgren, and many current advocates of methodical approaches, Gagné has gone on record as stating that we probably cannot teach people to become better problem-solvers. This is because of his belief that one cannot teach thinking skills in a vacuum – each problem involves its own content and context, for if it does not, we have moved towards the kind of routine exercises discussed at the beginning of this section. Having solved a problem we have learned something, but we have not become a better problem-solver *per se*. Ausubel (1963) too, whilst accepting that training in problem-solving within a fairly narrow and well defined subject discipline might achieve some success, is at great pains to point out the transfer problem, raised in Chapter 1 and discussed more thoroughly in Chapter 7.

One aspect of problem-solving in mathematics is that often the problems are divorced both from the mainstream subject matter and also from the real world. Such puzzles may contain great interest for some children, but others may not see the point and be demotivated. Such puzzles are unlikely to produce knowledge or rules which are useful or applicable elsewhere. It has been a common feature of research into problem-solving and discovery that subjects have been presented with problems which are almost frivolous or whimsical. This has advantages in a controlled experiment, for it is then most likely that all subjects start with the same knowledge of the situation – namely nil. It has also often produced interesting results. However, what can be deduced about problem-solving in a novel situation may not apply within school subjects.

## Suggestions for further reading

Byers, V. and Erlwanger, S. (1985) 'Memory in mathematical understanding', *Educational Studies in Mathematics*, 16, 259–81.

Howard, R. W. (1987) *Concepts and Schemata*. London: Cassell.

Nunes, T. and Bryant, P. (1996) *Children Doing Mathematics*. Oxford: Blackwell.

Resnick, L. B. and Ford, W. W. (1984) *The Psychology of Mathematics for Instruction*. Hillsdale, NJ: Lawrence Erlbaum.

Skemp, R. R. (1976) 'Relational understanding and instrumental understanding', *Mathematics Teaching*, 77, 20–26.

## Questions for discussion

1. To what extent is the provision of formula lists and books and other means of reducing memory load justifiable in mathematics?
2. How essential is relational understanding in learning mathematics?
3. Justify the algorithmic content of your mathematics curriculum.
4. Choose a unit of mathematics and analyse it in terms of memory load, algorithmic content and conceptual demand.

# Chapter 3

# Could We Enhance Learning Through Optimum Sequencing?

## Behaviourism

How do children best learn multiplication tables? Is it by 'sung' repetition (chanting)? Or do they learn best by investigating number patterns from knowledge of additions? Do they learn best by practising correct responses for given stimuli, such as random products presented on flash-cards? Or is a mixture of methods best? Mathematics teachers are likely to hold a variety of views on the best methods to use. Many adults will recall learning by chanting, and it is still used, but as the predominant method of learning tables it has been out of favour for many years. At the opposite extreme, investigation of number patterns and relationships, without other methods which involve repetition, may not fix products and factors in the memory. We do want children to 'understand' why $7 \times 9 = 63$, but we also hope that the stimulus

$$7 \times 9$$

will produce the instant response

$$63$$

However one defines behaviourism, it is likely that some of the practices of teaching associated with behaviourist learning theories will be used in the teaching of elementary arithmetic such as multiplication tables.

How should we define behaviourism? Different authors appear to use different definitions, so it is not easy to present a definition with which all interested parties would agree. Early behaviourist psychologists trained animals to exhibit required patterns of behaviour to prove that conditioning worked, so conditioning might be assumed to be an important feature of behaviourism. One very well known experiment was carried out by Pavlov, who conditioned dogs to salivate in readiness for eating on merely hearing the ringing of a bell. More recently, Skinner conditioned rats and pigeons to perform particular actions, usually in order to obtain food. Skinner claimed: 'Once we have arranged the particular type of consequence called a reinforcement our techniques permit us to shape up the behavior of an organism almost at will' (reported in Lysaught and Williams, 1963, p. 6). It seems that Skinner was suggesting that what could be achieved with animals could be achieved with humans; people could also be conditioned to exhibit the required behaviour. This seems a worrying claim – but how true is it?

One problem with trying to define behaviourism is that precise definitions may have changed over time. In a developing discipline one would expect newer theories to extend or amend older theories. For this reason, reading the literature brings to light a variety of technical terms, not only 'behaviourism' but also 'associationism' and 'connectionism', all of which appear to describe behaviourist-type beliefs. There are undoubtedly differences between the strict definitions associated with these technical terms, but it is not appropriate or necessary to discuss these here. A useful, simplistic definition of behaviourism as it has applied to education is that it is the belief that learning takes place through stimulus-response connections, in other words that all human behaviour can be analysed into stimulus and response.

It is also difficult to trace when the theory of behaviourism emerged, just as it is difficult in the history of mathematics to say when calculus was invented. Thorndike was certainly an important, and early, associationist instigator of ideas but perhaps one should look much further back, for example, to Herbart one hundred years before Thorndike. A comprehensive consideration of the development of behaviourist-type learning theories will be found in Bigge (1976). More recent neobehaviourists, like Gagné, appear to hold very different views from those held earlier. Gagné (1985, p. 2) expressed his views about learning as follows:

> Learning is a change in human disposition or capability, which persists over a period of time, and which is not simply ascribable to processes of growth. The kind of change called learning exhibits itself as a change in behavior.

Whatever the best definition of behaviourism, an important belief running throughout its development has been in the effectiveness of stimulus-response learning. As a result of a particular stimulus the required response is elicited.

$$S \text{ leads to } R$$
$$\longrightarrow$$

Given an appropriate question (stimulus) from the teacher, or from a book or programme, the correct answer (response) is obtained. Learning proceeds, slowly but surely, through a sequence or chain of stimulus-response links. The effectiveness of the programme depends on the quality of the sequencing as well as the stimuli. However, feedback, reinforcement and reward also have important places in the application of the theory. It might be a sufficient reward for a learner to receive instant feedback as to whether a particular response is correct, and this should then promote the desire to be presented with the next stimulus. A cycle of learning is thus generated, depicted in Figure 3.1.

Thorndike (1922) postulated a number of laws which have promoted discussion and debate ever since, and two are summarized here. Although these laws were

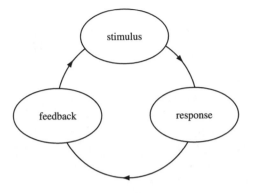

**Figure 3.1**

proposed many years ago it is interesting to consider how acceptable they are today in the teaching of mathematics.

(1) *The law of exercise*
*The response to a situation becomes associated with that situation, and the more it is used in a given situation the more strongly it becomes associated with it. On the other hand, disuse of the response weakens the association.*

The aim of learning multiplication tables through chanting could be considered to fit this exactly. Furthermore, much of the teaching of mathematics has traditionally consisted of the teacher demonstrating a method, process, routine or algorithm to be used in particular circumstances, followed by the class attempting to solve routine questions using the set procedure. Often the teaching will have incorporated some question and answer, yet the pupils will have been firmly steered towards the intended goal. The Cockcroft Report (1982) drew attention to this, in paragraph 243. Exposition by the teacher followed by practise of skills and techniques is a feature which most people remember when they think of how they learned mathematics. Even if we do not fully believe that practice guarantees perfection many of us might still believe that practice is the best way to set about it. We are seeking to establish a strong bond between the stimulus (the question-type) and the response (the application of the method of solution leading to the correct answer). This appears to be a direct application of the law of exercise. Teachers will know only too well, however, that many pupils subsequently appear to suffer severe weakening of this bond, assuming a bond existed in the first place. (The behaviourist term 'bond' still survives as 'number bond' in some literature describing addition combinations.) It is possible to teach pupils how to add two fractions together by practising the algorithm only to find that in the end-of-year examination, several months later, most pupils demonstrate only that they cannot respond correctly. The addition of fractions is carefully chosen here, because it is taught and re-taught throughout the years of schooling, subsequent to having been first introduced around the age of ten years. After revision, many pupils can once more cope for a while, but by next time round a year later many will have forgotten again. Disuse of the response does appear to weaken the association – but was the association really firm enough in the first place? Is disuse of the response the only reason for failures in responding? This apparent weakening of association would be explained by cognitive psychologists in a different way from how behaviourists explain it.

(2) *The law of effect*
*Responses that are accompanied or closely followed by satisfaction are more likely to*
*happen again when the situation recurs, while responses accompanied or closely followed*
*by discomfort will be less likely to recur.*

Certain of the things we do as teachers also appear to suggest some acceptance of the law of effect, though there are many ways in which satisfaction for a pupil can result from a response. Ideally, a correct response should automatically produce satisfaction, because it feels good to be right, and the pupil ought to be reinforced. However, many teachers find it necessary to provide extrinsic motivation. Hence, there are often rewards for good work, such as prizes, merit marks, gold stars and the like, on the assumption that they will help to persuade pupils to persevere. Poor work, on the other hand, may result in punishment, and certainly in low marks, producing discomfort and theoretically resulting in no recurrence of unsatisfactory work. Although recent research confirms the potential value of rewards in motivation, the effects of such an approach to education are not all beneficial. Pupils often look for the line of red ticks or a complimentary word rather than for advisory comments intended to improve understanding and attainment. On the other hand, a line of red crosses provides negative reinforcement; most children would wish to avoid this happening, though without comments from the teacher there is little chance that the pupil will improve.

So far, the question which forms the title of the chapter has not been addressed. Although behaviourism has now been explained in terms of stimulus-response connections, and 'practice makes perfect' is a widely-held belief, there is more to the theory than that. The optimum sequencing of learning units and materials is also important to behaviourism. Two important examples of the careful sequencing of learning material are considered later in this chapter, namely programmed learning and learning hierarchies. However, before that, it is appropriate to look at the place of objectives in teaching and learning mathematics.

## Objectives

It is common practice nowadays to plan lessons, topics and courses using published or written objectives as a starting point. This is a relatively recent development in the history of formal education. Here, we must distinguish between aims and behavioural objectives. An appropriate broad aim for a mathematics lesson could be: 'To study Pythagoras' theorem', but this needs to be made much more specific when clarifying what is actually to happen in the classroom. Hence, an appropriate behavioural objective might be: 'Given the lengths of the two shorter sides of a right-angled triangle, the pupils will be able to calculate the length of the longest side'. This tells us clearly what it is expected the pupils will learn in the lesson. The need for objectives in planning instruction was summed up by Mager (1975, p. 5): 'When clearly defined objectives are lacking, there is no sound basis for the selection or designing of instructional materials, content, or methods'.

It is open to debate as to whether objectives are necessarily associated with the behaviourist approach to instruction. Gagné (1975, p. 72) appeared to assume that objectives were part of his neobehaviourism, and explained the place of objectives as follows:

To define and state an objective for learning is to express one of the categories (or sub-categories) of learning outcomes in terms of human performance and to specify the situation in which it is to be observed.

Mager (1975, p. 23), however, wrote:

During the early sixties we talked about behavior, rather than about performance. This . . . [was] . . . unfortunate . . . people were put off . . . thinking that objectives necessarily had to have something to do with behaviorism . . . Not so. Objectives [do] . . . describe . . . behavior, [but only] because behavior is what we can be specific about.

Whether objectives are part of behaviourism is not vital in the context of this book, but objectives could be essential to the efficient sequencing of material to be learned. Behaviourist teaching methods should demand optimum sequencing.

One way in which objectives have been associated with behaviourism lies in the fact that objectives were widely discussed in connection with the programming of learning, itself a product of the behaviourist approach to education. Mager's own early book (1962) was entitled, *Preparing Objectives for Programmed Instruction*. Lysaught and Williams (1963) included, in their book on programmed instruction, an extensive discussion of the preparation of objectives. Early work, based largely on logical reasoning, led to the drawing up of taxonomies of educational objectives, for example by Bloom *et al.* (1956) and by Krathwohl *el al.* (1964). Considerable attention has subsequently been given to methodologies for the preparation of teaching objectives.

Writers seem to be generally agreed on why objectives are important. It is claimed that objectives:

(a) provide the teacher with guidelines for developing instructional materials and teaching method;
(b) enable the teacher to design means of assessing whether what was intended has been accomplished; and
(c) give direction to the learners and assist them to make better efforts to attain their goal.

It is not surprising that, because of (a), considerable emphasis is often placed on objectives in the training of new teachers. It is also not surprising that, because of (b), it is now expected that new examination schemes are prefaced by clear objectives for the course – not an easy thing to achieve. It is further suggested in (c) that it is advantageous if learners are clearly aware of course objectives. It would be false to claim that this is always the case, and so it may be one way in which we are failing to capitalize on opportunities presented by using objectives.

What should an objective look like? Is 'the pupils will understand probability' a suitable objective? Many people would prefer such a vague statement to be regarded as a broad aim. For the teacher, objectives provide a basis for instructional planning, for the conduct of teaching and for evaluating pupils' learning at the end, so the objectives need to be devised with these three points in mind. For the student, objectives might be expected to contribute to motivation and to provide feedback at the end. The distinction between aims and objectives could well depend on the words used, and considerable discussion has taken place about, for example, verbs which are open to many interpretations, such as 'know', 'understand', 'appreciate', 'enjoy', 'believe' and 'grasp', as opposed to other verbs which are open to many fewer interpretations, such as 'identify', 'calculate', 'sort', 'construct', 'compare' and 'solve'. Under no circumstances could: 'be able to understand mathematics', be acceptable as either an aim or an objective, because it is too vague and ill-defined. On the other hand: 'develop a liking for mathematics', could be a very worthy broad aim, though it is not specific enough to be an objective, and it makes no mention of expected changes in behaviour. One example of a strictly defined behavioural objective is: 'given any two natural numbers, each less than or equal to 100, the pupils will be able to write down the sum'. In this we have great precision, it refers to behavioural outcomes, the teachers and pupils alike know where they are going, and the examiner knows what sort of question to set to assess the progress of the pupils. The more detailed example of the difference between broad aims and more specific objectives given below is concerned with mensuration.

## Aims for a topic on mensuration

1. To develop an understanding of the mensuration of certain basic shapes, and hence also a wide variety of composite shapes.
2. To ensure that pupils have an adequate knowledge of the appropriate units involved and that they know and can use relevant formulas.

## Objectives for a topic on mensuration

1. Pupils will know that the *perimeter* is the distance around the boundary of a shape.
2. Pupils will know that, in the case of a circle, the perimeter is called the *circumference*.
3. Pupils will know that the *area* is the amount of surface contained within the perimeter.
4. Pupils will know the names of, abbreviations for, relative sizes of and relationships between the *units of length* mm, cm, m, km.
5. Pupils will be able to *measure* lengths using the units mm, cm, m.
6. Pupils will know that areas are measured in *square units* and will know the names, abbreviations for, relative sizes of and relationships between $mm^2$, $cm^2$, $m^2$, $km^2$.
7. Pupils will be able to *calculate the perimeters* of rectangles and triangles and also composite shapes based on these.
8. Pupils will be able to *calculate the areas* of rectangles, triangles, and composite shapes, using $A = 1 \times b$ (rectangle) and $A = \frac{1}{2} \times b \times h$ (triangle).
9. Pupils will be able to *calculate the circumferences* of circles using the formula $C = \pi d = 2\pi r$.
10. Pupils will be able to *calculate the areas* of circles using $A = \pi r^2$, and hence will be able to calculate the areas of composite shapes involving circles.

Even then, are these objectives specific enough? For example, with what degree of accuracy do we wish pupils to be able to calculate the areas? From what number sets will lengths be drawn — will they always be whole numbers or are fractions allowed? What degree of complexity will be involved in the composite shapes? How do we introduce the various formulas and should we formulate objectives concerned with the derivation of, for example, $\pi r^2$? Have we missed out other essentials which might cause problems when we try to teach? For example, do we need objectives concerned with clarifying how we use the formula $A = \frac{1}{2} \times b \times h$, for many errors are committed in handling this? Readers may be able to think of other questions.

One problem which has emerged is that the derivation of complete, detailed, unambiguous and absolutely specific objectives is itself an elusive objective to have. As Gagné and Briggs (1974, p. 94) wrote, in connection with their systematic approach to forming objectives:

> When instructional objectives are defined in the manner described here, they reveal the fine-grained nature of the educational process. This in turn reflects the fine-grained nature of what is learned. As a consequence, the quantity of individual objectives applicable to a course of instruction usually numbers in the hundreds. There may be scores of objectives for the single topic of a course, and several for each individual lesson.

This is certainly the case with the objectives for mensuration given above. Such objectives make better sense when they are allocated, one or two at a time, to individual lessons. The following list of objectives taken from a statistics course forms a good basis for discussion. Although an age range was specified (11–12 years), statistics and probability are now taught in most age ranges, and so the list is a relevant one for most mathematics teachers to consider. Are these objectives appropriate? Are they clear and unambiguous? Are they sufficiently fine-grained? Are they appropriate to individual lessons? Are they sequenced appropriately?

*Pupils should be able to:*
carry out a simple census to find facts from a small, well defined population; draw a random sample from a small population;
sample from distributions such as those given by throwing dice;
generate random numbers and use random number tables;
obtain their own data by counting and measuring and use other sources of such data;
draw up their own frequency tables by tallying and read them;
draw and read bar charts for discrete data and for continuous data with equal class intervals;
read pictograms;
draw simple pie charts;
read time series;
find the mode, median, mean and range of a small set of discrete data;
assign probabilities in the equally likely case;
assign probabilities to the random selection of one item from a finite population;
use finite relative frequencies to estimate future probabilities;

find the probabilities of simple combinations of elementary events by addition; draw simple inferences from bar charts and tables.

One of the most detailed examinations of how to prepare instructional objectives has been carried out by Mager (1975), and it provides a very helpful guide for teachers who wish to think carefully about objectives. Issues such as the refinement of objectives through the use of (a) additional conditions, (b) criteria of acceptable performance, (c) sample test items and (d) the avoidance of pitfalls are all considered in detail. For example, a simple objective might be: 'The pupils will be able to multiply together two 3-digit numbers'. The following could then form an additional condition: 'Without the use of a calculator'. An objective which also involves a criterion of acceptable performance might be: 'With the aid of a calculator, the pupils will be able to divide 1-, 2- and 3-digit numbers by 1-, 2- and 3-digit numbers and express their answers to three significant figures with a 90 per cent success rate'. Sample test items are usually obvious, for example: 'The pupil will be able to solve linear equations in one unknown, e.g. solve for x in the following: (a) $3 + 5x = 15$, (b) $3x - 2 = 8$'.

Since objectives are now generally included with the syllabuses and specifications for external examinations, an interesting exercise for mathematics teachers is to look critically at the objectives associated with familiar external examinations and to assess their value in the teaching–learning–assessment cycle.

## Programmed learning

One of the ways in which behaviourist-type approaches to instruction have influenced teaching methods has been in commending the programming of learning. Some people take the view that enthusiasm for programmed learning waxed for a time in the past and has now most emphatically waned, and one would certainly not find much obvious evidence of it in today's schools. There was, however, considerable interest in it around the 1960s, and it would be wrong to write it off as one of the bandwagons of the day because the advantages sought through the programming of learning material demand consideration. Programmed learning in schools in the 1960s was based on books or booklets, or perhaps on cheap, hand-cranked, teaching machines. Ideally, programmed learning needs to be machine-orientated, but although purpose-built teaching machines did exist at that time they did not reach the schools. Nowadays we have computers, so teaching programmes may be presented on screen and pupils may respond via a keyboard or mouse. The remaining problem is still a major one, however, and that is writing the computer software to present the material.

It must be pointed out, before moving on, that computers are being used in schools nowadays in many ways, not only in the 'old-fashioned' sense of programmed learning. Computer-assisted learning is itself a huge field of study, and there are many modes possible of which the programming of educational material is only one. The computer may be used, for example, as a magic blackboard, to provide simulation exercises, to allow exploration and discovery and to provide a database for investigation and deduction, to name just a few possibilities. In the context of this chapter, however, the computer will only be considered in its role in programmed learning.

The section of programmed learning material in Box 3A is from a textbook by

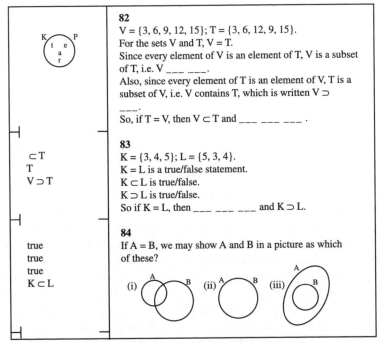

**82**

$V = \{3, 6, 9, 12, 15\}; T = \{3, 6, 12, 9, 15\}$.

For the sets V and T, V = T.

Since every element of V is an element of T, V is a subset of T, i.e. V ___ ___.

Also, since every element of T is an element of V, T is a subset of V, i.e. V contains T, which is written V ⊃ ___.

So, if T = V, then V ⊂ T and ___ ___ ___ .

**83**

$K = \{3, 4, 5\}; L = \{5, 3, 4\}$.

K = L is a true/false statement.

K ⊂ L is true/false.

K ⊃ L is true/false.

So if K = L, then ___ ___ ___ and K ⊃ L.

**84**

If A = B, we may show A and B in a picture as which of these?

(on the left margin answers):

⊂T
T
V ⊃ T

true
true
true
K ⊂ L

**Box 3A** Reproduced with permission (Young, 1966).

Young (1966, p. 41), and it clearly illustrates some of the problems inherent in the construction of such books. Where should pupils ideally write their responses to questions? Where should the correct answers ideally be revealed to the pupils? How can cheating be prevented? How is the interest of the pupil to be maintained? How can the programme cater for different abilities? What is the role of the teacher? And, beyond such practical problems, how valid is the theory which supports the programming of material in a form like this?

There seems to have been considerable optimism, in the 1960s, that the programming of educational material had an enormous amount to offer to school teachers. Lysaught and Williams (1963, p. 1) began their excellent book on programmed instruction as follows:

In the Blue Ridge mountain city of Roanoke, Virginia, pupils in the eighth grade of the local schools in a single term all completed a full year of algebra, normally reserved for the first year of high school in other parts of the country, and only one child in the entire Roanoke school system failed to perform satisfactorily on a standardized examination. At Hamilton College, Clinton, New York, nobody fails the logic course any more; moreover, the average of grades has risen markedly. At the Collegiate School, New York City, a private elementary and secondary institution for boys that long has maintained high scholastic standards, students are now progressing more rapidly in modern mathematics than ever before. These diverse achievements are neither accidents nor as unrelated as a casual reading might suggest. Through them runs a common element. In each instance, classroom teachers have been utilizing the techniques of programmed learning, a method of pedagogy that increases the learning rate and proficiency of pupils and students.

The most famous name in the programmed learning movement in the United States, where it has been practised with perhaps more conviction than anywhere else, was probably that of the behaviourist psychologist B. F. Skinner. Nowhere is the connection between conditioning and programmed learning clearer than in his claims. Skinner's beliefs were confirmed for him through his enormous success in training animals using methods of conditioning, and many criticisms have been levelled at the theory for this reason. Why should we believe that, because rats and pigeons can be conditioned to perform intricate movements in order to receive food, we can and should educate humans in a behaviouristic way? Yet Skinner believed that the possibilities for human learning were enormous. As we have seen earlier, an important element of Skinner's theory was the practice of reinforcement, and the belief that, through reinforcement, the behaviour of humans could be shaped as desired.

Reinforcement has always been an important part of formal teaching. Early in the twentieth century reinforcement was largely based on fear – of incurring the wrath of the teacher, of punishment, or of ridicule. Even today some aspects of the behaviour of children in school are based on their desire to avoid unpleasant consequences, and not on any desire to learn. Skinner was concerned that children were not learning in any positive sense, but that they were learning only to avoid the consequences of not learning. Dienes (1960) has also pointed out that learning motivated by gold stars, house points, merit marks or even to gain a high position in the class is not good education. Praise and encouragement from the teacher can, however, be a very good form of reinforcement, though it is inevitably spread very thinly across the class of pupils, so that any one pupil is unlikely to receive such reinforcement more than once in a lesson. Given the realities of life in today's schools it may be unrealistic to expect that all punishment intended as reinforcement, and all extrinsic rewards used as encouragement, will eventually be phased out. But Skinner's ideal, that all individual pupils will receive constant and rapid feedback of results and will, as a result, need no further form of reinforcement is not one that we can dismiss lightly.

Teachers would be likely to agree that reinforcement, through efficient feedback of results to pupils, is important. Skinner's view would be that even this might not be enough if feedback were delayed, that even a short period of time between response and reinforcement could destroy all positive effects. Normally, in our schools, it takes many hours, sometimes days, before pupils receive feedback for written work like homework. This view of the importance of instant feedback is not necessarily accepted today as a universal rule, and a contrary view is that the quality and nature of the feedback matter more (see Hartley, 1980, for an introduction to this), but the belief in the immediacy of reinforcement was a part of Skinner's justification for programmed learning and teaching machines.

Skinner was also critical of the unskilled way in which pupils were introduced to new knowledge, and, in particular, the way in which they were expected to cope with sequences of material that were aimed at presenting groups or classes with chunks of material. Each pupil ideally needs to proceed through a programme of work which is individually tailored to meet his or her needs. For Skinner, the theory was that each pupil requires every step forward to be small enough for that individual to accept readily. A possible counter-theory is that some pupils, at some times, may learn best through being plunged into a problem situation which is some way removed from their current state of knowledge and understanding. Learning then takes place through finding ways of relating the new situation to the current state of knowledge and understanding. Many teachers will feel that Skinner's theory is the safer one to accept, at least for many of the children they teach, and for much of the time. It is, of course, impossible to say which is correct, as each might apply in different circumstances, or with different pupils, but these represent contrasting views which teachers have to acknowledge. Skinner's opinions about step-size were critical to his approach to programmed learning.

It is interesting to record, in passing, that another of the conclusions that Skinner drew from his critical consideration of school learning had little to do with the programming of learning and was more akin to cognitive approaches to learning. Skinner noted that children gain reinforcement through practical approaches to learning, through interaction with their environment, and through manipulating real objects. Some teachers would feel that rigid programmed learning is at the opposite end of a spectrum of learning styles from the active approach. Yet Biggs (1972) included programmed discovery as one of five different kinds of discovery in her commendation of discovery learning. Perhaps programmed learning and active participation in learning are not irreconcilable. Skinner believed that the application of programmed learning via suitable teaching machines did provide an active approach in which the pupil had to be at least moderately creative in composing a response, as opposed to selecting a response from alternatives.

According to Bigge (1976), programmed instruction as advocated by Skinner requires the subject matter to be broken down into small, discrete steps and carefully organized into a logical sequence. Each new step builds on the preceding one:

> The learner can progress through the sequence of steps at his own rate and he (she) is reinforced immediately after each step. Reinforcement consists of his either being given the correct response immediately after registering his response or his being permitted to proceed to the next step only after he has registered the correct response. (Bigge, p. 133)

The example in Box 3B is taken from Lysaught and Williams (1963, p. 108).

In general, both appropriately small step-size and appropriate reinforcement are difficult to achieve for all pupils as individuals without the use of teaching machines. Skinner explained this as follows:

> As a mere reinforcing mechanism, a teacher is out-of-date – and would be even if he (she) devoted all his time to a single child. Only through mechanical devices can the necessarily large number of contingencies be provided. (Bigge, pp. 136–7)

Such devices (electronic not mechanical) now exist in large numbers as computers. Teaching machines did exist in the 1960s but were not particularly versatile or adaptable and, although used in the armed services, did not have any real impact on our schools, presumably for reasons of cost. The hand-cranked 'machine' which schools had to be content with only survived an initial novelty interest in the 1960s. However, the principles governing the presentation of material in programmed learning are the same whatever the means of presentation, whether by machine or by textbook.

Programmed learning involves the presentation of a sequence of stimuli to a pupil in the form of 'frames'. A single frame should contain any necessary information and

S. *Quad* means four. *Lateral* refers to side. A *quadrilateral* always has four sides. A square would be one type of quadrilateral. The figures below are all _____ because they have four sides.

R. quadrilaterals

---

S. A rectangle [                    ] is a quadrilateral because it always has _____ sides.

R. four

---

S. A rectangle is one type of _____ because it has _____ sides.

R. quadrilateral
four

---

S. A square is a type of _____ because it has _____ sides.

R. quadrilateral
four

---

S. All figures that have four sides are known as _____ .

R. quadrilaterals

**Box 3B**   Reproduced with permission (Lysaught and Williams, 1963).

then demand interaction, perhaps as a response to a question. The programming device used must provide a means for the pupil to respond. A textbook, worksheet, hand-cranked 'machine' and some mechanical machines would very likely demand this response to be written on paper, on the page of a book, or perhaps on a roll of paper passing through a machine. A computer naturally demands a response via the keyboard or mouse. An example of a single frame is given in Figure 3.2.

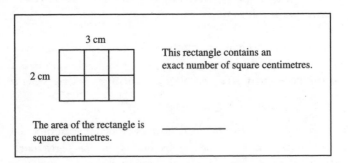

**Figure 3.2**

Having responded, the pupil moves to the next frame, at the same time receiving feedback about their response to the previous frame. The most elementary form of programmed sequence is a linear one, in which no deviation from a predetermined sequence of frames is possible. This is clearly not always satisfactory, as there is no concession to the different needs of the pupils, and it does not accord with Skinner's ideal. With more versatile equipment, variations on a linear theme can be introduced (see Lysaught and Williams, 1963), ultimately leading to the idea of branching and looping within a programme. In computers, there is no limit to the complexity of branching which may be used, save that imposed by the time required to prepare the software. Not surprisingly, attempts to implement branching programmes in textbook form have not been all that successful.

The mode of computer-assisted learning based on programmed learning is often referred to as 'instructional'. Because free responses are difficult to cope with it is common to find that pupil interaction is via multiple-choice or 'yes/no' or 'true/false' choices. As we have seen, this is not really what Skinner intended. Whatever the complexity, enormous flexibility is theoretically possible, and the computer can act as a teacher-substitute on a one-to-one basis. Thus, pupils do not have to expose their errors and learning difficulties to anyone. Another advantage for teachers is that pupils will not see a correct answer before making a response, which is something that cannot be guaranteed when using programmed learning texts.

Research into the value of instructional computer-assisted learning has raised questions about the assumptions behind the place of feedback. Simple knowledge of results may not be enough. What may be much more important is the location of errors and the provision of information to the pupil which allows such errors to be corrected. It may therefore be important not that the step-size is so small that errors are avoided, but that the stimuli set out to bring misconceptions to light as a first step towards correcting them. Furthermore, feedback can be passive, merely informative, or it can be active in that it requires the participation of the learner. A common form of feedback is when the computer will not proceed until the correct key is pressed, but this has to be terminated sometime and, if concluded by an instruction or message after which the next frame is presented, again the student can choose not to read it. Active feedback is in the form of further questions which demand further responses. The further questions are intended to be those the student should be asking (see also problem-posing in Chapter 5). One interesting study (Tait *et al.*, 1973) suggested that less able pupils particularly benefited from active feedback. For more able children it did not appear to matter as much.

To sum up, advantages claimed for programmed learning include the following:

- learning is individualized;
- pupils are responsible for their own learning;
- pupils work at their own rate;
- interaction between learners and material is constant;
- pupils only have to cope with one stimulus at a time;
- learning material is correctly sequenced;
- learning material is correctly paced;
- each idea must be mastered in order to progress;
- pupils receive instant feedback;
- pupils are motivated to learn;
- there is little problem of pupil anxiety;
- a range of pupil abilities may be accommodated.

Such an impressive list should suggest to any experienced educator that there must be corresponding disadvantages. These include:

- motivation generated by working with other pupils is missing;
- inspiration generated by ideas from other pupils is missing;
- pupil might choose to work too slowly;
- pupil might unwittingly choose inappropriate routes through the programme;
- material might not be sufficiently challenging;
- material might hold some pupils back unnecessarily;
- learning programmes are extremely time-consuming to prepare;
- some kinds of learning experiences cannot be presented in programmed form;
- there might be too much dependence on the honesty of the pupil;
- material might lack essential interest and might not motivate;
- learning might be promoted better when there is some anxiety in the pupil;
- it might not be possible to accommodate the full range of pupil abilities.

As part of a curriculum, programmed learning has strong claims for a place. Some obvious uses are for individuals with special needs (for example, enrichment for rapid workers, revision and repetition for slower workers and for new pupils), for pupils who have missed work through illness, or as a revision course. Now that we have computers in our classrooms we need to carry out a continual appraisal of the place of instructional programs in our teaching of mathematics. This, however, will not be the only way in which we will wish to make use of the particular advantages of the computer in the mathematics classroom.

## Learning hierarchies

Let us imagine that we wish to teach the multiplication of fractions to a class (why we should wish to do that is not our concern at the moment). Having defined our objective in behavioural form, for example: 'the pupils will be able to find the product of any two rational numbers', we then have to determine what is our starting point for the sequence of instruction. What are we assuming that the pupils already know? In our list we might be tempted to include all aspects of work with fractions which traditionally come before multiplication. Our list might, therefore, look something like this:

1. Products of natural numbers
2. Knowledge that 'of' and '×' are equivalent
3. Definition of a fraction
4. Equivalence of fractions
5. Lowest common denominator
6. How to change a mixed number into an improper fraction and vice versa
7. Comparative size of two fractions
8. Sums and differences of fractions.

Our list of prerequisite skills and knowledge, however, is intended to enable us to check that the pupils' understanding is adequate, and to revise material where necessary. We do not want to be side-tracked into revising what is not essential in order for pupils to attain the objective, so the above list may contain irrelevant items. For example, do we really need to revise sums and differences of fractions? Also, can we take it for granted that some items in the list are so elementary (for example, products of natural numbers) that they do not need to be revised? Only when we have clarified both our objectives and our starting point can we begin to work out a sequence of instruction, which we might decide is as follows:

1. Finding a proper fraction of a whole number
2. Finding an improper fraction of a whole number
3. Finding a proper fraction of a proper fraction
4. Finding a proper fraction of an improper fraction
5. Finding an improper fraction of a proper fraction
6. Finding an improper fraction of an improper fraction.

But is this the correct teaching sequence? Are there alternative teaching sequences? Should 3 come before 2, for example? Which comes first, 4 or 5? How do we decide on the correct teaching sequence?

More than likely, teachers will make certain decisions as to the order of instruction according to intuition and preference. They may teach one order at one time and a rather different order at another time. But decisions of this sort do have to be made, and all of this comes before decisions are made concerning the detail of how the instruction is to be carried out. Indeed, all of the steps along the road to the attainment of the ultimate objective may be regarded as prerequisite knowledge, each step requiring a clear statement of the objective. We could then hypothesize the existence of a sort of pyramid of stages, with the ultimate objective at the top, such as in Figure 3.3. A hierarchy of this kind is often very important for a teacher of mathematics to have in mind. If the teacher does not correctly identify the base line

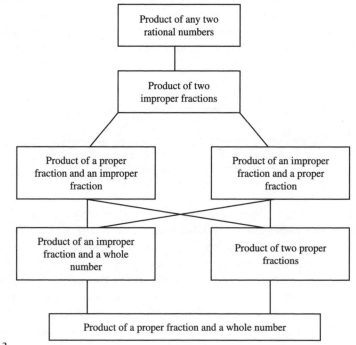

Figure 3.3

of the pyramid then some pupils will be lost right from the start. If the teacher does not identify all of the stages in the pyramid, and omits some, pupils could become confused somewhere in the middle of the hierarchy. If the teacher does not break down the steps into ones that are small enough for the pupils to cope with, many pupils will be unable to keep pace. Additionally, the teacher needs to check whether the objectives for each stage in the hierarchy have been attained before moving on to the next stage.

The theory of learning proposed by Robert Gagné is a more sophisticated and tightly controlled elaboration of this model. Gagné suggested that children learn an ordered, additive, sequence of capabilities, with each new capability being more complex or more advanced than the prerequisite capabilities on which it is built. We have considered one such analysis, concerned with multiplying fractions. At a higher level one might hypothesize that in order to be able to solve quadratic equations by factors, necessary prerequisites would include being able to solve linear equations, being able to find squares and square roots, and being able to factorize. At a lower level still there would be many more prerequisites concerned with ideas such as equality, products and quotients, sums and differences. A teacher preparing to teach how to solve quadratic equations might decide to revise some of the more advanced prerequisites but would probably take for granted that the children would be able to cope with the more elementary ones. These common sense considerations suggest two other features of Gagné's theory, first that there is a variety of different kinds of prerequisite, some more advanced than others, and second that the more elementary prerequisites can be ignored in devising a learning hierarchy.

A learning hierarchy, according to Gagné, is therefore built from the top down. We begin by defining the capability which is the ultimate objective at the apex of the pyramid. This must be defined in terms of behavioural objectives, for example: 'pupils will be able to convert rational numbers in fractional form into decimals'; or: 'pupils will be able to find the sum of any pair of directed numbers'. The next stage is to carry out a detailed task analysis by considering what prerequisite capabilities are required in order to be able to attain the ultimate capability (Figure 3.4). Then, it is necessary

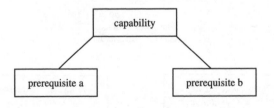

**Figure 3.4**

to repeat the procedure, by defining what prerequisites are required in order to attain the more elementary prerequisites (labelled a and b, see Figure 3.5).

Much of the research carried out by Gagné and his colleagues has been concerned with whether the hypothesized prerequisites were necessary and sufficient. If pupils possess prerequisites a and b can they always be taught the ultimate capability? Can pupils who do not possess either a or b or both be taught this final capability? If pupils possess the final capability, is it always found that they possess both a and b? To carry this out at all levels of a hierarchy is very time-consuming, but Gagné's research has produced many such fully-tested hierarchies (see Gagné, 1985). As one might expect

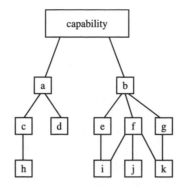

**Figure 3.5**

in education, however, results do not always correspond perfectly with theory. For example, one is likely to find that there are pupils who do possess the final capability but do not possess both a and b. One might also find occasions when pupils can attain a or b without specific teaching in the process of receiving instruction on the final capability. One is therefore forced into the conclusion, as defined by Gagné (1985, p. 128), that:

> a learning hierarchy . . . describes an *on-the-average* efficient route to the attainment of an organized set of intellectual skills that represents 'understanding' of a topic.

Another problem is that there seems little likelihood that tested learning hierarchies can be defined for all topics which might at some time be taught in mathematics. There is even less likelihood that busy teachers can involve themselves in devising and testing hierarchies. But as a general idea, used in a more loosely-defined manner, there must be some relevance to the idea of learning hierarchies in formal instructional situations.

It is important, in a consideration of Gagné's views, to realize that his theory incorporates a view of 'readiness for learning' to which not all teachers would subscribe. Quite simply: 'developmental readiness for learning any new intellectual skill is conceived as the presence of certain relevant subordinate intellectual skills' (Gagné, 1985, p. 130). Let us consider a typical conservation task (conservation tasks are described in more detail in Chapter 4) with liquids poured from one shape of container into another, pictured in Figure 3.6. A child is ready to learn any particular capability, in this case conservation of liquid, if all the prerequisite capabilities have

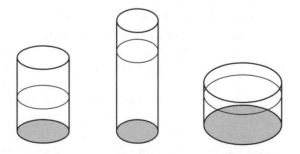

**Figure 3.6**

been mastered, and readiness depends on that alone. It is interesting to compare this view of readiness with that of Piaget. Piaget's view is that being able to perform such conservation tasks correctly depends on the stage of cognitive or intellectual development of the child, which is in itself defined by the fact that certain general logical processes have developed in the mind.

Gagné's theory of learning also incorporates views on the transfer of learning. The intellectual capabilities of a child do not remain specific; for example if, based on appropriate learning hierarchies, learning of conservation has taken place with both rectangular containers and with cylindrical containers, then the skills common to both situations will promote the generalizing of skills into other specific situations. Once a wide range of specific skills has been learned, for example in conservation, all other conservation situations will be that much easier to master. It then becomes possible to classify children as, in this case, 'conservers'.

The learning hierarchies of Gagné suggest that different prerequisites may be of different qualities, that there is, in fact, a hierarchy of *types* of learning. Let us consider Pythagoras' theorem, i.e. the sum of the squares of the lengths of the two shorter sides in a right-angled triangle is equal to the square of the hypotenuse (illustrated in Figure 3.7). The statement $a^2 = b^2 + c^2$ is clearly a rule of some kind (which applies

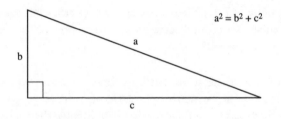

$$a^2 = b^2 + c^2$$

**Figure 3.7**

only to triangles when they are right-angled). A rule is a statement of a relationship between qualities. The relationship and the qualities both involve conceptual learning, for example, squaring, area, equality, summation, triangle, right-angle, length, side, angle. The concepts themselves involve discrimination, between lengths and areas for example, or between squaring and doubling, and they also involve classification, what it is that is common to all triangles, for example. At quite a low level squaring involves products, and the most efficient way to find products is to know the multiplication tables. The learning of multiplication tables is likely to involve some elements of stimulus-response learning whatever one's beliefs about how tables should be learned.

It is therefore possible to draw up a linear hierarchy of types of learning which might apply to mathematics. The well known list by Gagné is summarized in Figure 3.8. There are many examples one can give for each of these types as they relate to mathematics. At the lowest level much of the early number work might involve predominantly stimulus-response learning, for example, learning number names and symbols and their ordering, knowledge of number bonds and of products, multiples and factors. Gagné has suggested also that learning to use mathematical instruments and equipment falls into this category. The association of names with ideas, objects or processes may also be learned in much the same way, for example, 'octagon' (eight sides, octopus), 'triangle' (three angles, tricycle). 'Cube' may be learned from the

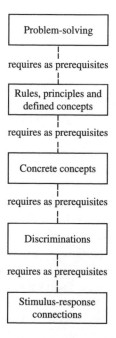

**Figure 3.8**

common domestic items, sugar cubes and stock cubes. 'Kite' may be learned through association with kites which fly. Ideas for which word and other associations do not exist (for example, 'rhombus') are much more difficult to learn.

The ability to discriminate is as important in mathematics as in any other subject. From the very early stages of being able to discriminate between numbers of beads, counters or other objects held in the hand – is it five or is it six? – to discriminating between Dx, dx and δx, mathematics is full of subtle differences and similar symbolisms. The symbols for the four basic rules, +, −, × and ÷ possess remarkable similarities, so that if a teacher is careless in writing them the child can have great difficulty in discriminating. When children learn about angles they have to be able to associate the correct term – acute, right, obtuse or reflex – with the correct picture or magnitude. Many children struggle to come to terms with the difference between $2x$ and $x^2$, though there may be conceptual difficulties here as well as purely discriminatory problems. Properties of objects, such as the cube, need to be discriminated – edge, face, vertex, surface, area, volume, length, mass, weight. At a higher level still, such similar arrangements of letters and numbers as $3x^2$, $\Sigma x^2$ and $5C_2$ need to be mastered and discriminated.

Mathematics is said to be very conceptually based, yet it is sometimes difficult to define exactly what we mean by a concept (see Chapter 2). There are hierarchies of mathematical concepts, some being of a 'higher order' than others (Skemp, 1971). One might claim, for example, that multiplication is a higher order concept than addition because multiplication, as repeated addition, depends on addition and cannot be learned before addition. In a different sense, number may be regarded as a higher order concept than natural number. It is necessary to learn what we mean by natural numbers, zero, fractions and decimals, negative numbers, integers, rational numbers, irrational numbers and real numbers in order to allow a mature concept of what we mean by 'number' to develop. Of course, young children will use the word 'number' when they mean, in the mathematician's terms, 'natural number', these being the only sort of numbers they have encountered. Their concept of number is a limited one.

There is probably an element of conceptual understanding in nearly all that we introduce in mathematics, from the beginnings of number work like multiplication tables and from elementary spatial work like identifying triangles and rectangles, through more complex ideas like sine and cosine to advanced procedures like differentiation and integration. The idea that readiness depends only on mastery of prerequisite concepts is not one which finds automatic favour with many teachers of mathematics. The concept of place value is very difficult for some children and yet comes so early in the logical hierarchy of mathematical concepts that it is difficult to accept that the problem only arises because concepts taught earlier have not been mastered. Learning to cope with place value is a long, slow process for many pupils. At a higher level, the concept of ratio appears to depend on so little in the way of obvious prerequisites, and yet ratio and proportion are not adequately mastered by many pupils by the time they leave school.

Principles are basically rules or laws. Gagné included 'defined concepts' within this category, that is, concepts which cannot be learned directly from concrete situations but require a definition. One example used by Gagné is 'diagonal'. He appeared to claim that it is necessary to state a definition, namely that a diagonal is a straight line which connects non-adjacent vertices of a polygon or polyhedron. Yet it is not always clear whether a concept is 'concrete' or 'defined'. Fractions (rational numbers) can be defined as ratios of integers; they can also be defined as parts of wholes (then mixed numbers are problematic); or they can be defined as operators (see Gattegno, 1960). Few people would claim to have learned what fractions were from such a definition. The same is true with the concept of 'diagonal' – it is likely to be learned best from concrete considerations. The definition is a summary which comes later after many examples have been encountered. Principles may cause some of us less of a problem, particularly scientific principles like the gas law $P = RT/V$. Here adults can clearly see that there is an association of concepts, though when children learn what the law really means it normally involves much more than being told about the relationship. It involves experimentation and measurement in order to observe that the relationship holds. It may be possible for more mature learners to accept principles without experimentation, but many teachers believe that children benefit from a concrete approach.

One might consider that one principle of mathematics is that 'equations remain valid if you do the same thing to both sides'. As a working rule for a particular stage of children's education this is very useful. It may present difficulties later (see Skemp, 1971), but many teachers use it with pupils around eleven or twelve years old. But again, it is doubtful that children would accept this rule as a statement without being able to construct it from concrete examples of what it means with familiar concepts like numbers. In terms of Gagné's analysis, it seems that we must classify Pythagoras' theorem as a principle or rule. But no teacher would introduce the rule without investigation, using numbers, squares of numbers and areas. The commutative law of multiplication is only defined as a rule once it has been found to hold in many numerical situations and one can generalize from it. So although principles (rules, defined concepts) might nominally be regarded as of a higher level of learning than concrete concepts this says nothing about the way principles might be learned.

Most people would agree that problem-solving can legitimately be regarded as the ultimate in terms of types of learning. It requires what we call 'thinking', and is dependent on a large store of knowledge and capabilities. One has first, however, to satisfy oneself that it is a form of learning. By problem we mean a question which requires some originality on the part of the learner for its solution, that is, it requires the learner to put elements of prior learning together in a new way. Having solved such a problem, something has been learned (see Chapters 2 and 5).

Gagné's contribution to the study of how learning takes place and how it can be organized is a substantial one. In its entirety it may have recruited few disciples in Britain, but it is worthy of study. Elements of it will turn out to be part of the approach of many teachers to lesson planning and presentation. In particular, the careful sequencing of material to be learned is likely to enhance the quality and quantity of learning. This sequencing, however, is not likely to be all that is required in the planning of learning experiences. Davis (1984, p. 21) suggested some of the major dissatisfactions with behaviourist approaches to learning in: 'learning mathematics by . . . routine is dull and unmotivating; learning it creatively is exciting and interesting (at least for many people)', and 'mathematics is too complex and too vast to learn by rote'. Skinner, however, maintained that behaviourism had been much maligned by educationists, and that many of the standard criticisms were unfounded (Skinner, 1974, p. 5): 'the contentions represent . . . an extraordinary misunderstanding of the achievements and significance of a scientific enterprise'. The alternatives to behaviourism, in terms of theoretical bases for planning education, are developed in subsequent chapters.

## Suggestions for further reading

Gagné, R. M. (1985) *The Conditions of Learning*, 4th edn. New York: Holt, Rinehart and Winston.

Hartley, J. R. (1980) *Using the Computer to Study and Assist the Learning of Mathematics*. Leeds: University of Leeds Computer Based Learning Unit.

Mager, R. F. (1975) *Preparing Instructional Objectives*. Belmont, CA: Fearon.

Skinner, B. F. (1961) 'Teaching machines', *Scientific American*, 205, 90–102.

## Questions for discussion

1. What is the place of stimulus-response and rote learning in a mathematical education today?
2. Assess the learning objectives for a mathematics course which you teach in terms of comprehensiveness, specificity, lack of ambiguity and overall value.
3. Define the learning objectives for a unit of mathematics and prepare a draft learning hierarchy to guide teaching.
4. What is the value of instructional computer-assisted learning programmes in mathematics teaching today?

Chapter 4

# Must We Wait Until Pupils Are Ready?

## Alternative views

Once children have learned the meaning of addition and subtraction of natural numbers and are sufficiently skilled in carrying out the two operations, the thoughts of the teacher naturally turn to multiplication. Is there any reason why we should not press on immediately with multiplication? Are the pupils ready? Later still, having learned about natural numbers and mastered all the standard operations on them is there any reason why we should not introduce our pupils to negative numbers and zero, and begin work on operations on integers? Is there any more to readiness for new mathematical ideas than adequate mastery of the mathematics which underlies the new ideas upon which they must be built?

The view that readiness for learning is simply 'the presence of certain relevant subordinate intellectual skills' (Gagné, 1985) was considered in Chapter 3 as being one interpretation of an aspect of behaviourist approaches to education. There are, however, alternative views around. Such alternative views have to be considered seriously when one acknowledges the learning difficulties experienced by pupils. If, for example, we treat fractions as an extension of the idea of number, as rational numbers in fact, it might be thought that pupils are ready for fractions once natural numbers have been adequately mastered. Yet many pupils struggle with operations on fractions for the whole of their school life, from the moment the ideas and techniques are introduced. Could such pupils really have been ready when we tried to teach them about operations on fractions? If we take an alternative view of the place of fractions in the curriculum, and regard them as part of a study of ratio and proportion, and acknowledge the difficulties inherent in a study of ratio and proportion, as illustrated in Chapter 1, it should not surprise us that doubts are raised about introducing operations on fractions as early as we often do. But what makes pupils ready for a study of ratio and proportion? Do many pupils struggle with ratio and proportion solely because we have failed to identify and teach all of the relevant subordinate intellectual skills? And how do we know when students are ready for the concept of real numbers (see Orton, 2001)?

The obvious major alternatives to behaviourist views of readiness are developmental views. Simplistically, developmental approaches are likely to state that a pupil is only ready when the quality of thinking and processing skills possessed by the learner matches the demands of the subject matter. Furthermore, such thinking and processing skills are heavily dependent for their development on maturation, but may also depend on environmental factors such as quality of schooling, home background, society and general cultural milieu. It is interaction between the maturing child and all aspects of the environment which makes the required development possible. Developmental views achieved prominence through the publication of the work of Jean Piaget and his colleagues at Geneva, and these views have become both better understood and modified with the passage of time. Many seeds of mathematical knowledge sown in our classrooms on the assumption that the earth is ready for cultivation appear instead to fall on stony ground. Developmental views attempt to explain this phenomenon, and the best place to begin to consider them is with a study of what is relevant from the work of Piaget. It needs to be stressed at the outset, however, that although Piagetian theory may be interpreted as containing views on readiness, many would say that the readiness issue is not the most important aspect of the theory.

## Piaget and readiness

Piaget's theory of intellectual development was based on results from experiments with children using the clinical or individual interviewing method described in Chapter 1. These experiments were carried out over a long period of time, commencing some 70 or more years ago, and were very numerous and varied in both nature and content. Many of the experiments investigated the understanding of mathematical content and concepts. Piaget himself came from a background in the biological sciences, and his view of learners as growing and ever-changing organisms is the underlying basis for his developmental approach to learning theory. It should be pointed out that Piaget never claimed to be a learning theorist as such, but the extent to which his theory has been applied to education suggests that it is not inappropriate for others to view his work as providing theoretical bases for learning. Piaget's experimental work was so extensive that it is possible only to select a very small part to illustrate both the emergence of the theory and the importance for learning mathematics. A suitable part is a selection of experiments concerning conservation.

One conservation experiment was based on containers of beads. Two equal quantities of identical beads were counted out into two identical containers, thus reaching the same level in both containers which were intended to be seen by children as totally equivalent. The beads from one of these two containers were then tipped into containers of a very different shape, firstly into a container which was both wide and shallow, and secondly into a container which was both tall and narrow (see Figure 4.1). At each stage of rest the child was asked whether there were the same number of beads in the two containers currently holding the beads. Piaget, and others who have repeated the experiment subsequently, noted that many children gave responses which, to an adult, would be considered strange, unexpected and incorrect. The younger children tended to express the view that the number of beads changed according to the shape of the container, and that, for example, there were more beads in the tall, narrow container than in the original. What is more, when tipped back

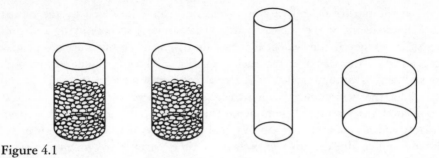

**Figure** 4.1

into the container in which they had first been placed there was once again the same number of beads as in the untouched original container. Testing children at a variety of ages led Piaget to conclude that children's first ideas are likely to be that the number of beads changes, in fact to deny conservation. Eventually, after a period of time which can be confusing to the observer (in that the children sometimes accept conservation and at other times do not), the adult opinion is finally expressed and conservation is consistently admitted.

A different experiment, but another approach to conservation, was to use liquids instead of beads, and one might regard this as the continuous equivalent of the discrete beads. Nowadays, lemonade or orange squash might be used in order to motivate and capture attention, perhaps through promise of a drink later. The questioning procedure, however, has always basically been the same as for the beads. Thus, equal quantities of liquid were poured into two identical containers. Alongside were containers of different shapes, taller and narrower than the original, or wider and shallower (see Figure 4.2). Pouring the liquid into these other containers was likely to

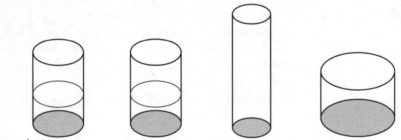

**Figure** 4.2

produce the same responses as for the beads, thus suggesting that the younger children were not accepting conservation. Older children, however, gave responses which were of the kind one would expect an adult to give.

A third version of the conservation experiment was originally based on modelling clay, but modern-day researchers would use plasticine. Starting with two balls, accepted as being equal in every way (mass and shape) one was rolled into a sausage shape under the constant gaze of the child. Having agreed initially that there was the same amount of plasticine in both balls, younger children would be likely to claim that the sausage, or perhaps the ball, now contained more plasticine. Older children would, however, generally give responses which suggest that they accepted conservation.

Piaget's view of results from conservation experiments, and from a very large number of other experiments which revealed a change in children's beliefs about the world at around the same age, was that the structure and nature of intellectual behaviour changed, that the children had moved on to a significantly different stage of intellectual development. In the case of conservation the critical age for this change appeared to Piaget to be around seven years old, though one would naturally expect some variation, perhaps from six to eight years old. The acceptance of conservation was not the only change in intellectual capability at around this age, suggesting that the critical feature was not some specific new understanding, like what happens when plasticine is moulded, but was a wholesale change over a comparatively short period of time into a radically different way of thinking and of seeing the world.

Piaget suggested that there were a number of such radically different stages in intellectual development. Thus, he also used experiments which he claimed revealed a significant change in the nature and quality of thinking at other times in life. A number of experiments appropriate to a change later on involved the ideas of ratio and proportion. One such task was adapted and used subsequently by Hart (1981) and was based on eels whose lengths were in a known ratio and whose appetites were said to be proportional to their lengths. In one version of the experiment the eels were fed with 'discrete' items of food, meatballs for Piaget and sprats for Hart, and the pupil was required to calculate the number needed to feed each eel. Thus, given eels of lengths 5, 10 and 15 cm and given that the 10-cm eel needed four meatballs, the pupils would be asked how many meatballs each of the other eels would need. In another version of the experiment eels were fed with 'continuous' items, biscuits for Piaget and fish fingers for Hart. Given that the 10-cm eel needed a biscuit of length 6 cm the pupils would be asked what length biscuit would be required for the other eels. The pattern of results obtained by Piaget, and its interpretation, has been discussed in detail by Lovell (1971a). From the point of view of the present discussion, Piaget used his results of proportionality experiments and many other experiments of a scientific or mathematical nature, to theorize that the ability to handle proportion was dependent on the pupil progressing to a more advanced stage of intellectual development.

From Piagetian theory we may therefore extract a clear view of readiness. Children are not ready for mathematics which depends on a grasp of conservation if they have not reached the stage of intellectual development at which conservation is accepted as a part of the way the world works. Pupils are likewise not ready for mathematics which depends on understanding ratio and proportion if they have not reached the stage at which the essence of proportionality can be mastered. Well-informed readers might feel that the above outline of aspects of Piagetian theory and the link with the readiness issue has been over-simplified. It is, for example, perhaps unlikely that Piaget would ever have presented the issue as it has been presented above, if only because the interpretation of his work in terms of implications for the mathematics curriculum has always been left to others. The justification for presenting the issue so simplistically is that it is precisely the way others have interpreted the results.

It is now appropriate to mention briefly the stages of intellectual development which Piaget proposed. For convenience four major stages are listed below though, for Piaget, some of these stages incorporated substages, and some stages have subsequently been allocated simple subdivisions by other educationists. In fact, different reviewers of Piaget have even grouped the stages and substages in slightly different ways, so it is possible to find authors referring to Piaget's five stages, or to four stages, or even to three. The four stages included here are:

1. The sensori-motor stage
2. The pre-operational stage
3. The concrete operational stage
4. The formal operational stage.

Piaget himself subdivided the pre-operational stage into preconceptual and intuitive. Early concrete, late concrete, early formal and late formal subdivisions have been used from time to time by others. All children, according to Piaget, pass through these stages and in the defined order, that is, they successively reveal those characteristics of intellectual activity which he spelled out for the stages.

From the point of view of learning mathematics the consequence should be that, if a child is known to be operating at a particular Piagetian level, if it is known at what stage they are functioning, there is no possibility that they will be able to cope with any mathematics which depends on capabilities associated with a subsequent stage. For example, acceptance of conservation is not a characteristic of the child's thinking before the concrete operational stage. Indeed, according to Piaget, a number of thinking skills emerge and develop with the onset of concrete operational thought, including class inclusion, reversibility, combination and separation, arranging in order and relative position, all of which might be very important in moving from an informal and intuitive approach to mathematics, involving little more than the manipulation of objects and materials, to mathematics as a thoughtful paper and pencil activity. A major problem with this interpretation, however, is how do you identify at what stage a particular child is operating? Is it even possible to identify a stage and label a particular child in this way? However, it is interesting to note that the age of seven has traditionally been given particular significance and importance in English education. Without the benefit of Piagetian theory suggesting an important intellectual development at around the age of seven we have seemingly traditionally classed children under seven as infants and children over seven as juniors. What is more, the approach to learning in the past would have likely changed, with infants spending their time learning through playing, and juniors being expected to cope with a more formal approach.

The two separate components of the term 'concrete operations' both require comment. The term 'operation' is common to three of the Piagetian stages listed earlier and, to Piaget, 'operation' possessed a precise meaning. Operations were to be thought of as actions, but carried out in the mind, and the operations were organized into a system. At the concrete operational stage these operations included combining, separating, ordering, and so on, operations which have been described earlier. The term 'concrete' must not be thought of as implying that mathematics teaching always requires concrete apparatus until the full emergence from the concrete operational stage. The concreteness of the operations depends as much on actions carried out in the mind on the basis of prior knowledge of, and familiarity with, relevant underlying concrete manipulations. Thus, in a new learning situation, physical activity with actual objects is likely to be important at the concrete operational stage, but only up to the time when the child is able to replace such actual physical manipulations with corresponding mental activities. Concrete referents are always likely to be important at the concrete operational stage but should not be required all the time. Although there has sometimes been misunderstanding about the relationship between the term 'concrete operational' and the use of concrete apparatus in the classroom, the usual error made in mathematics teaching has not been to overuse apparatus, it has been not to have apparatus as reference material sufficiently often. There are, of course, many people who cannot accept that such stages of intellectual development as described by Piaget have any meaning. However, the need for concrete referents in teaching mathematics to most pupils for much of their school life does appear to exist independently of any acceptance or non-acceptance of Piagetian theory.

In learning mathematics, Piaget's theory would suggest that the ability to cope with abstractions depends on the emergence or development of formal operational thinking. Apart from proportionality, there are many mathematical topics and ideas with which teachers know that many of their pupils will have difficulties because of the level of abstraction required. The whole of algebra as generalized arithmetic is dependent on abstraction from relatively more concrete numerical relationships. It is well known that algebra is found to be difficult by many pupils, and some develop such an intense dislike of it because of this that it colours their whole attitude to mathematics. To these pupils there is no real meaning underlying the use of letters. Perhaps many pupils are not ready in the sense that we, the teachers, are always eager to press on to the next topic and we introduce algebraic ideas too soon and too quickly. Piagetian theory also suggests that it is only at the formal operational stage that one might expect dependence on concrete referents to recede into the background. We know that our most able pupils have little need for concrete apparatus as they move into and through the secondary school though, again, we are always likely to assume that they need the support of concrete ways of thinking less than they perhaps do. Eventually the manipulation of symbols as an abstract exercise does become more comfortable, but only for a proportion of our pupils. It seems that the majority are never ready for most of the algebra we would like to be able to teach. Formal operational thinking, to Piaget, allows hypothesis and deduction, it allows logical argument, it allows reasoning in verbal propositions. It is important to emphasize, however, that for Piaget these more adult intellectual pursuits only become possible with the onset of the formal operational stage, they do not become certain. In other words, adults might also need to function at a more concrete level, and often a practical introduction to a new idea is helpful, like using interlocking cubes to investigate number series.

The implications for learning mathematics are clear. Many mathematical ideas require the kind of thinking skills which Piaget has claimed are not beginning to be available until the onset of the formal operational stage. It does not matter how carefully and systematically the teacher might try to build up a pupil's capabilities and knowledge – it is impossible to introduce concepts dependent on formal operational thought before the pupil has moved into that stage. The pupil is not yet ready for such abstract ideas. Pupils might, of course, be able to grasp the beginnings of an abstract idea in an intuitive or concrete way, but they cannot appreciate the idea as the teacher does. Explanations by the teacher will fail to make any impact unless such explanations are dependent only on skills available to pupils at the concrete operational stage.

Up to the present moment no attempt has been made to state the ages at which children move from one Piagetian stage to another, apart from the references to 'around seven' for the arrival of concrete operational thinking. There are many problems with trying to relate Piaget's stages with ages. Clearly, pupils do not pass suddenly from one stage to the next – there must surely be a period of transition between any two stages. One of the problems with Piagetian theory is that it might appear that children are in transition for much more of their childhood than they can be said to be identifiably operating within a particular stage. Yet the idea of continual transition cannot be reconciled with Piagetian stage theory. Another problem is that it is difficult to identify categorically at which stage a particular pupil is operating at a particular moment in time. It is interesting in this context to speculate on how the Piagetian theory of intellectual growth compares with physical growth, for example in terms of height. Children do go through periods of rapid physical growth and other periods of much slower growth. For example, in the years just before puberty many children appear to grow relatively slowly for a considerable period of time. Then, in adolescence and particularly noticeable in boys, there is often a period of amazingly rapid growth before it slows again as adulthood is approached. It almost seems as if there are stages in physical growth. It must be a possibility that children experience periods of rapid intellectual development and periods of much slower development. This need not, however, imply that such relatively stable stages in intellectual growth are qualitatively different in the way that Piaget has suggested. Nor has there been in the past any clear evidence to suggest that changes in intellectual development from one Piagetian stage to the next are related in any way to periods of rapid physical growth. However, there are physiological changes taking place throughout adolescence within the brain (see Winston, 2003), and further evaluation of these developments could eventually throw more light on changes in learning capabilities.

Since Piaget first outlined his theory that intellectual development takes place in stages, and at the same time related the stages to ages, the literature has been dogged by too optimistic a view of the rate of development in most pupils. Piaget suggested that the development from pre-operational thinking to concrete operational thinking took place around the age of seven, but there must be wide variation from pupil to pupil. Extensive research has suggested that those characteristics which Piaget described for the formal operational stage do not begin to emerge until fourteen or fifteen years of age in many pupils. This is much less optimistic than Piaget's original suggestion of eleven years of age, which seems to accord only with very able pupils, such as those with whom he mostly worked. There are undoubtedly differences between pupils of the same age and categorical statements about the age when pupils move from one stage to the next are not helpful. Cockcroft (1982) drew attention to this feature when he suggested a seven-year difference for a particular place value skill (referred to in Chapter 1). The only description of intellectual development which would make sense to most teachers is one that takes this seven-year difference phenomenon into account. Figure 4.3 illustrates the likely relationship between Piagetian stages and ages seen through the eyes of a mathematics teacher, though this diagram must not be taken as prescriptive. Omitting any reference to Piaget's stages, and using the sloping lines merely as markers, the diagram would probably not cause offence to those who are unhappy about stages.

It is necessary to comment on a number of features of this diagram. First, the discrepancy between the most able and least able widens with increase in age. That is, the difference in intellectual capability between the most able and the least able in a particular year group is considerable and growing, particularly in the upper junior and

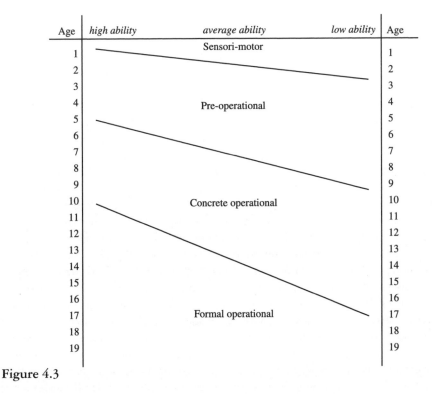

| Age | high ability | average ability | low ability | Age |

**Figure 4.3**

secondary schools. In comparison, the growth in intellectual capability from one year to the next for any individual child is relatively small. Secondly, at the extremes of the ability range it is difficult to know what to do with the sloping subdivision lines. A few children, including those with severe brain damage, make very little progress intellectually and do not fit into the implications of the scheme shown in Figure 4.3. Likewise, at the other extreme, a very few children seem capable of such rapid intellectual development that it is doubtful that the diagram accommodates them too. Thirdly, a considerable proportion of sixteen-year-old school-leavers have not reached the formal operational stage. Whether they ever do is not known since very little cognitive-development research evidence exists concerning such individuals. Taking into account the importance of motivation and intellectual activity in learning it seems very likely that some of the population might never develop those abilities outlined by Piaget as being characteristic of formal operational thinking. Finally, the diagram, in its simplicity, gives the impression of sudden change from one stage to the next. This, clearly, does not happen.

## Accelerating learning

From the preceding outline of Piagetian stage theory, itself only a part of the totality of Piaget's developmental theory, it might be thought that one implication is that there is little anyone can do to accelerate learning in others. This is not necessarily the case. Piaget's theory is not solely concerned with maturation; it is more fundamentally about action and interaction. Even when engaging in abstract mathematics our thought processes are founded on previous actions. Here there is a hint of the fundamental philosophical distinction between Piaget and the behaviourist tradition. To Piaget, it is not a case of pouring knowledge into an empty vessel (a simplistic interpretation of behaviourism). Knowledge has to be constructed by each and every learner, hence different children must be expected to learn differently from the same learning experience. Interaction with the world outside the individual child carries the implication that an enriched environment might help to accelerate learning but only to the extent that the child can benefit through his or her constructive efforts.

Piaget's background as a biologist ensured that he regarded intellectual development in the same way as any aspect of growth, and in particular as involving self-regulation. When new ideas impinge on existing ideas it can happen that they create conflict. A situation of disequilibrium can therefore emerge, and this must be resolved. As a living being a child must reconcile any disturbance to the stability of his or her mental state. Piaget referred to this phenomenon under the description 'equilibration', and there are many who regard this aspect of Piagetian theory as the most important. Equilibration implies equilibrium in the same sense as in the natural sciences. It implies not a state of rest but a state of balance, a state for which the system is striving. In connection with equilibration Piaget introduced two helpful ideas, namely assimilation and accommodation. Assimilation refers to the taking in, the acceptance or absorption of, new ideas. Accommodation refers to what might be necessary in the way of modification and amendment to previously held ideas in order for assimilation to be possible. These two aspects of equilibration occur together and are generally inseparable. Equilibration, in the form of assimilation and accommodation, is relevant to all learning, but a few mathematical examples are appropriate.

We introduce young children to the idea of number. The children must master ideas of 'oneness', 'twoness', 'threeness', and so on, and must comprehend the implications of the usual counting sequence 'one, two, three . . .'. They must also absorb all relevant terminology and symbolism, must appreciate both cardinal and ordinal aspects, must learn how to apply the four rules, involving the use of place value to organize our recording and manipulation of numbers, and all of this takes a long time. Over many years, children build up a view in their minds of what we mean by number and what a number is. This undoubtedly necessitates continual equilibration. Subsequently we introduce fractions. At the time of introduction there might be no suggestion that fractions are themselves also numbers, but eventually we hope that what is regarded by the child as a number is very much extended and modified from our original implication that 'numbers' $\equiv$ 'natural numbers' (possibly including zero). In assimilating the ideas that fractions are (rational) numbers, that improper fractions are still fractions and are numbers, that integers are numbers, that there are other (irrational) numbers, that the idea of real numbers is a valuable one, at each step the previously held view of what 'number' means requires modification. Assimilation cannot take place without accommodation, and accommodation might not be easy. In a trivial way we can appreciate this because in puzzle situations, when asked to 'give a number between 1 and 10', the almost universal assumption is that the number required is a whole number or natural number. There is a strong tendency to think only of natural numbers when adults are requested to provide 'a number', so perhaps many of us have still not accommodated fully to a more mature view of number.

Another mathematical example involves equations. When equations are introduced they are inevitably linear equations, and techniques for solving linear equations are introduced and practised. The subsequent introduction of quadratic equations might well raise problems of accommodation. What we mean by 'equation' is certainly extended and methods appropriate for solving various kinds of equations need to be assimilated. The accommodation problem might be that techniques appropriate to linear equations no longer work; pupils certainly sometimes try to use them, however, showing that there are residual accommodation difficulties. Once a broader, more general, view of 'equation' is arrived at through the gradual introduction of a variety of different kinds of equation, there might be little problem when any further kinds of equation are introduced. Mastery of a broad view of equations as incorporating linear, simultaneous, quadratic and trigonometric should lead, for those who continue beyond this point, to minds which are open enough to accommodate logarithmic, exponential and differential equations.

At a higher level still, there is a widespread belief that velocity is proportional to force and also that force always acts in the direction of motion. These views arise through construction by the individual on the basis of observation of the world. They are, however, incorrect, and it took mankind many thousands of years to arrive at contemporary agreed views. It should not be a surprise that such beliefs are prevalent, nor that they are very resistant to teaching. It is even possible to find individuals who show mastery of the mathematics (and physics) in the classroom but whose views outside the classroom revert to the popular incorrect notions. This is a situation where accommodation might even require complete eradication of previously held views. It even seems as if the correct laws can be assimilated and yet incorrect laws continue to survive alongside. The individual must arrive at a state of mental equilibrium, even if that means one law for the classroom and another for the real world.

There are issues raised by the concept of equilibration which relate to the acceleration of learning. Is it possible, for example, to accelerate learning by setting out to avoid some occurrences of disequilibrium? Is it wrong to introduce pupils to the concept of a simple balance as a support to solving linear equations on the grounds that the comparison with balancing weights works less well or not at all when we move on to quadratic equations and differential equations? Skemp (1971) has referred to the problems of using inappropriate 'schema' which are not applicable beyond a certain type of mathematical situation. The Nuffield Mathematics Project (1969), in introducing integers, criticized such devices as temperature scales which took children some way into a study of integers but had to be rejected when it came to multiplication and division. Unfortunately, it is not easy to find illustrations which are better than thermometers (in many countries) for introducing integers and balances for introducing equations. When these devices subsequently fail, however, disequilibrium may follow, and a struggle to achieve equilibrium must follow, unless the pupil decides it isn't worth the effort.

There is a contrary view, namely that deliberately placing a child in a state of mental disequilibrium generates the constructive activity required for accommodation, and learning is more permanent than if ideas are presented passively. Evidence from using apparatus as a basis for experiment and discussion in mechanics learning suggests that the presentation of conflict which needs to be resolved can lead to successful learning with motivated students. Given a loop-the-loop toy as an aid to studying motion in a vertical circle (see Figure 4.4) students have been observed to

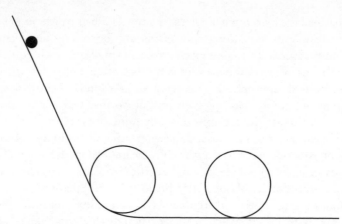

**Figure** 4.4

propose theories based on intuition which were incorrect, but which could be tested and thus found wanting (Williams, 1985). The conflict between incorrect theory and observed results in this situation led the students to new theory and experimentation and eventually to the acceptance of the universally accepted laws. Such learning is likely to be more successful and permanent than any attempt to present the correct law without active involvement. Further examples of incorrect theories which might lead to useful and constructive conflict experimentation are: that the completion of a vertical circle depends on the steepness of the approach track, and that the object needs to be released from a point on the approach track level with the top of the circle in order to complete a circle.

The views of Bruner concerning learning are relevant to a consideration of the acceleration of learning. The following statement from Bruner (1960b, p. 33) is well known: 'We begin with the hypothesis that any subject can be taught effectively in some intellectually honest form to any child at any stage of development'. This certainly appears, on first reading, to be a complete contradiction of any suggestion that particular topics may be assigned an absolute level of difficulty according to Piagetian stages of development. One experiment described by Bruner (1966) involved comparatively young children learning about quadratic expansions, not normally taught until at least age thirteen, by using some of the equipment suggested by Dienes (1960), illustrated in Figure 4.5. It was first necessary to ensure that the children accepted the dimensions of the small square (actually a cuboid but commonly referred to as a square!) as $1 \times 1$ and that they accepted that, since we did not know its length, a suitable name for the strip was '$x$' (dimensions $1 \times x$). The dimensions of the larger square are then $x \times x$. Naturally, the introduction of these notions is not simple, but Bruner claimed that they were eventually accepted by the children. The

**Figure** 4.5

experiment then proceeded via the construction of squares larger than $x \times x$ by putting appropriate materials together. Figure 4.6 shows some such larger squares. The introduction of notation to record these results then became necessary, and this again was not simple, but was achieved through such steps as, 'one $x$-square plus two $x$-strips plus one unit square', to 'one $x^\square$ plus two $x$ plus one', and finally to '$x^\square + 2x + 1$', which could then also be equated with $(x + 1)^\square$.

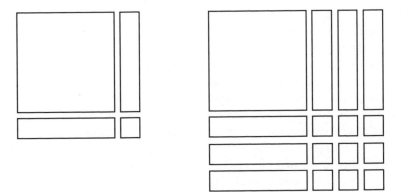

**Figure 4.6**

At all stages, because so many new ideas were being considered, particularly involving the use of notation, time for both discussion and reflection were important. At the end the children, it was claimed, had learned some mathematics several years in advance of what might have been expected. The ideas that

$$(x + 1)^\square = x^\square + 2x + 1,$$
$$(x + 2)^\square = x^\square + 4x + 4,$$
$$(x + 3)^\square = x^\square + 6x + 9,$$
$$(x + 4)^\square = x^\square + 8x + 16,$$

and the studies of number patterns which could emerge, leading to further generalization, are all very advanced for young children. The method can eventually lead to the practical demonstration of the use of the distributive law in more general cases like

$$(x + 2)(2x + 3) = 2x^2 + 7x + 6.$$

It is important to note that the children concerned had not been introduced to the ideas in the way which would be considered normal for, say, fourteen-year-old pupils. This would have been impossible if only because the symbolism would not have been available. However, in an intellectually honest way appropriate to their stage of development they had been introduced to a much more advanced mathematical idea than is normal at their age. The question must arise as to whether the results of the experiment are in any way in conflict with the kind of conclusions about the acceleration of learning which one might draw from Piagetian theory. There was no suggestion in the results of the experiment that children had learned advanced mathematics in a formal way and were able to use the ideas and relate them to other aspects of formal mathematics. So in stating that proportionality, for example, is an aspect of mathematics which requires formal operational thinking it is implied that we mean reasonable facility in the use of equality of ratios in arithmetic manipulative situations. The idea that because one measure is larger another must be comparably larger would not be considered a sufficient indication that metric aspects of proportion were understood.

Certain other aspects of Bruner's experiment have led to criticism by mathematics teachers. In terms of practical applicability in the ordinary classroom there was no suggestion from Bruner that teachers might be able to use the procedure without assistance and with an entire class of 30 or more pupils. The original experiment reported by Bruner and Kenney (1965) involved only four children, with six adults available in the role of teachers! The four children were only eight years old but were in the IQ range 120–130 and came from middle-class professional homes. The classroom environment was as favourable as is possible, in terms of the availability of concrete resource materials, suitable work assignments and, of course, opportunity for question and discussion with adults. One must accept the results for what they are – the results of one experiment which show what might happen under particularly favourable circumstances. One must therefore be cautious about assigning absolute levels of difficulty to topics in the mathematics curriculum. There are almost certainly alternative ways into mathematical topics which are appropriate for young pupils which particular circumstances might make possible.

The Schools Council Bulletin (1965) recorded accounts of work carried out by some ten-year-old pupils. In one particular instance one child was so motivated by a study of gradients that he pursued the idea to the beginnings of differentiation and integration. Other children became involved in what was an intellectually honest and justifiable approach to elementary calculus taking into account the stage of development of the children. It is, of course, possible that those pupils who took the lead in the investigations were intellectually amongst the most able in the class. However, that does not contradict the view that the assignation of absolute levels of difficulty to particular mathematical topics is not easy and might be dangerous and unhelpful. The issue of readiness for learning is a very complex one. We should certainly not use general statements about stages of development to justify not looking for appropriate ways of helping children to learn mathematical ideas, just as we should not present mathematical ideas to pupils in such a way as to persuade them that mathematics is not for them.

## Curriculum implementation

The work of Piaget has probably been more influential than has the work of any other theorist in terms of mathematics curriculum development in Britain, particularly at the primary level. This is in stark contrast to the situation in the USA where the behaviourist tradition was not seriously questioned before Bruner began to inject new ideas from cognitive psychology, some of which were influenced by the work of Piaget. One illustration of the impact in England and Wales is the Schools Council Bulletin (1965) referred to in the previous section. Although this publication was principally a practical guide for teachers, it included a chapter on research into the way children learn. There were many references to Piaget in that chapter and the impact that the work of Piaget was having on those concerned with improving the primary mathematics curriculum at that time is illustrated by the following extracts (pp. 5–9).

Piaget set himself the task of finding out . . . how the principles of conservation and of reversibility, as applied to numbers and to spatial thinking, develop in the minds of young children. The two principles are fundamental to all mathematical (and logical) thinking.

. . . understanding cannot be taught nor does it come by itself, independently of experience . . . This does not mean that there is nothing the teacher can do except wait for the dawn of understanding. He can provide the kind of experience which will assist the child to move from intuitive to operational thinking.

Children learn mathematical concepts more slowly than we realized. They learn by their own activities.

Although children think and reason in different ways they all pass through certain stages depending on their chronological and mental ages and their experience.

The report of the Mathematical Association (1970) on primary mathematics included an appendix on 'Understanding and mathematics' which incorporated much of the spirit of Piaget within a broader review of what was known about learning. Caution was recommended, however, in the application of any interpretation of Piagetian theory, as is shown in these two extracts (p. 153):

Although these stages . . . have been broadly substantiated by a large number of research workers, we should show due caution in accepting them as a permanent feature in childhood development;

. . . it is important not to discourage experiment, in the belief that what has been found is an unalterable feature of childhood development. We have only to compare the thinking of primitive adults with that of educated children in industrial societies to see the vast changes which are possible.

Piagetian views provided the underlying rationale for the book by Lovell (1971b) prepared as a guide for teachers of young children. The two extracts below would be found acceptable by many teachers today, even though certain aspects of Piagetian theory have received considerable criticism (p. 17):

There appears to be a danger that some mathematical ideas are introduced too early to children, or that there is insufficient appreciation on the part of professional mathematicians that many of the ideas they would like to introduce to elementary school pupils are understood only in an intuitive and not in an analytic sense by the children.

It is not in any sense suggested that the child must always be 'ready' for a particular idea before the teacher introduces it. The job of the teacher is to use his professional skill and provide learning situations for the child which demand thinking skills just ahead of those . . . available to him . . . When a child is almost ready for an idea, the learning situation provided by the teacher may well 'precipitate' the child's understanding of that idea.

The distinction between 'ready' and 'almost ready' might be considered too subtle to be useful, but the message that the teacher does have a role to play and that it is not appropriate to sit back and wait is clear.

The early 1960s to the late 1970s was a time of curriculum experimentation in school mathematics and a considerable number of curriculum projects sprang up in Britain. The only project which overtly expressed a Piagetian view was also the only major project aimed at younger pupils, and that was the Nuffield Mathematics Project. The title of the first publication which introduced teachers to the work of the project was *I Do, and I Understand* (1967). The words of the title themselves reflected the Piagetian message, though it was claimed that the title formed part of a Chinese proverb. This particular book included a discussion on how children learn and contained reference to stages of learning, to active learning and to the role of interaction with the environment. Among the many publications for teachers produced by Nuffield (1970, 1973) were three, *Checking Up* (*I, II* and *III*), which provided teachers with Piagetian tests which could be applied to pupils in order to ascertain readiness in terms of the stage of development. The authors were at pains to point out that the tests were put on trial in schools before publication, as was the other material of the project, and that the original ideas came from the work of Piaget. The *Checking Up* books also included a sort of time chart of conceptual development, particularly through the concrete operational stage, showing which ideas needed to be developed before other concepts could be mastered.

In *I Do, and I Understand* there were references to readiness, in relation to development through stages, and to the slow rate of intellectual development:

> Any attempt to hurry children through this stage of development [concrete operations] is liable to lead to a serious loss of confidence. They will discard real materials themselves at the appropriate moment . . . and eventually, when faced with a problem, will ignore all available materials and approach it abstractly. (p. 9)

Those who are familiar with the material of this Nuffield Project, however, cannot fail to have speculated on how a project which was apparently so heavily influenced by Piaget could include, for example, the approach to integers through ordered pairs (Nuffield, 1969). The reasons for doing this were explained, and a variety of practical or game-type activities were suggested to help in introducing this approach to integers, but they could not wholly compensate for the fact that, in the end, abstraction of quite a high level was required.

The Cockcroft Report (1982) contained many references to aspects of learning but showed no real enthusiasm for Piaget's stage theory or for any views on readiness which might be said to follow from Piaget. Both understanding and rate of intellectual development are recurring themes, however, as reflected by these extracts (pp. 100–110):

> . . . it is not possible to make any overall statement about the mathematical knowledge and understanding which children in general should be expected to possess at the end of the primary years;

> . . . the curriculum provided for pupils needs to take into account the wide gap in understanding and skill which can exist between children of the same age.

The review of research, carried out for the Cockcroft Committee by Bell *et al.* (1983), contained a section on research relating to stages of intellectual development and to the work of Piaget. This was an important section because it clearly revealed ways in which subsequent research to that of Piaget has raised doubts about the value of the idea of stages in relation to learning mathematics. Criticisms and current attitudes to aspects of the work of Piaget and to readiness are considered in the next section of this chapter.

## Critical evaluation

The work of Piaget was originally welcomed as being helpful in relation to curriculum design and to the planning of learning activities and experiences for children, but a body of criticism has grown up subsequently. Given the complexity of human learning and the comparative youth of educational psychology in the history of mankind it would have been very surprising if criticisms had not appeared. Any major theory which appears to fit experimental data is likely to lead us forward towards widely acceptable theories about learning but may not provide the ultimate answer. In accepting that there have been criticisms of Piaget's work it is important to realize that many have been concerned with particular aspects, some relatively trivial. We must not necessarily reject every aspect of the theory because certain parts do not stand up to close inspection.

There has been criticism of many of the tasks used by Piaget on these grounds:

- many questions are not meaningful to the children – either they do not relate to the world in which the child lives or they do not motivate;
- some questions might be regarded as ridiculous or frivolous for the above reason or because they contain questionable statements;
- the complexity of instructions in some questions, that is the language demands, are too much for some pupils;
- some questions are not sufficiently free from context variables to produce results, from different backgrounds, which are comparable;
- some questions, particularly those devised to test formal operational thinking skills, are too difficult even for most adults.

Other, more substantive, concerns have also been expressed. Some of the many criticisms are now considered in more detail.

One difficulty of task construction is to devise a question which is both meaningful and mathematically appropriate, and which is fair to every child. The task devised to expose a child's competence in handling ratio and proportion based on the eating habits of eels is an interesting example. In the Piagetian version (translation) eels eat meatballs and biscuits (Lovell, 1971a), but in the Concepts in Secondary Mathematics and Science project (CSMS) version (Hart, 1981) the eels eat sprats and fish fingers. The whole situation, in both cases, is artificially contrived to set up a particular mathematical task. This is common in mathematics teaching, but could be one reason why some pupils can find mathematics unpalatable and divorced from the real world. It is hoped that children will play along with us under such circumstances, but do they, and could results be affected by differing attitudes? What of those children whose knowledge of biology is such that they cannot accept that eels would eat biscuits, or cannot accept that eels have mouths which are big enough to eat sprats? The particular stretching of the imagination required in this question is unimportant, but the general principle is not. Are the results of research sometimes distorted because some pupils do not or cannot accept the situations?

Another Piagetian question concerns two fields each containing a cow and in which houses are to be placed. In one field houses are to be spaced randomly but in the other the houses are to be lined up, in terraced format. At all times when questions are asked there must be the same number of houses in each field. The basic question is whether each cow has the same amount of grass to eat, and this question is to be put for a variety of different numbers of houses. Results have been as intriguing as those for the conservation tasks described earlier, but children do tend to agree that the two cows have the same amount of grass to eat when there are no houses or just one house in each field. With more houses than one, younger children are inclined to deny conservation. However, there is a complication to the situation, appreciated by some children. Cows have a tendency to churn up the ground around buildings, thus killing off the grass. Would this happen round the houses in the question? If it did there *would* be less grass to eat in one field than in the other! This feature could be considered even more relevant if there were to be more than one cow in each field. The question is arguably not equally fair to all children, and is clearly open to varied interpretations, so either way results might be distorted.

Yet another Piagetian task involves wooden beads in a box. Most of the beads are brown, but a small number are white. The question is whether the box contained more wooden beads or more brown beads. Results have suggested that many children were unable to answer correctly. The question, however, is one that most adults would puzzle over, not because they could not answer the question but because they might not believe that the questioner had expressed it correctly. It is unusual, and to some extent ridiculous, to ask a question comparing the number of objects in a set with the number of objects in a subset of the set. The description of the application of the test by Piaget suggests that he was at great pains to try to ensure that the question was understood. But there is still a nagging feeling that the unusual and unexpected, even unacceptable, nature of the question might have seriously influenced the results.

The above examples illustrate how difficult it is to produce or invent a question which is acceptable from all points of view and upon which one can base general conclusions about intellectual development. There have been many experiments carried out to test Piaget's conclusions using alternative language or situations but based on the same ideas. Results from such experiments have thrown serious doubt on aspects of the conclusions drawn by Piaget. Yet it must be admitted that no alternative experiment has ever produced results in which all children across a wide age range have answered correctly. What has normally happened is that the proportion of children answering correctly has been different, occasionally very different.

Many of these issues have been discussed by Bryant. Another ability required for mathematical development not previously considered here and which Piaget had claimed was not present until the onset of concrete operations was the ability to make transitive inferences. A simple task involving transitivity might be based on three quantities A, B and C, for which direct comparison showed that $A > B$ and $B > C$. Piaget concluded that pre-operational children could not deduce that $A > C$. Bryant's discussion of this issue (Bryant, 1974) is well worth studying. Bryant was particularly concerned that Piaget had not taken into account alternative reasons for the failure of young children to make transitive inferences. A very real alternative reason was considered to be that young children could not keep in mind the two earlier comparisons, A > B and B > C, which is essential before inferencing becomes possible. Memory training involving such relationships did, indeed, produce a higher success rate. Bryant also took into account the possibility that children might state the correct conclusion for the wrong reason, that is, because A is the larger in A > B and because C is the smaller in B > C, any relationship involving only A and C must have A as the larger and C as the smaller. In conclusion Bryant stated (pp. 47–8): 'This experiment demonstrates conclusively that young children are capable of making genuine transitive inferences . . . Piaget's theory about logical development must, to some extent, be wrong'.

The Piagetian task involving beads and brown beads has been investigated by McGarrigle and the conclusions are reported in Donaldson (1978). McGarrigle invented an experiment based on toy cows, three of them black and one white. When laid on their sides the cows were described as 'sleeping'. He was then able to compare the standard Piagetian form with a version which introduced greater emphasis on the total class – 'Are there more black cows or more sleeping cows?' The cows were all sleeping in both versions of the experiment. With six-year-old children the success rate increased from 25 per cent to 48 per cent with the introduction of the word 'sleeping'. This illustrates the kind of influence particular variations can exert on test results. In another experiment black and white toy cows and horses were arranged on either side of a wall, as in Figure 4.7. The children were asked a number of questions, including, 'Are there more cows or more black horses?' Only 14 per cent of children answered this correctly. Donaldson concluded from the results and the accompanying comments of the children that they were comparing the black horses with the black cows. Children's own interpretations of the language used in framing questions clearly can affect results and conclusions drawn from such results can be distorted (see Chapter 9).

Cows

| B | B | W | W |
|---|---|---|---|
| B | B | B | W |

Horses

**Figure 4.7**

Piaget has also been criticized for his lack of concern about sampling. Generally his experiments were tried out on very small numbers of children, seemingly often a few comparatively clever children from the immediate locality. As a biologist, however, he may have been very content in working with a few readily available subjects. Biologists often have to be content with very small samples in experimental work. Conclusions drawn on the basis of work with small samples must be cautious, but the information which is obtained can have genuine value. Many experiments based on Piagetian tasks have been replicated by others in many countries around the world using much larger samples including children spanning the whole range of all relevant variables like age, ability and social background. Because this criticism has been addressed by others, inadequate sampling is therefore not a substantive issue.

A much more substantial criticism of Piagetian theory concerns the idea that human intellectual development occurs in stages in which qualitatively different thinking structures may be detected. Many critics have drawn attention to the weaknesses of such a theoretical position. There is just too much variation to make the theory useful, particularly in terms of prediction. There is considerable evidence that individual children cannot easily be categorized as being at a particular stage of development. For example, in one subject area they might reveal complete competence in tasks which are considered to require formal operational thinking, yet in another subject area they might reveal no higher than concrete operational responses. Even in the same subject area, say conservation, they might behave on some tasks as if they are at the concrete operational level but on other tasks their behaviour might indicate only pre-operational thinking. One day they might answer a particular task correctly, suggesting capabilities associated with a particular Piagetian level, but on the next day, on what is seemingly an exactly comparable task, their reaction might suggest they have not reached that level. Piagetian theory acknowledges this phenomenon in two ways. Firstly, between any two adjacent stages there must be a period of transition when such phenomena will arise. Secondly, some element of confusion of the sort described above, referred to by Piaget as 'décalage', is accepted because humans will always be prone to respond with a degree of variability. Many modern critics, however, are unhappy that the variability seems too great to support a theory which is of any real use. They would not necessarily reject any suggestion that intelligence or cognition develops throughout childhood, that maturation of the central nervous system plays a part and that the quality of interaction with the environment is an important contributory factor. They are unhappy with the idea of development in identifiable stages.

Another criticism arises in the accusation that Piaget's theory is only illustrative and not confirmatory (Brown and Desforges, 1977). The data may be considered to fit the theory but there is no other way to prove the theory. Certainly, any theory which can only be supported in this illustrative way cannot be regarded with complete satisfaction, yet it is likely that human progress in many areas of science has depended on such assumptions. It would be interesting to research into the history of science with a view to establishing how many theories were originally developed solely because they fitted the available data. More abstract proofs can only be sought once the data has suggested a hypothesis.

Piaget's work has also been taken to imply a consistent order in the acquisition of mathematical concepts, and the time chart contained in the Nuffield *Checking Up* books has already been mentioned. Cross-cultural studies, however, have generally not confirmed consistency of order. It is possible that there are elements of order, that length must come before area, for example, but there are also many indications that in different cultures the order is not the same as in Western culture. Piaget's theory does, however, acknowledge the vital effect of interaction with the environment in its widest definition. The role of experience is much more crucial than any constant order theory can acknowledge. It is, for example, often suggested that any differences in spatial and mechanical ability between boys and girls is because of differences in the environment in which the two sexes are reared. This is an hypothesis which cannot easily be proved or disproved but it cannot be denied that this is an example of different environments within the same overall culture. Children from more rural and agricultural cultures tend to develop skills, knowledge and understanding required for survival and not develop other capabilities which those in an industrial society might take for granted.

All of the above reservations about aspects of Piagetian theory should suggest that attempts to apply Piaget either to the construction of the mathematics curriculum or to assessing pupil progress have not been successful. On the whole this has been the case. The only mathematics curriculum development project in Britain which has referred heavily to Piaget was the original Nuffield Mathematics Project. This project in itself received rather limited levels of support and interest from teachers, who tend naturally to be more interested in the practicalities of schemes of work and exercises for pupils rather than directly on the implications of Piaget for classroom implementation. The materials of the scheme were comparatively lacking in material of direct applicability to the classroom. More recently, in the 1980s, a new scheme entitled 'Nuffield Maths 5–11' (1983, for example) was produced as a revised and extended version of the primary section of the Nuffield Mathematics Project. The revision included removing any reference to Piagetian theory. The nearest messages one can find to those of the original Nuffield and to the Schools Council (1965) publication in terms of the influence of Piaget are that children learn at different rates and so will not reach the same stage simultaneously, and that young children learn by doing and by discussion.

Difficulties in relating to the Piagetian stage theory have been experienced by those who have researched into mathematical understanding on a large scale. Hughes (1980), writing about the Schools Council Project on the development of scientific and mathematical concepts in children between the ages of seven and eleven stated that (p. 94): 'The conclusions . . . confirm the doubts one has for the resolving power of Piagetian type tests'. The study was based on the responses of 1000 children to a battery of practical tests on the concepts associated with area, weight and volume. It developed (p. 88): 'as a result of the trend in the late sixties and early seventies for modes of teaching to be loosely based on beliefs about the conceptual development of children [basically Piagetian]'. The results exposed so much décalage as to make general statements about conceptual development, particularly of stages of intellectual development, completely inappropriate. The following extract sums this up (p. 92):

> Some children, at all ages, grasp one conservation concept in one test situation before grasping it in another; this is true from topic to topic and also between apparently fairly similar tasks in any one topic (say weight). From our research it is not possible to determine for certain which they will grasp first.

Reference to selected results of the work of the mathematics team of the CSMS project has already been made (Hart, 1981). This team also experienced difficulty in relating their findings to Piagetian theory. It had been hoped that the development of the understanding of mathematical concept areas 'could be described in terms of the demand (as related to) Piagetian levels of cognition', but this did not materialize. The problem was clearly stated:

> It was hoped that a child could be designated as being at a particular Piagetian level and, by looking at his performance on a maths test, the mathematical levels could also be described in Piagetian terms . . . we found however that the child's

performance varied considerably task to task and that we could not label a child as being overall at a certain Piagetian level. (Hart, 1980, p. 55)

Nevertheless, the terminology 'concrete operations', 'formal operations', is still apparently found to be useful by those reporting on empirical research, and by the many who write about child development and curriculum reform.

Work by Booth (1984) reflects the dilemma facing empirical researchers in relation to Piagetian theory. Reporting on the research project 'Strategies and Errors in Secondary Mathematics: Algebra' she draws attention (p. 95) to inconsistencies militating against 'the unqualified acceptance of the "unified stage" view of cognition which characterizes the Piagetian formulation'. At the same time the following points are also made (p. 95):

> the observed similarities in the nature of the informal methods used by different children, as well as the points concerning context and the generalized nature of algebraic representation outlined above, suggest some generality in cognition which requires explanation;

and (p. 91):

> Analysis of the *nature* of the difficulties which children have been observed to experience suggests a picture of conceptual growth which is generally not inconsistent with Piaget's description of the development from concrete to formal operational thinking.

Despite criticism, expected in the world of education, Piaget has acted as an inspiration to many who have produced alternative theories concerning cognitive development, for example, Ausubel, and also to those who have proposed ideas concerning mathematics learning, for example, Dienes. Shulman wrote (1970, p. 40), 'Many psychologists are seriously suggesting that [Piaget's] stature will eventually equal that of Freud as a pioneering giant in the behavioral sciences'. The influence of Piaget will certainly reappear in subsequent chapters of this book.

## Cross-cultural issues

The implication from the work of Piaget is that all children, all over the world, develop in substantially the same way. To Piaget, progression from one stage to another is achieved through a combination of maturation, interaction with the environment and equilibration, with equilibration being perhaps the most critical factor. But what is the comparative effect of these various factors? Might it be that the wider environment, which includes the social and cultural environment, plays a larger part than Piaget believed? It must be admitted that Piaget's theoretical constructs were produced within a Western cultural situation and on the basis of empirical work carried out with children brought up in such an environment. Berry (1985, p. 18) has summed up the criticisms of the assertion that development is invariant across different cultural and linguistic groups in writing: 'studies conducted in a variety of settings in Latin America, Africa, Asia and the South Pacific have raised serious questions about the validity of this assumption'.

Many cross-cultural studies have, in fact, been carried out, but a substantial number of them by Western research workers, who Piaget himself pointed out would find this kind of research very difficult, because such studies presuppose a complete and thorough knowledge of the language and a sophisticated understanding of the culture and society within which the research is to be conducted. The same point could, of course, be made about research with children from particular subcultures within Western society, and not only ethnic subcultures. Dasen (1972, p. 29) reported that: 'A number of studies show that both non-Western and low socio-economic class Western children lag behind in their concept development when compared with middle-class Western children.' Also, '. . . since Western science does not necessarily represent the form of thought valued in other cultures, nor in fact in some subcultures within the West, the Piagetian sequence is likely to be ethnocentric' (Dasen, 1977, p. 5). A particular issue is the one of language, namely whether the language used to communicate ideas allows the complete elaboration of concepts which have largely been derived through the medium of Western languages, and whether this communication is conducted in the first or a second language (see Chapter 9).

A major difficulty in making sense of the findings from cross-cultural studies has been the absence of adequate common ground, with each new study being perhaps in a new culture and with new tasks. Many studies, however, have deduced a 'time-lag' in the development of concepts. Such studies should not be interpreted in terms of cultural deprivation, with the development of the Western child being taken as the norm against which all other children must be compared. Concepts might develop together in a Western society but at different rates in another culture when that culture places a different value on the ideas or when one idea is more culturally relevant than another. The early study by Gay and Cole (1967) established that for the Kpelle of Liberia it was the requirements of everyday life which dictated which numerical estimation skills were most fully developed, and that with certain skills the Kpelle were better than American college students. Not all cross-cultural studies have adopted a strictly Piagetian framework, of course, but the results often throw light on the issue of social and cultural environment. Saxe and Posner (1983) have reported research carried out in the Ivory Coast which reveals that the children of merchants adopted more economical strategies of arithmetic problem-solving than children brought up in an agricultural situation, showing 'how individuals develop the symbolic skills that are most useful to them in their differing social contexts' (p. 303). There is some support, across many different cultural groups, for believing that concepts of number conservation develop similarly through the concrete operational stage, yet time-lags are still widely reported and there seems to be considerable variability in performance across tasks. Saxe and Posner claimed that, '. . . problematic for the Piagetian formulation is the lack of empirical support for the construct of stage' (p. 311). A further conclusion drawn from evidence from a wide range of cross-cultural studies by Saxe and Posner is that: 'the formation of mathematical concepts is a developmental process simultaneously rooted in the constructive activities of the individual and in social life' (p. 315). Solomon (1989) has similarly criticized Piaget's assumption of a solitary knower who must construct mathematical understanding, suggesting persistently that it is rather the case of an essentially social being for whom knowing number involves entering into the social practices of its use. Social practices (also discussed later in the context of the issues of Chapter 7) will inevitably vary according to cultural background.

In terms of readiness for learning, the underlying theme of this chapter, the issue remains somewhat unresolved. The view of behaviourists is found to be unsatisfactory by many teachers, yet the presence of prerequisite knowledge, suggested by Gagné and supported by the cognitive psychologist, Ausubel, is clearly important. There might well be a maturational factor in learning mathematics. The role of interaction with the environment is clearly important, and that environment comprises not only the immediate classroom or teaching environment but also extends to the wider social and cultural milieu within which children are educated (see Chapter 7). To a certain extent teachers are forced to keep an open mind on the readiness issue. It would possibly be detrimental to the cognitive development of pupils to assume too quickly and easily that they are not yet ready for a new idea. But experience of teaching would suggest that attempts to introduce new ideas will not always be successful, and we ourselves must be ready for that.

## Suggestions for further reading

Bryant, P. (1974) *Perception and Understanding in Young Children*. London: Methuen.
Copeland, R. W. (1979) *How Children Learn Mathematics*. New York: Macmillan.
Dasen, P. R. (ed.) (1977) *Piagetian Psychology: Cross-Cultural Contributions*. New York: Gardner Press.
Donaldson, M. (1978) *Children's Minds*. Glasgow: Fontana/Collins.
Rosskopf, M. F., Steff, L. P. and Taback, S. (eds) (1971) *Piagetian Cognitive-development Research and Mathematical Education*. Reston, VA: National Council of Teachers of Mathematics.

## Questions for discussion

1. Do you think that there is more to readiness than the presence of certain relevant sub-ordinate intellectual skills? Give reasons for your answer.
2. What do you understand by the terms 'concrete' and 'formal' and what are the implications for mathematics learning?
3. When are children ready to learn about fractions (rational numbers) and operations on them?
4. For any topic which you teach regularly, state what you need to take into account in deciding whether a pupil is ready to learn the topic.

Chapter 5

# Can Pupils Discover Mathematics for Themselves?

## Learning by discovery

All polygons with more than three sides have diagonals. A quadrilateral has two diagonals, a pentagon has five, a hexagon has nine, and so on (see Figure 5.1). Pupils may obtain at least some of these results for themselves by drawing. A table (Table 5.1) showing number of diagonals against number of sides reveals a number

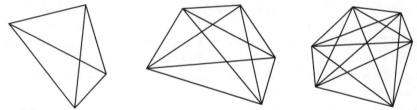

Figure 5.1

Table 5.1 Number of diagonals for polygons

| Number of sides | 3 | 4 | 5 | 6 | 7 | 8 | 9 | 10 |
|---|---|---|---|---|---|---|---|---|
| Number of diagonals | 0 | 2 | 5 | 9 | 14 | 20 | 27 | 35 |

pattern which may be used to extend the sequence and thus determine the number of diagonals for any given number of sides. It is also possible to use the pattern to obtain a formula linking the number of diagonals and the number of sides. Extension activities might include investigating the number of regions into which the diagonals dissect the polygon when (a) the polygon is regular, and (b) the polygon is irregular. The entire assignment may be given to children to work on for themselves. Any results obtained would not really constitute knowledge which all truly educated people must possess. Nor is it likely that such knowledge would ever be taught in an expository way. The assignment would not be given to children unless the teacher believed or was persuaded that taking part in an active way in a mathematical investigation, and perhaps discovering some mathematics, was worthwhile.

Some teachers of young children regularly use coloured rods to help with the introduction to the counting of (natural) numbers. It is sometimes claimed, by advocates of the use of such apparatus, that simply playing with the rods takes the children a very long way towards mastery of number relationships (see Figure 5.2). The children discover that a certain pair of different coloured rods arranged in a 'train' is equivalent in some way (length) to a third rod of yet another colour. They might also discover that the rods may be arranged in a staircase of equal steps.

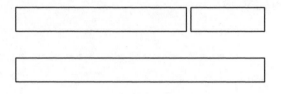

**Figure 5.2**

There is clearly an extent to which some mathematics may be discovered by children, and it is often claimed that learning is the more thorough and complete for having been obtained by this means rather than by exposition. However, there is also an extent to which the teacher may need to intervene in order to introduce first the appropriate language, then to help clarify the thinking, and then to introduce symbolism and recording methods. Nevertheless, the children can have considerable control over their own learning. Unfortunately, experience suggests that some children may be able to discover disappointingly little, and so the teacher may then feel obliged to try to give detailed guidance. Certain number relationships, for example, still do constitute knowledge considered essential for a truly educated person, so if nothing is discovered the teacher might well feel inclined to try to hasten learning by telling the child in some direct or indirect way. On the other hand, it is questionable whether a child who cannot discover anything at all can benefit much from expository teaching either.

Words such as 'discovery', 'investigation', 'activity' and 'problem-solving' have become very much a part of the language we now use in talking about mathematics teaching. Many pupils today, however, are still taught largely by exposition and are given little opportunity to learn by discovery. Some teachers, when they themselves were pupils, were given almost no chance to discover mathematics, though some educators in every generation have believed that exposition alone was unlikely to be effective, particularly with younger pupils. With more able and older pupils teachers of mathematics have, in the past, often been able to avoid criticism with only minimal use of methods other than exposition and practice of skills. At the present time, however, there is now much more pressure on teachers to use more active approaches. Supporters of the use of discovery, investigations and problem-solving have probably never been absent from the educational scene, but paragraph 243 and associated elaboration in the Cockcroft Report (1982) has given a boost to their cause. There is still a degree of vagueness about terms such as 'discovery', 'investigation' and 'problem-solving' which some would say does not matter much in a general discussion of the issues. It is the spirit of active rather than passive education, they would claim, which is at the heart of the matter.

Shulman (1970) wrote of a new psychology of learning mathematics which, to a large extent, was based on discovery learning. The main advocate of discovery learning in the USA around 1970 was Jerome Bruner. Shulman described the origins of the theory of learning by discovery as a mélange of Piaget and Plato. It was the work of Piaget, interpreted in mathematical education as supporting interaction with the environment leading to individual insight, which was a major factor in justifying a discovery approach. In the USA this was a relatively revolutionary idea for many teachers, given the previous domination of educational practice by behaviourist learning theory. It is interesting to speculate, however, whether behaviourism need necessarily rule out discovery, and indeed the idea of programmed discovery will be considered later. Bruner's pioneering work in encouraging discovery learning in the USA was certainly significant for a considerable time and developments in Britain around the same time also reflected similar interest in more active approaches.

The Schools Council Bulletin (1965) contained a number of references to learning by discovery at the primary level, for example:

> Mathematics is a discovery of relationships and the expression of the relationships in symbolic (or abstract) form. This is no static definition, but implies action on the part of the learner of whatever age and whatever ability. It is the fact that mathematical relationships can be discovered and communicated in such a variety of ways that puts mathematics within reach of children and adults of all abilities. (p. 9)

A central message of the Bulletin was that teachers must teach primary mathematics by means of as much active involvement as possible, using practical activities with equipment and apparatus whenever possible, and by this means children would discover and would need to be told much less. The principal author of this bulletin, Edith Biggs, has also written separately about discovery (Biggs, 1972), and one interesting feature was her use of 'discovery', 'investigation' and 'active learning' in an almost synonymous way, reflecting an earlier point of this chapter. Another feature was her claim that discovery methods gave pupils the opportunity to think for themselves, and develop their capabilities to the full. In addition, such methods generated real excitement for mathematics which, given the binding relationship between cognitive and affective factors in learning, no doubt contributed to the greater realization of potential.

Different authors have attempted to classify discovery methods. The five described by Biggs (1972) provide a good means of reflecting on this issue, and they were: fortuitous, free and exploratory, guided, directed and programmed. At one extreme, fortuitous discovery certainly cannot be planned. It happens, but no learning programme can be built around it. At the other extreme, programmed discovery has a feeling of contradiction about it. The intention in programming a unit of work is to try to ensure that learning does take place. The unit of work entitled 'Fibonacci Fractions' (p. 74) is an example of an attempt of this kind.

The 'Fibonacci Fractions' unit of work should provide an example of a discovery programme at the level of the reader. Successful completion of the unit cannot be guaranteed with any individual learner, but successful completion does imply discovery of some mathematics, assuming the knowledge was not already held. The learning sequence is more than guided – it is heavily directed and could be considered to be virtually programmed, although it might not pass a Skinnerian test of what constitutes programmed learning. Unfortunately, the lack of activity implicit in the

---

### FIBONACCI FRACTIONS

You have already met the Fibonacci sequence

$$1, 1, 2, 3, 5, 8, 13, 21, 34, 55, 89, 144, \ldots$$

The numbers in this sequence may be used to form Fibonacci fractions, for example,

$$\frac{1}{1}, \frac{1}{2}, \frac{2}{3}, \frac{3}{5}, \frac{5}{8} \ldots$$

(1) Write down the next ten fractions in this sequence.

(2) Use your calculator to convert all fifteen terms into decimals.

(3) Draw a graph to show the value of the decimal for each term of the sequence.

(4) Describe, as fully as you can, what you notice about your sequence of decimals and, in particular, what would happen if you went on to 20, 50, 100 or more terms.

Now look at the alternative sequence of fractions,

$$\frac{1}{1}, \frac{2}{1}, \frac{3}{2}, \frac{5}{3}, \frac{8}{5} \ldots$$

(5) Write down the next ten fractions in this sequence.

(6) Use your calculator to convert all fifteen terms into decimals.

(7) Describe, with the aid of a graph if necessary, what you notice about this sequence of decimals.

(8) What is the relationship between the fifteenth terms of the two sequences? What do you think is the relationship between the limits of the two sequences? (There are two relationships, one based on difference and the other involving reciprocals.)

(9) Use your two relationships to write down a quadratic equation, the solution of which is the exact value of the limit of one of the sequences.

(10) Solve the quadratic equation to find the exact value of this limit and then determine the limit of the other sequence.

---

unit renders it boring to some students. Others find it interesting and revealing, which confirms the existence of individual differences between learners.

Near the other extreme, discovery which is free and exploratory might follow from the investigation entitled 'Rectangles'.

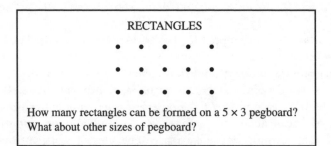

### RECTANGLES

How many rectangles can be formed on a 5 × 3 pegboard?
What about other sizes of pegboard?

---

There is no guarantee that anything other than numerical information (which may or may not be correct) will be discovered from the 'Rectangles' investigation. Further, there is much more of a burden for the teacher if it is important that correct conclusions do result from free and exploratory activity. For this reason, with a firm eye on the syllabus and forthcoming examinations, teachers might be happier to allow free and exploratory investigation if the results do not constitute essential knowledge. Where mathematical results are important many teachers would undoubtedly support teaching methods which they believe come closest to guaranteeing that pupils gain the requisite knowledge. Despite the missionary work of a few, and despite its inadequacies, teachers generally favour exposition under such circumstances. Edith Biggs, and other advocates of investigational and discovery learning, have been at pains to point out that examination syllabuses can be completed and all required results learned thoroughly via active learning methods, but it still seems the majority of mathematics teachers have yet to accept this view.

The value of discovery has been the subject of debate and some disagreement amongst educational psychologists. Gagné and Brown (1961) claimed to have established that guided discovery was the best method (of those used) to promote the learning of certain rules. There is not much other evidence from research to support any particular view about the value of discovery methods. Ausubel (1963) argued that guided discovery only seemed the best method because it had been compared with rote learning. He went further and claimed that there was just no evidence that discovery of any kind was a more effective teaching method than meaningful exposition. Ausubel did, however, agree that discovery is important in promoting learning with young children, and both Gagné and Ausubel agreed that active learning methods are more important for younger pupils than for older. Yet guided discovery is quite popular with some teachers. They believe the pupils are better motivated by an active approach, and perhaps by a challenge, but the teacher may justifiably step in at any time.

The enthusiasm for discovery learning generated by Bruner led to a public and published debate with Ausubel, and both their viewpoints are important. The main points recorded by Bruner (1960a) in favour of learning by discovery were as follows. Firstly, discovery encouraged a way of learning mathematics by doing mathematics, and encouraged the development of a view that mathematics was a process rather than a finished product. Secondly, discovery is intrinsically rewarding for pupils, so that teachers using discovery methods should have little need to use extrinsic forms of reward. These two points carry great weight. A more debatable third issue concerns whether pupils can be genuinely creative, which was certainly implied by Bruner. Practical difficulties were acknowledged, namely that one could not wait for ever for pupils to discover, and that the curriculum could not be completely open, so discovery would often need to be to some extent guided or directed. Some pupils might even find their inability to discover extremely discouraging. It was, of course, up to the teacher to make the kind of judgements necessary to circumvent these difficulties.

Ausubel (1963) attempted to temper the missionary zeal of Bruner because he feared excessive or inappropriate use of discovery. He suggested that discovery was not the only way a teacher could generate motivation, self-confidence and a desire to learn, because expository teaching, at its best, was just as capable of exciting and inspiring pupils. Discovery could seriously demotivate when nothing was discovered. Further, any suggestion that discovery learning implied creativity was questionable, for pupils can rarely be genuinely creative, and guided discovery was hardly creative at all. No research evidence was available which conclusively proved that discovery learning was superior to expository learning in terms of long-term learning gains. Certainly there was need for discovery methods with young children but discovery was not at all valuable for most learning at the abstract stage of cognitive development. Discovery, after all, could use up too much time. Practising mathematics as a process was not the main priority for school learning. It was much more important, for example, that pupils should learn the substantial body of knowledge which was essential for survival in a complex society. Since there was no possibility that pupils could re-create the whole of that knowledge, teacher intervention in a more or less direct way was frequently necessary.

Whether teachers are persuaded more by Bruner or by Ausubel, discovery learning was definitely adopted by some of those involved in curriculum development in mathematics in the 1960s and 1970s. Discovery was an important feature of the Madison Project in the United States of America. Davis (1966) drew attention to the place and value of discovery largely through examples of pupils' discoveries. The Madison Project claimed to use an additional discovery technique which they described as 'torpedoing' in which, once pupils thought that they had discovered a pattern, relationship or rule, an example was injected which did not fit, which caused the pupils to think again. In a sense, this is an example of deliberately creating a state of mental disequilibrium, in order to encourage the twin processes of assimilation and accommodation. It is not clear, however, that 'torpedoing' was sufficiently successful in promoting learning for it to be seriously advocated as a worthwhile technique to be used on a large scale.

In Britain, discovery methods were generally actively encouraged at the primary level through the work of Edith Biggs and also through the original Nuffield Mathematics Project. Chapter 5 of *I Do, and I Understand* (Nuffield, 1967) described the meaning and importance of discovery learning within the project. Some teachers may remember the early stages of secondary curriculum reform in the 1960s for the emphasis on changes of content. In the first report of the Midlands Mathematical Experiment (1964, p. 12), however, we find: 'We are continually being surprised by what children *can* do, provided that it grows out of their peculiar experiences. Our job is to recognize mathematics in the children's activities and utilize it'. From 1968 onwards, the A-H series of the School Mathematics Project included experimental and investigational sections. More recently, in the wake of the Cockcroft Report (1982), there have been developments aimed at ensuring that secondary school mathematics curricula do involve an element of active learning leading to discovery.

However, the efficacy, or otherwise, of discovery methods has always been under debate. The issue was commented on by Davis (1984, p. 371), as follows:

> one cannot compare, say, 'discovery teaching' with 'non-discovery teaching' . . . one can only compare *some specific attempts to do 'discovery' teaching, vs. some specific attempts to do 'non-discovery' teaching*. One or both may be done very well, or moderately well, or badly, or even very badly . . . One has NOT compared 'discovery' and 'non-discovery' *teaching in general. But that is the way the results are invariably interpreted.*

In this respect, discovery is no different from the subject of much other educational research. Supporters of discovery learning may therefore, rather than accepting evidence, be accepting a belief, summed up by Biggs (1972, p. 240):

> I believe this method [discovery] is the best way to give our pupils real excite-ment in mathematics. I believe too, that it is only when we give our children a chance to think for themselves that they realize their full potential.

Research, in any case, usually attempts to measure only cognitive development, or what has been mastered. Gains in attitude to mathematics and increased awareness of the nature of the subject are not easily measured. Who knows what long-term benefits might accrue if discovery were to be used much more than it is, particularly at the secondary level where the balance, up to now, has been very much in favour of more passive instructional methods of learning mathematics?

## Gestalt psychology

Discovery learning depends on a child making connections and seeing relationships without having to have them explained by the teacher. Consider the 'Quarter-Circle Problem'. Here, the child must see through the information in the diagram and realize that the length of XY is equal to the length of the other diagonal of the rectangle, which is a radius of the circle. Such insight is frequently required in problem-solving.

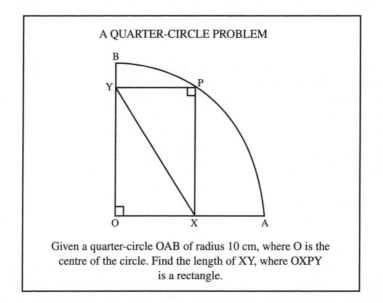

A QUARTER-CIRCLE PROBLEM

Given a quarter-circle OAB of radius 10 cm, where O is the centre of the circle. Find the length of XY, where OXPY is a rectangle.

Insight was acknowledged by Gestalt psychologists as being vital to independent learning. The essence of Gestalt psychology has always been that the mind (and not necessarily just in humans) attempts to interpret incoming sensations and experiences as an organized whole and not as a collection of separate units of data. If the underlying structure is immediately perceived in a meaningful way the learner is better able to proceed to the solution of the problem. We, as teachers, can help our pupils by providing experiences in which the structure is evident or by guiding or directing pupils to the structure. Gestalt psychology originally developed in Germany, and the word 'Gestalt', roughly translated, means 'form' or 'shape'.

The leading mathematical Gestalt psychologist, throughout the period of the development of the theory, was Max Wertheimer. Scheerer (1963, pp. 2–3), commenting on Gestalt psychology, reported on Wertheimer's famous parallelogram example as follows:

Suppose a child who already knows how to get the area of a rectangle is asked to find the formula for the area of a parallelogram. If a child thinks about it, Wertheimer said, he will be struck by the fact that a parallelogram would look like a rectangle were it not for the fact that one side has a 'protuberance' and the other side has a 'gap' [see Figure 5.3] . . . Then he realizes that the protuberance is equivalent to the gap; if he moves the protruding corner to the indented side, the figure is converted into a rectangle of the same base and altitude. Hence the formula is the same as it is for a rectangle.

**Figure 5.3**

Thus, although trial and improvement might be involved in solving problems, where a problem has a relatively clear structure it helps to point the way to a solution.

There are four principles of Gestalt psychology, which may be summed up as follows:

1. The *principle of proximity*, which explains why humans tend to organize elements which are close (spatially or temporally) as a unit.
2. The *principle of similarity*, which predicts that elements which have a similar structure are perceived together.
3. The *principle of good continuation*, which explains why humans tend to perceive smooth curves rather than curves which have breaks or sharp angles.
4. The *principle of good form* by which, in a complex diagram where there are many possible configurations embedded, humans tend to perceive only those configurations which form closed shapes, such as triangles, quadrilaterals and circles.

The fact that humans tend to perceive a configuration as a whole has a drawback in that a specific structure or order is imposed on the mind which may prevent the definition and use of crucial elements of a problem. To overcome this imposed structure a reorganization of the elements is needed, which then hopefully enables the individual to comprehend how the elements fit together, thus achieving what Gestaltists termed *structural understanding*. For the parallelogram example, structural understanding occurs when the shape is perceived as equivalent to a rectangle. Both Wertheimer and Katona (1940) attempted to show that structural understanding produces greater success than rote learning, but others have criticized aspects of their methodology. Nevertheless, both of these Gestalt psychologists helped to promote greater understanding of knowledge organization as a key factor in cognitive psychology.

Wertheimer (1961) also recorded the well known story of Gauss who, as quite a young child, is reputed to have found a simple solution to the problem of summing any set of consecutive natural numbers. Given, for simplicity, $1 + 2 + 3 + 4 + 5 + 6 + 7 + 8 + 9 + 10$, insight into the structure might bring to light that $1 + 10 = 2 + 9 = 3 + 8 = 4 + 7 = 5 + 6 = 11$, and hence the sum is $5 \times 11 = 55$. Longer sums, or sums

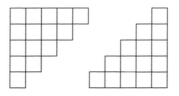

**Figure 5.4**

involving larger numbers, may be obtained in a similar way. Some children might benefit from a pictorial cue to help bring the structure to light (see Figure 5.4). When put together, the two staircases reveal that

$$2(1 + 2 + 3 + 4 + 5) = 5 \times 6$$

and hence, in general,

$$2(1 + 2 + \ldots + n) = n\,(n + 1).$$

Whether many pupils are capable of the kind of insight reputedly shown by Gauss is an open question. What is clearly suggested by Gestalt theory is that demonstration of a result by the teacher might not lead to insight for the pupil. Exposition of how to calculate the area of a parallelogram, perhaps based on proving congruence of the two small triangles, will not necessarily ensure that the pupils understand why it is required that the triangles should be proved congruent. Insight comes as an aspect of the discovery process. The situation needs to be structured so as to make the necessary discovery as certain as possible. The insight gained may then be transferred, and areas of triangles and trapeziums understood.

Gestalt theory acted as the spur for Catherine Stern in the invention of her structural apparatus. Stern, in fact, dedicated her book (Stern with Stern, 1953) to Wertheimer. The Stern structural apparatus was devised to enable children to discover arithmetic for themselves through the prompting of insight which the equipment fostered. It was not enough to learn number by counting – the relationships between numbers needed to be made explicit. Thus, coloured rods were used as the basis, and these rods were segmented to enable pupils to see how many 'unit' rods were equivalent to a particular rod, and to see the difference in value of any two rods (Figure 5.5).

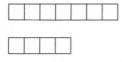

**Figure 5.5**

## Structural apparatus

Simple learning support materials consisting basically of rods and blocks have been used in classrooms for many years, and long before Stern used Gestalt theory as a theoretical support for her advocacy of their use in a structured form. The terms 'manipulative' and 'structural apparatus' have both been used in educational publications to describe such apparatus, though the very words suggest the two terms ought to mean different things. The term 'manipulative' suggests any object which is intended to be handled by the children in a learning situation, but 'structural apparatus' must surely suggest that there is some inbuilt structure to the equipment, perhaps a structure which is intended to reflect and therefore direct the children towards an equivalent mathematical structure. Throughout the last few centuries there have been many different forms of apparatus, even of structural apparatus. There is evidence that earlier educational pioneers, such as Tillich (born 1780) and Froebel (born 1782), advocated the use of concrete equipment in the teaching of elementary number, though this equipment might not have possessed the degree of structure inherent within some of the apparatus developed since that time. For both Tillich and Froebel, however, it did seem that much more than the provision of beads, counters and other unitary equipment was recommended. In particular, the Tillich equipment was concerned with a concrete approach to place value, an idea which was taken up in the mid-twentieth century by Dienes. Froebel claimed that arithmetical relationships and processes will unfold naturally in children's minds if their home and school activities help them to form concepts before they are asked to deal solely with symbols, and he provided rods and blocks to support this unfolding in the classroom. Montessori (born 1870) also used a variety of forms of apparatus, including rods similar to Stern (but bigger), bead bars, counting frames, apparatus for multiplication and division, fraction equipment, and equipment for learning about indices and for studying algebra. According to Resnick and Ford (1984, p. 108), at least some of the Montessori materials 'represent an attempt to teach place value concretely through the systematic use of colour coding and a carefully planned sequence of manipulative materials'. Those of us who have attempted to help children to grasp the essentials of place value can take comfort from the fact that it may not be our fault that pupils often struggle. Eminent educational innovators such as Tillich and Montessori clearly felt compelled to produce materials and equipment intended specifically to support the learning of this essential concept.

There was a surge of interest in structural apparatus in the 1960s, perhaps for a number of reasons. Firstly, there was greater awareness of the work of Piaget, which brought with it the suggested importance of the construction of understanding from activity and from interaction with the learning environment. Secondly, there was growing interest in discovery learning, as a kind of theory concerning how children might be able to learn more effectively. Around this time, also, the use of equipment generally was being greatly encouraged and supported through the work of the Association for Teaching Aids in Mathematics (later to become the ATM). Many schools in Britain thus procured some Stern apparatus, or some Cuisenaire kits, or some of the Dienes equipment, or indeed even some of the other kits such as Unifix. The ones mentioned specifically here together illustrate the point that different apparatus was indeed devised to emphasize different structures. Unifix essentially consists of *cubes* which may be slotted together to form rods. The Stern apparatus, as mentioned earlier, is based on *segmented rods*, so that eventual use of a number line for addition, for example, makes sense (see Figure 5.6). The Cuisenaire equipment

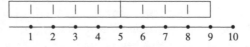

Figure 5.6

consists of *unsegmented rods*, so the numerical relationships have to be learned with the aid of the colours of the rods and in relation to their lengths (whereas the Stern rods allowed children to count the number of units on each rod). It was claimed by Cuisenaire that children grasped essential elementary number concepts better if there was no assistance from segmentation. A further advantage intended from Cuisenaire is that any rod may more easily be defined as the unit, and then shorter rods become fractions. The Dienes Multi-base Arithmetic Blocks (MAB) are different yet again, consisting of small (unit) *cubes*, segmented $1 \times n$ *rods* rather like the Stern rods, $n \times n$ *flats* and $n \times n \times n$ *blocks* (larger cubes), illustrated for base five in Figure 5.7. The Dienes MAB apparatus was originally available in all number bases from two to ten, and the structure it was intended to illustrate is clearly place value. The MAB apparatus was, of course, just one of the types of apparatus which Dienes introduced (or reintroduced) to mathematics (see Chapter 10).

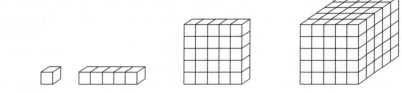

**Figure 5.7**

Modern equivalents of the original apparatus kits are of cheaper plastic, and are more colourful, more attractive to handle, and can provide for more flexible use, for example when based on *interlocking cubes* such as Multilink. With such cubes the teacher needs to build or create the structure, so that with one class the cubes might be assembled as rods and used in the way Stern advocated, and with another class they might be built up into multibase apparatus like Dienes MAB. What must be weighed in the balance, however, are the advantages of cheap and flexible interlocking cubes on the one hand, and the disadvantages of the loss of purpose-built apparatus which requires no prior assembling on the other. With Stern, Cuisenaire and Dienes MAB the structure is in evidence right from the start and, unlike interlocking cubes, the apparatus is not going to collapse or disintegrate when being used, thereby destroying the very structure which is being illustrated.

Throughout the last 40 years or more, sceptics have suggested that the structural apparatus movement of the 1960s was merely another educational bandwagon. At the moment, there is some evidence that teachers in Britain who believe they are under overwhelming pressure from the demands of the National Curriculum are rejecting the use of apparatus as being too time-consuming (Threlfall, 1996). At the same time, some express the view that the equipment doesn't work anyway, though their evidence for this is likely to be anecdotal and their application of the apparatus unknown. Whatever the pressures of teaching, the critical questions remain as they always have, namely (1) do children learn better with or without the support of apparatus, and (2) how should apparatus be used in the classroom in order to achieve the objectives of greater understanding and enlightenment? Cockcroft (1982), in recommending the use of apparatus throughout the whole of the primary school, and into the secondary school for some pupils, suggested that practical work provides the most effective means by which understanding in mathematics can develop. The case for providing children with concrete support for learning mathematics, because they often struggle without it, clearly accepted by respected and prominent educators throughout the 1800s and 1900s, was thus given an official seal of approval. The case for using such support materials is surely just as strong as ever now, so how do we address the criticisms?

The case for using structural apparatus would be overwhelming if research evidence showed that it was clearly beneficial. Unfortunately, and typically with education, it is not as simple and clear cut as that. Some of the research of the 1950s and 1960s certainly suggested that there were immediate gains, but there was usually little evidence of long-term benefits. Two or three years afterwards, any advantages gained through a project based on using structural apparatus had usually disappeared. What many of these studies also revealed very clearly are the difficulties inherent in carrying out educational research. If an experimental group is being compared with a control group, how can one ensure that the two groups are exactly comparable, and that either group is completely denied any input other than what they received from their 'official' lessons? And how can one be sure that any measured effect is independent of the effects introduced by particular teachers? Also, what sort of test should be used at the end of the experiment to ensure a fair comparison between the effects of two very different experiences? One additional well known complication with research studies is that teachers who wish to take part in an experiment in teaching and learning are often stimulated by the whole idea and are very keen to see it succeed. Furthermore, their enthusiasm is conveyed to the pupils, which makes them more enthusiastic in turn, and so learning may be enhanced through enthusiasm. Under such circumstances, any measured gain is therefore likely to be the outcome of an inseparable combination of the effects of new materials and methods and the total involvement of the teacher and the pupils. It is also well known that the most likely significant variable in trying to improve learning is the quality of the teaching.

The problems with evaluating the effectiveness of apparatus do not end there. In the years both before and since the Cockcroft Committee lent its support to the use of structural apparatus, serious concerns have been expressed about the effectiveness of its use, and these need to be addressed. The main conclusion must be that simply providing children with apparatus is often not enough, because the children will not necessarily see any connection between the bricks and the sums. Holt (1964), writing on his experiences of using Cuisenaire rods with children, tells of his delight in having discovered apparatus which could be used to reflect the way numbers worked – but his dismay on realizing that he already knew how the numbers behaved, and that was why he was able to see the connection so clearly. Unfortunately, as he explained, it is not so clear for many of the children:

> We want the rods to turn the mumbo-jumbo of arithmetic into sense. The danger is that the mumbo-jumbo may engulf the rods instead. It doesn't do any good to tell [her] to look at the rods if she doesn't believe that when she looks she will find the answer there. She will only have two mysteries to contend with instead of one. (p. 87)

Dearden (1967, p. 146) expressed similar doubts when he stated that, 'in some mysterious way, a special potency is thought to inhere in . . . apparatus such that if children play with it or manipulate it, significant experiences must be had, and important concepts must be abstracted'. For Dearden, the essential flaw in the claims for using apparatus was the assumption that children would perceive for themselves the structure that the apparatus embodies. Hart (1989, p. 142), on the basis of research data, expressed the problem thus:

> Many of us have believed that in order to teach formal mathematics one should build up to the formalization by using materials, and that the child will then better understand the process. I now believe that the gap between the two types of experience is too large.

She went on to provide a striking example of why the provision of apparatus might not be helpful to understanding the intended mathematical ideas:

> Consider ... the case of a class of 8-year-olds who used Unifix blocks to do subtraction questions building up to the algorithm involving decomposition. A valid and much used method of solving $56 - 28$ was to set out 56 as five columns of ten bricks and six bricks and then to use 28 as a mental instruction. This was followed by the removal of three of the tens, returning two units (broken off one of the tens) to the table. Finally, the collection still left on the table was counted. This (method) . . . has very little connection to the algorithm, which is supposed to result from all the experience with bricks.

The conclusion we must draw is that apparatus is not a panacea which, if provided, will solve problems of learning elementary number concepts. Dearden (1967), stressed the importance of the role of the teacher in being much more than the hovering provider of materials, or the structurer of an environment from which new concepts are supposed to be abstracted in the course of undirected activity. Thus, the teacher needs to question, discuss, hint, suggest and instruct what to do to find out. It is perhaps significant that the Cockcroft Committee (1982, p. 84) were careful to expand on the simplistic view that apparatus was important:

> such work (with apparatus) requires a considerable amount of time. However, provided that the practical work is properly structured with a wide variety of experience and clear stages of progression, and is followed up by the teacher by means of questions and discussion, this time is well spent.

Thus, it is clear that, far from providing the teacher with materials that children can learn from without any teacher input, the provision of apparatus places great demands on both lesson planning and classroom implementation.

Dickson *et al.* (1984) reported many studies to support the view that the rules of arithmetic are forgotten if not supported by understanding and that understanding is best facilitated with the help of concrete materials. Threlfall (1996) has provided a detailed and timely reminder of all the benefits which might accrue from the use of apparatus. At the same time he points out that the apparatus will not show its full value if it is used inappropriately, for example, in supporting calculations: 'to use the apparatus to get answers is to obscure its purpose and prevent it from having its true value, which is to bring meaning to arithmetic', and, 'if there are children who cannot do the calculations without the apparatus, they should not yet be doing such calculations' (pp. 10–11). Hart (1989) pointed out that it is very important that children understand the connection the apparatus is intended to support, and that teachers need to devote considerable time and attention to explaining the connection under consideration. Furthermore, even when we do attempt to relate the practical activities to the abstraction, we must not expect all of the pupils to understand this connection immediately – in other words they will not necessarily all be 'ready'. The evidence available to us about disappointments when apparatus is used does not add up to the conviction that practical work with apparatus is a waste of time. Rather, it suggests that: (1) our expectations in the past have perhaps been unrealistic, (2) the mere provision of apparatus is usually not enough, (3) the issue of readiness is still clearly also relevant, (4) it is not easy to organize learning situations so that all the pupils may use the apparatus to develop their thinking, and (5) it is not always easy to know what to do and say as we move around assisting the children to progress.

## Problems and investigations

The desire to help learners to become better problem-solvers is a frequently expressed aim of education, and not only of mathematical education. Although it has been claimed (Anderson, 1985; Newell and Simon, 1972) that all cognitive activities are fundamentally problem-solving in nature, we do need to be clear what is usually meant by problem-solving in mathematics. First, we must suggest that there are different kinds of problems in mathematics, one possible classification being into routine practice problems, word problems (see Chapter 9), real-life applications and novel situations (see also Chapter 2). It is the last of these four which is usually what is meant when discussing problem-solving. Gagné (1985, p. 178), who classed such problem-solving as the highest form of learning, defined it as 'a process by which the learner discovers a combination of previously learned rules . . . [which can be applied] . . . to achieve a solution for a novel problem situation'. Here, the word 'rule' is being used in a way similar to that in which Descartes used it as anything which has been proved or established on a previous occasion. Other researchers have attempted to study problem-solving by using the idea of 'states'; at the outset a task is in a particular state, it is hoped to attain a different state, but there is no obvious direct way to journey from the initial state to the final state. Some people believe that solving problems is the essence of mathematics learning, even to the extent of considering that the body of knowledge, which others regard as mathematics, is merely the set of tools available for the active process of problem-solving. This process, it can be claimed, is a creative act of striving for a goal (specified or unspecified) based on discovering new ways of combining or uniting prior learning. Thus, insight is likely to be required in solving novel problems. Johnson and Rising (1967) declared that: 'learning to solve problems is the most significant learning in *every* mathematics class'. They gave five reasons for this: it is a way of learning new concepts, it is a way of discovering new knowledge, it is a meaningful way to practise computational skills, it is a way of stimulating intellectual curiosity, and it is a way of learning to transfer concepts and skills to new situations. Problem-solving studies have produced an immense bibliography (see, for example, Hill, 1979). Lester (1977) suggested that research into human problem-solving has a well-earned reputation for being the most chaotic of all identifiable categories of human learning. Although this should warn us to be careful about drawing conclusions, it could be said that almost any category of studies of human learning is prone to produce inconclusive results!

The description 'investigation' has appeared in the literature on learning mathematics much more frequently in the last thirty years. The exact distinction between an investigation and a problem has rarely been clarified by advocates of their inclusion in the curriculum, and it is still not always clear what is meant when either is being discussed today. Disappointingly, Cockcroft (1982) and Her Majesty's Inspectorate (1985) both chose not to distinguish between them. Both words encompass the idea of active participation in learning on the part of the child, and to some people that is all that is important. Others suggest that we really ought to try to define the distinction in order that we can make it clear to our pupils exactly what we are requiring of them in a particular task. Of the two, 'problem' has a more static feel about it, though activity is involved in striving for a solution. 'Investigation' has an active feel about it, though an investigation could, presumably, incorporate a problem or might lead to a problem. There is some suggestion in the words that a problem has a definite end-point, and is thus essentially a convergent process, whether there is a solution or not, whilst an investigation might offer much more openness, and is likely to provide scope for divergence. Frobisher (1994) has discussed the issue of the importance of being clear about whether we are setting a problem (routine, word, real-life or novel) or an investigation. He has also provided suggestions about how convergent routine tasks may be converted into more open investigations, thus at the same time providing a hint as to what the difference between a problem and an investigation might be. The simplest kind of example concerns routine practice problems, for example:

$$
\begin{array}{r}
36 \\
+\,23 \\
\hline
59
\end{array}
$$

We might justifiably open this situation up by asking questions based on the property that there are six digits here, and although it is the 'answer' (59) which is required in a convergent problem, any one or more of the six digits might be the unknown(s). Thus we could create all kinds of tasks which are much more like investigations, for example based on finding the missing numbers in:

$$
\begin{array}{cccccc}
48 & 2X & 26 & 25 & 37 & AB \\
+\,2A & +\,1X & +\,3L & +\,1P & +\,TU & +\,BA \\
\hline
B9 & Y2 & 5M & 4Q & 9V & CD
\end{array}
$$

Opportunities to convert a convergent task into something which provides greater scope for investigation, inventiveness and creativity surely ought to be grasped, at least from time to time, if we wish to develop problem-solving skills. Also, although there might well be an important distinction between a problem and an investigation, it is clear that either or both may be developed from the same basic idea or situation.

Like other active approaches to learning, the use of problem-solving as a deliberately intended component of a mathematics curriculum involves a radical change of teaching approach from the more traditional exposition and practice of skills. The impression conveyed to learners at all levels by expository approaches to mathematics is that the subject necessitates a clean, logical, tidy sequence of statements and a tightly-controlled crystal-clear argument. We pursue this by such instructions as always working down the page, keeping the 'equals' signs directly underneath each other in a mathematical solution, providing suitable links between lines in an argument (for example, by using the symbol for 'therefore', or for 'implies'), and so on. Many learners may never appreciate that the process of establishing mathematical results, theorems and rules in the first place probably involved some very untidy activity indeed. It is this potentially untidy activity which those who are persuaded that the process side of mathematics is important are anxious to allow. Of course, the activity might turn out to be quite tidy, but the point is that we do not mind if investigations and problems lead to untidy recording. This does not imply that our approaches to active mathematics need be unsystematic, in fact it could be argued that we should always be attempting to promote systematic approaches to problem-solving. The point is that we have all frequently used the backs of envelopes to solve problems, but we can subsequently tidy up our solutions in order that others might read them (though it is better if they work them out for themselves!).

An early, extensive and famous, study of problem-solving in mathematics was carried out by Polya (1957), in which he suggested ways of improving the teaching and learning of problem-solving. In fact, he claimed that solving problems was a practical skill like swimming, and therefore both imitation and practice were needed if improvement was to take place. To some extent this might well be true, but the differences between mental and physical activity would suggest that this conclusion is too simplistic, and that the reality of developing problem-solving proficiency cannot be explained quite so straightforwardly. Wickelgren (1974) has subsequently followed in Polya's footsteps in trying to describe and explain how problem-solving skills may be developed. More recent research into human problem-solving abilities has drawn attention to comparisons with the use of a computer to solve problems. Problem-solving involves the processing of information, an activity for which computers are well suited, particularly when many possibilities need to be studied. A considerable proportion of current research in mathematics involves lengthy computer searches, as for example in the continuing attempts to identify larger and larger prime numbers. Such modern research perhaps confirms that problem-solving is still prone to be an essentially untidy activity, sometimes made to appear tidy only because most of the processing carried out by the computer remains concealed.

The essence of Polya's *How to Solve It* was the elaboration and justification of a self-questioning procedure to be carried out by the solver. This technique involves four stages: (1) understanding the problem, (2) devising a plan, (3) carrying out the plan and (4) looking back. The first stage must not be dismissed as trivial, for it includes such essential steps as drawing a diagram and introducing suitable notation, in addition to considerations like trying to decide whether the information provided is sufficient and whether it incorporates any redundancy. The last stage involves the final checking, but also includes extension considerations such as whether the result may be generalized and whether alternative, perhaps more economical, solutions might exist. The crucial and sometimes very difficult stages both to carry out and to explain are the middle two, particularly stage (2) for which inventiveness and insight might be required. In reality, the problem-solving process might involve circularity or looping, illustrated in Figure 5.8.

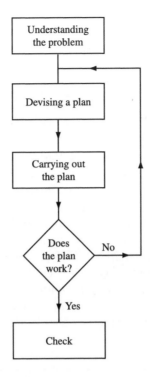

**Figure 5.8**

It is interesting that Hadamard (1945), drawing from writings and statements of famous mathematicians, himself included, also independently suggested that there were four stages in the solution of a problem. His stages were: (1) preparation, (2) incubation, (3) illumination and (4) verification. The first and last of these stages are clearly similar to those described by Polya. If there is a difference it must lie in the middle two stages where Polya's belief, that by practising a routine pupils and students can become better problem-solvers, might seem to be at variance with Hadamard's apparent implication that you almost have to sit back and wait for illumination. Of course, it could be said that the two were writing about different levels of problem-solving. Hadamard was writing more about the process of creating new mathematics whereas Polya was writing more with the ordinary mathematics student in mind. But even restricting ourselves to the school situation one suspects there is common ground in both. For particular students and for many problems the Polya routine might work, but there are likely to be other problems for which application of the routine does not automatically lead to a solution. Almost everyone has experienced being unable to solve a problem at a particular moment, even after much effort but, having slept on it, or having gone away to do something different, a fruitful idea has suddenly and unexpectedly come to mind. Unfortunately, this cannot be relied on either, for there are some problems which we never solve. The incubation and illumination sequence is, of course, very interesting from the point of view of studies of learning. The only tenable theory so far produced to explain sudden illumination is that the mind continues to search for meaning, to look for and try out connections, but at a subconscious level, thus it can produce ideas whilst we sleep and whilst we are doing other things. Sadly, this theory suggests that we might produce wonderful ideas whilst we sleep which never come to the surface when we reawaken! Winston (2003) suggests that it is necessary sometimes to clear and relax the mind, because when the mind is too full of 'noise' and bustle the tiny signal of an original thought cannot and does not stand out.

There have been other, similar, studies of problem-solving. Hadamard gathered his ideas from a number of sources, one such major source being Poincaré who suggested there might be a kind of aesthetic element in the process (see Poincaré, 1970). The subconscious mind never ceases trying out connections but the ones which emerge at the surface are the ones which are, in a mathematical sense, the most pleasing, elegant or even beautiful. This is not a theory which will enable us to teach our pupils to become better problem-solvers! Dewey (1910) also wrote about the problem-solving sequence. He outlined five stages, which were: (1) the presentation of the problem, (2) the definition of the problem in terms of, for example, distinguishing essential features, (3) the formulation of a hypothesis, (4) the testing of the hypothesis and (5) the verification of the hypothesis. The similarity with Polya's stages is striking, indeed Dewey's list looks like a forerunner. However, such stages are all very well, but what do they imply in relation to classroom practice? What do we actually have to do within each of these stages? What should our thought processes be? The 'Divisors' problem (often described as an investigation) might help us here.

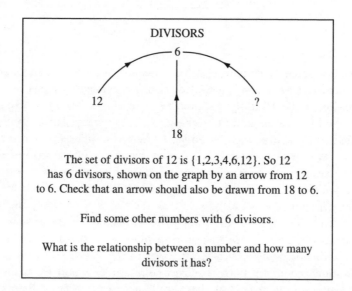

DIVISORS

The set of divisors of 12 is {1,2,3,4,6,12}. So 12
has 6 divisors, shown on the graph by an arrow from 12
to 6. Check that an arrow should also be drawn from 18 to 6.

Find some other numbers with 6 divisors.

What is the relationship between a number and how many
divisors it has?

This task first directs students to use trialling to find more whole numbers with six divisors, and numbers such as 20, 28 and 32 should emerge. Subsequently, in order to relate a number to how many divisors it has, in what is the main task, it is necessary to widen the search. Every whole number from 1 upwards needs to be investigated to ascertain how many divisors it has. In this way it will be found that 2, 3, 5 and 7 are examples of the many numbers with two divisors, and that 4, 9 and 25 have three divisors. Eventually, it should become apparent that tabulation might clarify matters still further. This entire first stage may be summed up as data collection leading to a systematic recording of results. Table 5.2 shows the resultant classification for the numbers 1 to 40. We are now in a position to look at the properties of the rows

**Table 5.2** Numbers and their number of divisors

| Number of divisors | Numbers |
|---|---|
| 1 | 1 |
| 2 | 2, 3, 5, 7, 11, 13, 17, 19, 23, 29, 31, 37 |
| 3 | 4, 9, 25 |
| 4 | 6, 8, 10, 14, 15, 21, 22, 26, 27, 33, 34, 35, 38, 39 |
| 5 | 16 |
| 6 | 12, 18, 20, 28, 32 |
| 7 | – |
| 8 | 24, 30, 40 |
| 9 | 36 |

of numbers, and certain features should be apparent immediately. Firstly, only one number (unity) has one divisor. Secondly, all the numbers with two divisors are prime. May we draw the conclusion that the only numbers with two divisors are the primes? Thirdly, all the numbers with three divisors are perfect squares. But some perfect squares apparently have more than three divisors (16 and 36, for example), so what may we deduce from that information? Many numbers have four divisors, but there is a confusing mixture here. Close inspection reveals that the perfect cubes 8 and 27 are present, but what are all the other numbers (6, 10, 14, 15, 21, 22, 26, etc.)? Will all perfect cubes have exactly four divisors? Why is there only one number for five divisors and one number for nine divisors? Why are there no numbers for seven divisors? Do any numbers exist which have seven divisors? The investigation started with data collection, then involved systematic tabulation, pattern-spotting, problem-posing, hypothesis formulation, and finally led to hypothesis checking. This particular investigation is very relevant to the ordinary mathematics curriculum, though it is not easy to carry the process through to what might be thought of as a final conclusion. Nevertheless, different ages and stages of pupils can all make some progress. The link with the stages suggested by Polya and others, however, seems to be somewhat tenuous.

This illustration of problem-solving in action is similar to the illustrations contained in the Joint Matriculation Board/Shell Centre pack *Problems with Patterns and Numbers* (1984). The main assumption underlying this pack seems to be that it is possible to teach children to become better problem-solvers. Included in the pack is a recommended routine to be followed when presented with a problem, namely:

Try some simple cases,
Find a helpful diagram,
Organize systematically,
Make a table,
Spot patterns,
Use the patterns,
Find a rule,
Check the rule,
Explain why it works.

This list of steps applies fairly well to 'Divisors', but only up to the stage of under-standing the patterns; finding a rule is then very difficult for pupils. Thus, even this one example suggests that any recommended routine is not likely to apply to all problems. Indeed, the JMB/Shell Centre routine basically only applies to the kinds of problems which subsequently appeared in examination papers, specimen questions and curriculum documents. In other words, this procedure works for a very limited range of problems, just as Polya's does. There must also be dangers with this kind of prescriptive approach to problem-solving. It gives a false impression of what problem-solving is about. It only helps pupils to solve particular kinds of simple problems. It even suggests that collecting numbers, tabulating and spotting patterns is the key to problem-solving. And it moves us away from openness and creativity and back towards using a learned routine, thus seeming to defeat the objective of setting problems and investigations. On the other hand, supporters could claim that it does provide a beginning, by setting out to enable pupils to experience solving one kind of problem. After all, in teaching we often have to be satisfied with one small step at a time.

What is not clear from the JMB/Shell Centre list is the importance of asking the right questions and seeking answers to them. Problem-solving is always likely to involve problem-posing. There could be valuable questions to ask oneself at all stages in the solving procedure. At the start, there might be simple clarification, for example, when asked to find how many squares there are on a chessboard. Does this task involve only the $1 \times 1$ squares, or are other sizes like $2 \times 2$ and $3 \times 3$ to be included? In finding sets of three numbers which fit the rule $x^2 + y^2 = z^2$ must the numbers be integers, or are other numbers allowable? What about complex numbers? These are 'clearing the ground' questions. Then, as with 'Divisors', questions will arise within the processes of collecting and ordering any data, such as what is it about 24, 30 and 40 which makes them have exactly eight divisors? Later on still, once a kind of rule has been found for each row, is it possible to sum the whole situation up with one all-embracing rule? At the end of an assignment, when the problem has supposedly been solved, there might still be the opportunity to pose extension problems. For example, in relation to Pythagoras' theorem, how does the rule change if the triangle is not right-angled? The geometrical illustration of the rule involves squares, but does it work for other shapes and, if so, which shapes? Is there a three-dimensional equivalent to Pythagoras' theorem? Does the rule work for cubes and higher powers as well as for squares? What would be the geometrical illustration for a rule like $x^2 + y^2 = z^2 + 1$? Brown and Walter (1983, p. 2) suggest that, 'problem-posing is deeply embedded in the activity of problem-solving . . . it is impossible to solve any novel problem without first reconstructing the task by posing new problems'. Perhaps it is more important to try to teach pupils to ask questions and pose new problems rather than to give them a routine to apply to a very limited range of problems.

Polya (1957) was probably the first to attempt to provide a list of suitable questions in his suggested problem-solving procedure. For each of his stages he outlined some questions which he thought the solver should ask, though not all of these questions are likely to turn out to be relevant to all problems. Some of those at his first stage have already been presented, though it is important to reiterate here the value of drawing a diagram (when appropriate) and introducing suitable notation. His longest list of questions is for the critical second stage. These include trying to relate the new task to previously solved problems, relaxing the conditions, trying to solve a truncated version of the problem, and using the data to see what emerges, to list just a few of the suggestions. Once the problem is solved, he recommends checking, looking for alternative ways of proving the result, trying out the procedure on other problems, and generally looking beyond the problem. Here is a problem (Polya, 1957, p. 237) on which this procedure may be tested. How well does it fit his routine?

> The length of the perimeter of a right-angled triangle is 60 cm and the length of the altitude perpendicular to the hypotenuse is 12 cm. Find the lengths of the sides of the triangle.

Brown and Walter (1983) also provided a list of questions to ask when solving a problem. It is too long to include here, but it incorporates issues such as whether there is a formula, whether there is a pattern, whether there are examples or counter-examples, whether a table would help, whether there is a range of answers, what the data suggests, and so on. What the work of Polya, Brown and Walter, Wickelgren, and many others indicate is the impossibility of being completely prescriptive. Problems are many and varied, and thus cannot be classified easily, so it should not be surprising that it is difficult to teach pupils how to solve them. Indeed, Brown and Walter admit they do not have a simple prescription, or even a complete list of suitable questions. Rather, what they are seeking to emphasize are both the importance of knowing what kinds of questions to pose and of accepting that different circumstances are likely to require different sets of questions.

Another issue related to pupils' active participation in problems and investigations concerns recording. What should we expect pupils to be writing down? What are the purposes of written recording, and what part do they play in the learning process? Traditionally, writing in sentences has not been a frequent activity of mathematics classrooms, but some recent and current investigative projects, such as those used for public examination purposes, expect the progression of steps and associated findings to be recorded clearly and set within descriptive writing. Morgan (1998) has discussed mathematical writing, and in particular the assessment of written reports of investigative work, very fully. There are many important issues and difficulties related to such assessment, but they are not our concern in this book. Mason *et al.* (1985a) have suggested that recording and writing up play a significant role in developing mathematical thinking. Common sense would support such views, given that writing down one's thoughts and conclusions does generally make them clearer and more open for reconsideration and possible improvement (c.f. the use of discussion – see Chapter 9). Thus, when pupils produce a written report, it should make it easier for the pupil to reflect, to check, to amend, and to understand what has been achieved. But is this how it works out in practice? Or do some pupils find the written recording a burden and a hindrance to learning? Are there significant differences in what can be gained from extended writing between boys and girls, between ethnic groups, or between pupils of different abilities? We need to know much more about the potential benefits and drawbacks of encouraging pupils to write extended reports or essays in mathematics, whether for investigations or otherwise.

A sometimes difficult but vitally important stage in solving some problems involves finding a rule from a pattern. Generalization is likely to be the key, an activity which was fully considered by Polya. A simple example of generalizing is in the search for a formula for the sum of the cubes of the natural numbers. Trying out simple cases systematically produces:

$$1^3 = 1$$
$$1^3 + 2^3 = 9$$
$$1^3 + 2^3 + 3^3 = 36$$
$$1^3 + 2^3 + 3^3 + 4^3 = 100$$
$$1^3 + 2^3 + 3^3 + 4^3 + 5^3 = 225$$

The pattern of the totals should immediately suggest squares, for $1 = 1^2$, $9 = 3^2$, $36 = 6^2$, $100 = 10^2$ and $225 = 15^2$. We now have a derived pattern, the numbers 1, 3, 6, 10 and 15, the first five triangular numbers, and these are the sums of consecutive natural numbers:

$$1 = 1$$
$$1 + 2 = 3$$
$$1 + 2 + 3 = 6$$
$$1 + 2 + 3 + 4 = 10$$
$$1 + 2 + 3 + 4 + 5 = 15$$

which then leads us to the generalization we really wanted:

$$1^3 + 2^3 + \ldots \ldots + n^3 = (1 + 2 + \ldots \ldots + n)^2.$$

Not all attempts to generalize in problem situations are as straightforward as this! And even this example based on familiar number patterns is difficult for most pupils below the sixth form. To complete the process a mathematician would now require a proof of the generalization. The usual sixth form method of proof for this result is induction, a method which many students, meeting it for the first time, regard with great suspicion. There is, for them, a feeling of having assumed the result which they were expected to prove and so, having made the assumption, the 'proof' cannot be a proof. This is an indication that barriers can occur in the mind, and that there can be hurdles which students can take a long time to surmount. There are, indeed, other well known barriers to problem-solving which are considered in a later section of this chapter.

If it is important that pupils learn how to solve problems, it is equally important that they learn about proof in mathematics. How do we set about proving results? What constitutes a proof? What different ways of proving are there? This is much too large an aspect of learning mathematics to tackle in a chapter on discovering mathematics, but discussion of pattern and proof will be continued in the next chapter. Polya's *How to Solve It* did include a discussion of all of the standard methods of proof in mathematics, which he calls induction, deduction, contradiction, counter-example, and working backwards. He also continued his work in two further books (1954 and 1962). Wickelgren (1974) based his work on the same premise as Polya, namely that problem-solving in mathematics can be learned, and indeed he was careful to acknowledge the pioneering work of Polya. An important aspect of Wickelgren's work is his claim that there are only seven types of mathematical problem, in the sense that in order to achieve a solution it was necessary to use one or other of the seven methods which he explained in considerable detail. Each of these seven methods, he claimed, needed to be practised, if one wished to become a better problem-solver. Wickelgren also included an enormous number of problems in his book, which should be of great interest to teachers of mathematics. In recent years many other books have been published which are concerned with helping teachers to take problem-solving into the classroom (see, for example, Burton, 1984).

## Obstacles and difficulties in problem-solving

There are a number of well known obstacles and difficulties which might hinder attempts to solve problems. These will be discussed with reference to the following six problems which the reader should attempt before reading on.

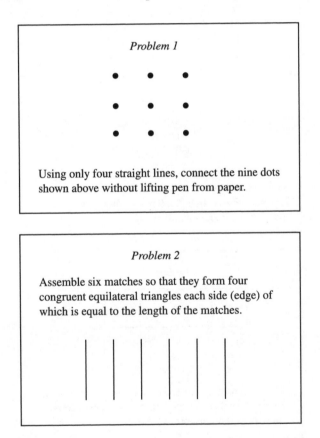

*Problem 1*

Using only four straight lines, connect the nine dots shown above without lifting pen from paper.

*Problem 2*

Assemble six matches so that they form four congruent equilateral triangles each side (edge) of which is equal to the length of the matches.

*Problem 3*

Four soldiers have to cross a river. The only means of transportation is a small boat in which two boys are playing. The boat can carry at most two boys or one soldier. How can the soldiers cross to the other side?

---

*Problem 4*

Given 3 containers ('buckets') and plenty of water, the task is to measure out a required amount.
Example: Given 3, 21 and 127 litre buckets, measure out 100 litres.

Solution: $100 = 127 - 21 - 3 - 3$.

Problems:

|   | *Buckets* | | | *Goal* |
|---|---|---|---|---|
|   | *a* | *b* | *c* | |
| 1 | 21 | 127 | 3 | 100 |
| 2 | 14 | 46 | 5 | 22 |
| 3 | 18 | 43 | 10 | 5 |
| 4 | 7 | 42 | 6 | 23 |
| 5 | 20 | 57 | 4 | 29 |
| 6 | 23 | 49 | 3 | 20 |
| 7 | 15 | 39 | 3 | 18 |

---

*Problem 5*

Given the sum

DONALD
+ GERALD
ROBERT

and the fact that D = 5, find what numbers the letters represent. Every digit 0 to 9 has a different letter, every letter has a different number.

---

*Problem 6*

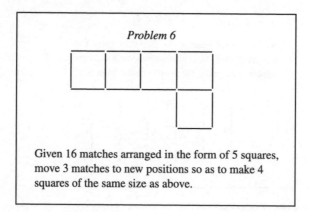

Given 16 matches arranged in the form of 5 squares, move 3 matches to new positions so as to make 4 squares of the same size as above.

---

The problems above, or variations on them, have been so widely used that it is difficult to know where they originated. They have been used, however, by a variety of researchers involved in investigating human problem-solving behaviour.

Very few people, including university students of mathematics, are able to solve Problem 1 within a limited time period. It is necessary to draw lines which go outside the shape implicitly defined by the nine dots (see Figure 5.9). It appears that most

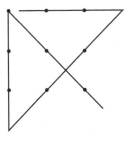

**Figure 5.9**

people work under the assumption that the four lines must lie entirely within the shape, yet no such restriction was stated in the question. The phenomenon was discussed by Scheerer (1963) as 'fixation', sometimes referred to as 'problem-solving set'. It appears that we are prone to making initial assumptions which are not included in the problem specification.

The second problem also brings to light another fixation. Most people try to arrange the matches on a flat surface and fail to appreciate the novel three-dimensional use which is required. The solution (shown in Figure 5.10) is to arrange the matches into a tetrahedron.

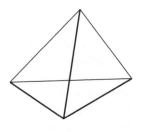

**Figure 5.10**

The third problem, sometimes rather less of a problem than the other two as far as mathematics students are concerned, depends on an iteration or cycle of moves. The fixation here is described by Scheerer as unwillingness to accept a detour when it appears that the achievement of the required goal is being unnecessarily delayed. The solution requires the two boys to row across, one to return with the boat, one soldier to cross in the boat, and the second boy to bring the boat back. That completes the first cycle, so the problem is solved after three more cycles. It appears that some people cannot surmount that barrier of 'undoing' what has already seemingly been achieved.

The barrier of fixation is a major discussion point in the paper by Scheerer (1963, p. 9) who wrote: 'If insight is the essential element in intelligent problem-solving, fixation is its arch enemy'. Fixation, however, is not the only possible barrier or difficulty. In Problem 4, all of the seven parts of the problem may be completed in a routine way using $b - a - c - c$. The inclination we all have, once we have settled into a routine, is not to look for another method. Thus we might fail to see that part 6 only requires $a - c$ and part 7 only $a + c$. In general, in mathematics, we are sometimes inclined to overlook a quicker route in our haste to apply an established routine. This particular barrier was described by Scheerer as 'habituation'.

There is yet another barrier to successful problem-solving, known as 'over-motivation'. Scheerer's explanation was that '. . . there is some evidence that strong ego-involvement in a problem makes for over-motivation and is detrimental to a solution' (p. 9). Thus, for example, when a pupil presents the mathematics teacher with a novel mathematics problem and then waits around to watch over the attempts at solution, a situation of over-motivation can arise! But this barrier, and the others mentioned earlier, must affect pupils too. Indeed, it is rather reminiscent of what professional sports teams experience when playing away in a cup-tie against supposedly inferior opposition!

Newell and Simon (1972) used Problem 5 to research how subjects attempted the task. They found that subjects who achieved the solution all followed very similar paths, based on processing the most constrained columns in order of emergence. Thus $T = 0, E = 9, A = 4, R = 7, G = 1, L = 8, N = 6, B = 3$ and $O = 2$. In this problem there is little need for much more than serial processing which places little demand on short-term memory. If, however, we tried to solve the problem by investigating the number of possible assignments of digits to letters we would find the demands of the search procedure unacceptable. In general terms, Newell and Simon suggested that we are willing to endure only a limited amount of trialling. So, in situations which involve a huge 'problem-space' it is necessary to isolate promising parts of the space, or to first find promising approaches with which we can cope.

The sixth problem is one of many variations on the theme of moving matches, sticks or other objects in order to achieve a specified transformation. The expected solution is shown in Figure 5.11. Katona (1940) used problems of this type in Gestalt studies of problem-solving. Of three methods used to try to promote successful problem-solving he discovered that the least effective was to demonstrate the solution and then rely on the solver remembering the procedure. Such a method is basically rote learning, and provides no connection to units of existing knowledge structured in the mind. A second method used by Katona was to make helpful statements like, for example, 'matches with double functions should be moved so that they have single functions', and, 'proceed by creating holes and generally loosening the figures'. This method was reasonably effective in promoting success but the best teaching method was to illustrate what changes would be brought about by particular moves of individual matches, such as moving one with a double function. It is interesting that both the second and third methods were based on providing limited guidance. The second was based on making verbal statements but the third, the most successful, was based on carrying out particular actions and forcing the student to try out particular moves and think about their effects.

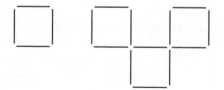

Figure 5.11

Newell and Simon (1972) have also pointed out difficulties in problem-solving which stem from the limitations of the human information-processing system. Firstly, we can only operate in a serial manner, one process at a time, and not on several processes in parallel. Secondly, whatever processing we do has to pass through our short-term memory, which has a limited capacity of around seven units of information

(Miller, 1956). Sometimes it might be possible to retain more in our short-term memory by chunking units of knowledge, but we are still limited. Thirdly, although we have apparently virtually unlimited storage capacity in long-term memory, there is the difficulty of committing knowledge to it. It takes a long time to do this in comparison with the very short time required for actual processing. It can also be difficult to do it unless we can link the new knowledge to existing knowledge. Retrieval of knowledge held in long-term memory is by no means automatic.

## Logo

Most teachers are now familiar with Logo as a computer microworld, within which children may discover mathematics. Seymour Papert, co-inventor of Logo as a computer programming language, was the original instigator of school activities, and pioneered the use of a mobile electronic 'turtle' which can trace out shapes on a classroom floor. Hence this often highly motivating school application of Logo is sometimes referred to as 'turtle geometry'. Papert gained his enthusiasm for active, discovery-type learning environments directly from Piaget, with whom he worked for five years. Summing up his impressions of Piaget's work at Geneva, he said he left, 'impressed by [Piaget's] way of looking at children as the active builders of their own intellectual structures' (Papert, 1980, p. 19), but he believed that the enrichment of the learning environment through the use of materials was of greater significance than Piaget had suggested. The task of drawing a regular pentagon without Logo requires some knowledge of angles, such as angles at the centre, interior angles, and exterior angles. By using a computer equipped with Logo facilities, however, children are able to explore the drawing of polygons, starting with squares and rectangles, and building up to more difficult constructions such as regular pentagons. Trial and improvement is clearly involved but, possibly because the computer is motivating, and because the computer removes much of the potential tedium of continuous trialling, children are able to construct their own polygons and develop their understanding of shapes and their properties.

Papert's approach to the application of Piagetian theory to education involved a mildly critical attack on the perceived implications of accepting the notions of concrete and formal thinking. Papert claimed that the boundary between the two could be moved, with the help of the computer, and that the computer can concretize (and personalize) the formal. The computer provides the additional advantage that the child's anxiety level is reduced, and the desire to obtain the correct solution is not so compelling. Working in an exploratory way with Logo not only guarantees many wrong attempts, producing merely impersonal and uncritical responses on the screen, it also encourages the process of 'debugging', claimed by Papert as an important life skill. Papert believed that the usual mathematics curriculum was meaningless to most children, but Logo allowed them to construct knowledge in a meaningful way.

Subsequent experience of using Logo in ordinary classrooms has, however, convinced many teachers that pupils cannot work entirely on their own in the way Papert seems to suggest is both possible and desirable, and that skilful teacher mediation between the child and the software is needed. There have also been some objections firstly on the grounds that Logo is too difficult, and secondly that it takes too much time. The first is best evaluated through studying the findings of the Logo Maths Project (Hoyles and Sutherland, 1989), and other research reports. There is no short answer to the second – save to say that so does all learning.

A very large amount of research into the use of Logo with children has now been carried out. According to Noss and Hoyles (1996), early Logo-based research tended to adopt a learning-transfer approach which invariably ended in trivial outcomes. Papert was never directly interested in using Logo to teach curriculum content, and believed that Logo programming was best seen as a means of fostering ways of thinking which would subsequently make it easier to learn content. Noss and Hoyles pursue this thought in drawing our attention to the potential outcomes of Logo as a curriculum priority, alongside the current ones of literacy and numeracy. This might be an exciting prospect to some, but busy teachers endeavouring to cope with an overfull curriculum are looking for more direct advice, which they might find in reports such as that of the Logo Maths Project. A major aim of this study was to encourage an interactive exploratory environment, in which pupils were allowed to work in pairs, thus having to learn to discuss and cooperate. Dependence on teachers was discouraged, pupils determined their own goals, and teacher inter-actions always attempted to push decision-making back to the pupils. Individual conceptual development was clearly observed as the feedback provoked recon-sideration of ideas, thus allowing pupils to move on from earlier conceptions. There were gender differences both in pupil approaches and in role demarcation, with boys favouring more well defined goals than girls, and boys being more competitive and generally less willing to share. Emotional resistance from past mathematical experiences was exposed, and misconceptions were brought to light. Logo also proved to be a natural and profitable context for generalizing and formalizing. Most importantly, the role of the teacher was clarified – the teacher is the pivotal mediator of the technicalities of the language, the mathematics embedded in the computer activity, the problem-solving processes and the connections between Logo and paper and pencil work.

## Suggestions for further reading

Biggs, E. E. (1972) 'Investigational methods' in L. R. Chapman (ed.) *The Process of Learning Mathematics*. Oxford: Pergamon Press.
Brown, S. I. and Walter, M. I. (1983) *The Art of Problem Posing*. Philadelphia: The Franklin Institute Press.
Papert, S. (1980) *Mindstorms*. Brighton: Harvester Press.
Polya, G. (1957) *How to Solve It*. New York: Doubleday Anchor Books.
Stern, C. with Stern, M. B. (1953) *Children Discover Arithmetic*. London: Harrap.

## Questions for discussion

1. Under what conditions are children able to discover mathematics for themselves?
2. Is problem-solving the essence of mathematics?
3. How should structural apparatus be used in helping children to learn basic number knowledge?
4. What obstacles to problem-solving have you observed amongst your pupils and students?

Chapter 6

# Is an Appreciation of Pattern Important in Learning Mathematics?

## Pattern in mathematics

In the previous chapter, we have seen how patterns can arise in classroom problem-solving situations. When this happens, the key to solving the problem may lie in finding a rule from the pattern. In learning mathematics, children are often encouraged to base their understanding on patterns, particularly of numbers, indeed pattern has frequently been claimed as a vital component of mathematics. Warwick Sawyer (1955, p. 12) stated that 'Mathematics is the classification and study of all possible patterns'. Sawyer's books have provided a wealth of ideas for teaching, and in many of his suggestions it is patterns that provide the insights. Edith Biggs pioneered investigative approaches to teaching and learning mathematics in primary schools in Britain, and in Biggs and Shaw (1985) we find: 'Mathematics can . . . be thought of as a search for patterns and relationships'. Williams and Shuard (1982), in a book that has become a classic of primary mathematics teaching, suggested that: 'the search for order and pattern . . . is one of the driving forces of all mathematical work with young children'. Such views about mathematics teaching cannot be ignored. Indeed, an analysis of the school mathematics curriculum immediately reveals how pattern is an ever-present strand. In the study of numbers, in the approach to algebra, in aspects of geometry such as symmetry, in graphs and calculus, and in many aspects of higher mathematics, there are patterns which can make the subject more meaningful. Figure 6.1 illustrates how pattern underlies and illuminates so much of school mathematics.

The vital issue from the perspective of this chapter is whether the patterns which underlie our curriculum really do help pupils to learn mathematics. There is some psychological support for pattern as one of the bases of all learning in that we, as a species, are said to depend on pattern in our attempts to comprehend the universe. In many aspects of life it seems we are attracted to regularity, and may even try to make sense of new situations by seeking or even imposing patterns and structures within them. A simple example of a pattern which is used to help children to make sense of the structure of our number system is the 100-square (Table 6.1). To most adults, the patterns and structures could not be clearer and more significant, but it takes children many years to come to such a mature understanding of all the patterns and relationships. In this chapter we look at some of the evidence of pupils' growing

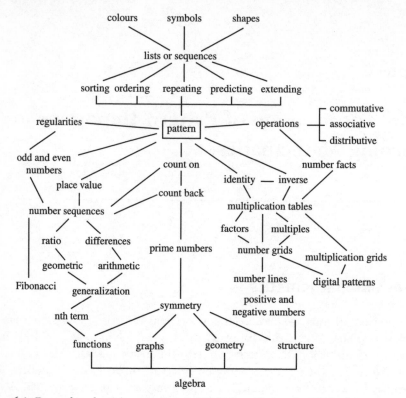

**Figure** 6.1 Reproduced with permission (Frobisher, L. *et al.*, 1999, *Learning to Teach Number*, Cheltenham: Nelson Thornes Ltd.)

**Table 6.1** The 100-square

| 1 | 2 | 3 | 4 | 5 | 6 | 7 | 8 | 9 | 10 |
|---|---|---|---|---|---|---|---|---|----|
| 11 | 12 | 13 | 14 | 15 | 16 | 17 | 18 | 19 | 20 |
| 21 | 22 | 23 | 24 | 25 | 26 | 27 | 28 | 29 | 30 |
| 31 | 32 | 33 | 34 | 35 | 36 | 37 | 38 | 39 | 40 |
| 41 | 42 | 43 | 44 | 45 | 46 | 47 | 48 | 49 | 50 |
| 51 | 52 | 53 | 54 | 55 | 56 | 57 | 58 | 59 | 60 |
| 61 | 62 | 63 | 64 | 65 | 66 | 67 | 68 | 69 | 70 |
| 71 | 72 | 73 | 74 | 75 | 76 | 77 | 78 | 79 | 80 |
| 81 | 82 | 83 | 84 | 85 | 86 | 87 | 88 | 89 | 90 |
| 91 | 92 | 93 | 94 | 95 | 96 | 97 | 98 | 99 | 100 |

awareness, understanding and use of pattern through the years of schooling, and how pattern may be used to support learning.

## Early concepts of pattern

Before we can use patterns to support mathematics learning we need to be sure that children appreciate and understand pattern and what we mean by pattern in mathematics. Perceptive parents who observe their pre-school children arranging toy cars or dolls or any other play objects in straight lines, and later perhaps in two parallel lines, and then maybe even in three parallel lines or more, ought to note that a structure is being imposed, and that this might convey interesting information about their children's talents. If similar objects are placed alongside each other in the lines this might be construed as an appreciation of symmetry. If a child is also using the lines to add up the numbers of objects, in twos or threes, or even more in the case of the parallel lines, this may well be an illustration of using patterns as a support to learning about numbers. There is no doubt that there is an extent to which many young children do appreciate patterns, and can begin to impose their own structures and patterns on objects around them. In the nursery environment, children are often provided with objects which lend themselves to patterning, for example, coloured bricks, threading materials, pegs and pegboards and mark-making materials. Colour is a particularly important basis for structuring at this stage. Her Majesty's Inspectorate (1989) claimed that some children will frequently impose a patterned structure on play materials. In a research study, Gura (1992) classified children who were observed in self-initiated play with wooden blocks into three groups, patterners, dramatists, and those who were happy to mix the two styles. This should not be taken as an indication of different preferences which will continue throughout life; it is merely an indication that spontaneous patterning activities do feature in the play activities of at least a considerable proportion of very young children.

The early National Curriculum of England and Wales included reference to pattern within the mathematics specifications for young children. The demands of the various curriculum documents have changed over the years, but they have at various times included reference to such activities as recognizing, describing, copying, re-creating and continuing patterns. However, what stands out clearly from these early curriculum demands is that the intention was that the teacher should control what the children do. The teacher is to provide the patterns and the children are expected to use them and learn from them. There is little or no indication that children should engage in free and open activities, such as making up patterns of their own, at least not before they have received a thorough grounding from activities provided by the teacher. Aubrey (1993), researching with children at the point of entry to formal schooling, found that the children had more difficulty with set tasks which involved some element of pattern than they did with other aspects of the number curriculum. What is more, on both copying and continuing simple repeating patterns, more than half the children were unsuccessful. Garrick *et al.* (1999, p. 16) suggest that guidelines:

> which place recognizing and copying the work of others before making patterns of their own devising, may well have underestimated the cognitive demands of this apparently simple activity of recognizing patterns, as well as failing to acknowledge the spontaneous pattern-making that often occurs without models.

Garrick studied children in the three to five age range, recording and commenting on their pattern-making activities over periods of time. The children, who were not 'advantaged' in any way, used objects such as beads, pegs and mosaic tiles, so that both spatial and colour organization of objects could be noted. She was able to conclude that, within this ordinary inner-city nursery, significant development took place in children's spatial structuring of materials, as they gained control of a number of linear and non-linear basic elements, such as proximity placing, symmetry, and finding and marking mid-points, corners and centre. Between four and five years of age the children developed increasing capabilities in utilizing the basic elements in more complex pattern-making. Similar and parallel development took place in relation to colour, the basic elements including chaining (for example, red, red, red, blue, blue, green, green, green, green, . . .), alternating (red, yellow, red, red, yellow, red, yellow, yellow, yellow, . . .), repeating (red, yellow, blue, red, yellow, blue, . . .), and placing symmetrically. A small number of children eventually began to integrate spatial and colour structuring in relatively complex ways. The younger children usually worked alone, but many of the older children regularly chose to work alongside friends, and ideas spread through working side-by-side, and by allowing the whole class to see finished products. Adult-initiated models were not only superfluous, being helpful only rarely and with a minority of the children, but there was more than a suggestion that too much adult input could undermine and limit children's individual explorations. Some children could work independently for long periods of time, and were highly motivated to develop both their thinking and their skills, whereas others were more dependent on peer group support and on the well-timed interventions of the teacher. Making the teacher the only source of pattern is likely to miss the potential which exists within groups of pupils. Nevertheless, the teacher has an important role in helping children to become more aware of the significant features of what they have produced, and in providing opportunities for the sharing of ideas.

As children progress through the primary school years, greater emphasis is placed by the curriculum on repeating patterns, particularly linear ones. The curriculum may only indicate that the intention is to develop ideas of sequencing and regularity, but there may be greater importance to this activity. There is an obvious link with everyday repeating patterns like the days of the week and the months of the year. There is the possibility that repeating patterns lead to ideas of length. And there is the claim that repeating patterns lead eventually to generalization and algebra. The question is whether children learn what we want them to learn. The official view seems to have been that devising a repeating pattern requires the creation of a rule and its consistent application, but is that what children do? Threlfall (1999) points out that the sequence ACABACABA . . . may be generated in at least three different ways. One method is rhythmic, and often children can be heard chanting as they create, another method is something like, 'if it is an A and the one before was a C, then the next must be a B', and finally there is using ACAB as a unit of repeat. Observation of children creating patterns also reveals that they frequently use filling in, as this example of placing pegs on a pegboard illustrates:

| First | R | R | R | R |
|---|---|---|---|---|
| Then | RB | RB | RB | RB |
| Then | RBG | RBG | RBG | RBG |
| Finally | RBGG | RBGG | RBGG | RBGG |

Here, all the red pegs were placed first, then all the blues, and finally all the greens. Thus, Threlfall suggests, the existence of a repeating pattern is no evidence at all that a rule has been created and applied.

Various studies have suggested that there are two strands to development in repeating patterns, one relating to the complexity of the patterns and the other to how the children are 'seeing' the patterns. Threlfall (p. 25) concluded from his research that, in relation to seeing the pattern, 'there seems to be a major developmental threshold, concerning whether or not the children are aware of the pattern as a whole being related to a unit of repeat'. Children must be able to refer to a unit of repeat (such as RBGG) to convince us that they have made this step; chanting should not be taken as evidence that the unit of repeat is appreciated, nor should it be accepted by the teacher. Wood (1988) and others have confirmed the developmental issue in suggesting that, from a Piagetian perspective, pre-operational children are limited in how they understand repeating patterns. Children can seem to be operating with a particular strategy when they are not, so we must be wary of drawing too firm a conclusion about a child's grasp of repeating patterns before we are absolutely sure. The danger is that children who have not surmounted this developmental hurdle by the time they reach the later primary years may at the same time have also moved beyond the stage in the curriculum where repeating patterns are studied. For their sakes, repeating patterns need to be included in the curriculum of the later primary years, and perhaps even beyond. There is also evidence that the two strands of pattern complexity and appreciation of a unit of repeat develop largely independently. It is important that the issue of whether a repeating unit is being fully appreciated is not overlooked as children create increasingly complex sequences.

Gray and Tall (1994) have declared that both procedure and concept may be important in mathematics, and that, emphasizing procedures leads many children inexorably into a cul-de-sac from which there is little hope of future development. Seeing a repeating pattern in terms of a unit of repeat involves both a conceptual aspect and a procedural aspect, in that the unit of repeat offers ways of both under-standing and creating a pattern. Gray and Tall have named this combination a 'procept'. The importance of the proceptual approach may be seen from the pattern of squares in Figure 6.2. This pattern enables many searching questions to be asked,

□ □ □ ■ ■ □ □ □ ■ ■ □ □ □ ■ ■ □ ...

Figure 6.2

such as, 'What colour would the 27th shape be?' or, 'What would be the position of the 19th white?', or 'If there were 32 squares, how many of each colour would there be?' Children with a procedural or rhythmic approach would basically have to count, a process which is subject to errors and which offers no means of checking for accuracy. On the other hand, a child with a unit of repeat approach would be thinking in fives (where each five = first three white, then two black), a method which is 'pre-algebraic'. Threlfall (1999, p. 30) concludes that:

For the whole of its mathematical potential to be realized, and to deserve its comparatively exalted status as 'pre-algebra', the approach of the child to the recognition and creation of repeating patterns needs to be developed to a 'pro-ceptual' one, in which the unit of repeat is 'seen' and can be processed both as a part of a pattern and as a composite of parts.

## Number patterns

As some of the concepts associated with pattern become more firmly established, number sequences become a major focus for study. One early number pattern which is emphasized in primary mathematics is odd and even numbers. To an adult, the odds and evens stand out very clearly from the 100-square (Table 6.1) but it seems that, for two-digit numbers, many children do not find it at all easy to distinguish odds from evens. Frobisher (1999) conducted an extensive study with primary children aged five to eleven years. The tasks allowed the children to place the numbers from 0 to 99 into one of the five categories: odd, even, neither, both and don't know. By the age of eleven only 86 per cent of the year group successfully recognized the odd and even nature of a single-digit number, never mind double-digit numbers. Zero was a particular problem across the entire age range, and it was clear that success in deciding that zero is an even number rose only very slowly with age. More than one in five children in every year group decided that zero was an odd number. Not surprisingly, therefore, there were difficulties in classifying the multiples of ten. A major problem for the children was that, instead of focusing solely on the units digit, the tens digit was always likely to be a distraction. One number, 21, was incorrectly classified by a majority of the children. Table 6.2 shows the percentages of correct responses for Year 6 pupils (age ten to eleven years), and many interesting features of the responses are apparent. Clearly, what seems to be a relatively simple classification to teachers is not at all straightforward for many pupils. Given that we think it is vital that children should be able to distinguish odds from evens, lesson time needs to be devoted to this topic throughout the whole of the primary school, and perhaps even into the secondary school for some pupils.

**Table 6.2**  Percentages of correct responses for Year 6 children

| Ten digit | Unit digit | | | | | | | | | |
|---|---|---|---|---|---|---|---|---|---|---|
| | 0 | 1 | 2 | 3 | 4 | 5 | 6 | 7 | 8 | 9 |
| 0 | 47 | 84 | 84 | 83 | 84 | 86 | 86 | 87 | 86 | 91 |
| 1 | 84 | 82 | 82 | 82 | 78 | 84 | 79 | 85 | 76 | 85 |
| 2 | 86 | 47 | 88 | 71 | 86 | 69 | 84 | 69 | 81 | 69 |
| 3 | 71 | 80 | 72 | 81 | 70 | 81 | 74 | 86 | 68 | 80 |
| 4 | 87 | 68 | 82 | 69 | 79 | 70 | 83 | 75 | 86 | 76 |
| 5 | 74 | 85 | 69 | 86 | 71 | 76 | 70 | 81 | 66 | 84 |
| 6 | 79 | 79 | 83 | 65 | 80 | 67 | 82 | 75 | 82 | 71 |
| 7 | 67 | 84 | 67 | 84 | 71 | 80 | 68 | 82 | 64 | 66 |
| 8 | 84 | 69 | 84 | 67 | 83 | 62 | 87 | 72 | 84 | 66 |
| 9 | 67 | 88 | 68 | 82 | 62 | 78 | 69 | 86 | 68 | 85 |

One way in which even numbers result from an arithmetic procedure is in the addition of 'ties', that is when both addends are the same, such as in 3 + 3, 4 + 4, and 7 + 7. There is evidence that the first addition facts to become knowledge retrieved from memory are the ties:

All the research evidence on children's recall of addition facts point to ties as the combination of pairs of numbers which are most readily known and are also the starting point for the derivation of many other facts. (Threlfall and Frobisher, 1999, p. 60)

Examples of derivation based on ties include arguing that $6 + 7$ must be 13 because $6 + 6 = 12$, or $8 + 6 = 6 + 6 + 2 = 12 + 2 = 14$. Other derivation strategies ultimately exist amongst children, however, for example $8 + 6 = 8 + 2 + 4 = 10 + 4$. Gray (1991) found that many children over the age of eight years were able to use derived facts extensively. Furthermore, it seems that teachers are often not aware of the extent to which derived facts are being used by children. The foundation for the use of derived facts is a thorough knowledge of the ties, so there are strong grounds for singling out ties for thorough classroom treatment. Derivation also depends heavily on being able to add and subtract 1 and 2, accurately and speedily, from any given number. Threlfall and Frobisher argue that the way to learn number facts is by means of the automatization of derived facts, and that this learning may be supported by the use of number patterns, such as with number strips, Cuisenaire rods, and diagrams:

Competence in addition facts is attainable if children have a knowledge and understanding of the workings of the number system, of the relationships between numbers and the principles of commutativity, associativity and inverse operations, all of which can be developed through observation and application of number patterns. (p. 65)

The only major alternative to this approach to learning number facts is rote learning. Many would say this has been discredited, but teachers are often tempted to resort to rote learning for basic number facts, perhaps because other methods seem slow in comparison. Rote learning of basic number facts can certainly seem effective at first, because the facts can apparently be learned quite quickly, if enough effort is applied. However, knowledge learned by rote frequently does not stand the test of time – it requires constant and regular reinforcement, and it therefore wastes time in the longer run if there is an effective alternative – and without regular rehearsal it is likely to disappear altogether. Rote-learned knowledge can also become distorted by 'interference'. This phenomenon is when errors in remembering occur through accidental association with similar facts, for example the common confusion between the answers to $7 \times 8$ and $6 \times 9$. Acquiring basic knowledge of number facts is too important to rely on ineffective methods. Whatever methods are used, children need to be equipped with reliable ways in which number facts can be retrieved. The use of derivation strategies, based on ties and supported by number patterns, is a good long-term strategy.

Number facts also include the multiplication tables, which many of us recall learning by chanting. It may be that chanting is an enjoyable social activity in its own right, and it may make some contribution to learning, but it is not likely to lead to true understanding on its own. In order to make sense of multiplication other methods are needed, and these are likely to incorporate emphasis on the patterns which multiplication tables reveal. Each separate table has its own patterns, and each needs to be dealt with separately, before an overall combined table such as Table 6.3 may be presented. Within this table we see not only all the multiplication tables, we

Table 6.3  Combined multiplication tables

| 12 | 12 | 24 | 36 | 48 | 60 | 72 | 84 | 96 | 108 | 120 | 132 | 144 |
|----|----|----|----|----|----|----|----|----|-----|-----|-----|-----|
| 11 | 11 | 22 | 33 | 44 | 55 | 66 | 77 | 88 | 99 | 110 | 121 | 132 |
| 10 | 10 | 20 | 30 | 40 | 50 | 60 | 70 | 80 | 90 | 100 | 110 | 120 |
| 9 | 9 | 18 | 27 | 36 | 45 | 54 | 63 | 72 | 81 | 90 | 99 | 108 |
| 8 | 8 | 16 | 24 | 32 | 40 | 48 | 56 | 64 | 72 | 80 | 88 | 96 |
| 7 | 7 | 14 | 21 | 28 | 35 | 42 | 49 | 56 | 63 | 70 | 77 | 84 |
| 6 | 6 | 12 | 18 | 24 | 30 | 36 | 42 | 48 | 54 | 60 | 66 | 72 |
| 5 | 5 | 10 | 15 | 20 | 25 | 30 | 35 | 40 | 45 | 50 | 55 | 60 |
| 4 | 4 | 8 | 12 | 16 | 20 | 24 | 28 | 32 | 36 | 40 | 44 | 48 |
| 3 | 3 | 6 | 9 | 12 | 15 | 18 | 21 | 24 | 27 | 30 | 33 | 36 |
| 2 | 2 | 4 | 6 | 8 | 10 | 12 | 14 | 16 | 18 | 20 | 22 | 24 |
| 1 | 1 | 2 | 3 | 4 | 5 | 6 | 7 | 8 | 9 | 10 | 11 | 12 |
| × | 1 | 2 | 3 | 4 | 5 | 6 | 7 | 8 | 9 | 10 | 11 | 12 |

may see much more, for example, in the 'diagonal' lines and in the positions of individual numbers (for example what do the positions of the number 24 reveal?). The point here is that number patterns can not only make a contribution towards the understanding and memorization of the basic number facts which all children spend many years attempting to master, they can also pave the way for more advanced mathematical ideas to be dealt with more fully in later years.

## The approach to algebra

Cockcroft (1982, p. 60) included the statement that, 'algebra is a source of considerable confusion and negative attitudes among pupils'. Teachers have always known this, particularly since the broadening of the mathematics curriculum some fifty years ago. Around this time, when the school leaving age was raised in Britain, first to fifteen years of age and then to sixteen, the curriculum for the majority of pupils naturally needed to be extended. Thus, it began to include many areas of mathematics like algebra which had previously only been taught to pupils in selective schools. Because of the acknowledged difficulties of algebra, there have been many attempts in recent years to find alternative routes into algebra which would be more meaningful, particularly for academically weaker pupils. One such route is the use of pattern. According to the Department of Education and Science (DES/WO 1988, p. 16):

Algebra develops out of the search for pattern, relationships and generalization. It is not just 'all about using letters' but can exist independently of the use of symbols. Work in the primary school on number pattern and the relationships between numbers lays the foundation for the subsequent development of algebra.

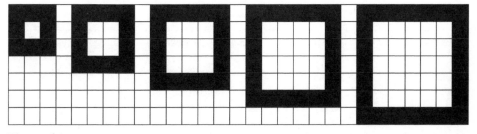

**Figure 6.3**

As we have already seen, the earliest number patterns encountered by children include counting numbers, even numbers, odd numbers and square numbers. Ultimately being able to understand $n$, $2n$, $2n - 1$ and $n^2$ as general terms for each of these sequences is thus considered to be a valuable step into algebra. Variations and extensions based on simple number patterns, such as arithmetic and geometric progressions, may be presented either as sequences or in some pictorial form, as shown in Figure 6.3. Here, the sides of the inner squares and the areas of the outer borders are related as shown in Table 6.4. Such a task might require pupils to continue each row of numbers, to explain the patterns in words or writing, and possibly to decide on a suitable general term for the inner and outer areas, first in words but eventually as a mathematical formula. Graph drawing is also supported by tables of numbers,

**Table 6.4**   Number patterns revealed by Figure 6.3

| Length of side of white square | 1 | 2 | 3 | 4 | 5 | . . . | $n$ |
|---|---|---|---|---|---|---|---|
| Area of black outer border | 8 | 12 | 16 | ? | ? | . . . | ? |

**Table 6.5**   Table of values for a straight line graph

| $x$ | −3 | −2 | −1 | 0 | 1 | 2 | 3 | 4 |
|---|---|---|---|---|---|---|---|---|
| $y$ | ? | −1 | 1 | 3 | 5 | ? | ? | 11 |

for example, Table 6.5, and the objectives here are likely to be to understand the pattern and thus find the equation. From the point of view of this chapter we need to know whether such approaches to algebra are successful.

An early enquiry into pupils' attempts to master patterns of numbers was conducted by the Assessment of Performance Unit (undated, pp. 417–19). Tasks were based on finding the next two terms in the following four sequences: (1) 1, 2, 4, 8, . . ., (2) 1, 3, 6, 10, . . ., (3) 1, 4, 9, 16, . . ., and (4) 1, 1, 2, 3, 5. The results are shown in Table 6.6. Clearly, even the fifteen-year-old pupils did not find all of the tasks elementary. The general comments about number patterns from the APU (p. 416), which many subsequent research studies have confirmed, were that:

Finding terms in number patterns gets progressively more difficult the further the terms are from those given in the question,

More pupils can continue a task than can explain it,

**Table 6.6**   Facility levels for APU questions (1978 to 1982)

| Question | Expected response | Age 11 (% correct) | Age 15 (% correct) |
|---|---|---|---|
| 1 | 16, 32 | 48 | 82 |
| 2 | 15, 21 | 60 | 77 |
| 3 | 25, 36 | 41 | 64 |
| 4 | 8, 13 | 14 | 37 |

Number pattern rules are described by a large proportion of pupils in relation to differences between terms,

Generally, oral explanations of rules . . . are given by more pupils than can write an explanation.

It is common for pupils to seek an explanation of a number pattern in terms of differences, and all subsequent research studies have confirmed this, even with adults. Differences are important in arithmetic progressions (for example, 4, 7, 10, 13, 16, . . ., with first differences 3), and both first and second differences might help in understanding quadratic sequences (for example, 1, 4, 9, 16, 25, 36, . . ., with first differences 3, 5, 7, 9, 11, . . . and second difference 2). However, differences may not enlighten other sequences, as the APU tasks illustrate. Thus an important conclusion we can draw is that pupils must be encouraged not to rely solely on differencing as a way of trying to understand a number pattern.

There are additional problems with differencing. Stacey (1989), Orton, A. and Orton, J. (1999), Orton, J. and Orton, A. (1996) and others have not only confirmed the widespread use of differencing, but have identified the methods used by pupils, some of which are inappropriate. Given a linear sequence like 1, 4, 7, 10, . . ., and asked for the 50th term, say, there are four common methods which pupils use. The first is to try to extend the sequence until a list of 50 terms is obtained, a procedure which is tedious and subject to errors. The second is to identify the difference (3, in this case) and then to multiply this by the number of terms, thus obtaining 150. The third is to try to shortcut the procedure in another way, by finding perhaps the fifth term (13) and multiplying this by ten, thus arriving at 130, or perhaps finding the tenth term (28) and multiplying by five, thus obtaining 140. The fourth method is some version of the correct analysis (for example, $1 + 3 \times 49 = 148$). The second and third methods, which are likely to yield incorrect answers, are in widespread use in the classroom. Teachers need to be aware of what is going on, even when pupils are legitimately using differencing, and need to challenge incorrect methods. It should also be noted that even those pupils who are able to obtain the correct answer by a formula method may not be able to write down the general term as $3n - 2$. Plenty of practice with number sequences leads to trying to determine the general term in some appropriate algebraic form, but it does not guarantee that a 'finished' formula will be obtained. Using patterns does not provide immediate insight into algebraic formulas.

Number patterns based on squaring are not surprisingly much more difficult for pupils to understand than linear patterns. It is easy to be misled by the fact that the rule for the square numbers (1, 4, 9, 16, 25, 36, . . .) can be grasped relatively easily, for even the triangle numbers (1, 3, 6, 10, 15, 21, . . .), which crop up so frequently in

**Figure 6.4**

mathematics, are difficult to generalize. Making sense of anything more obscure (for example, 3, 6, 11, 18, 27, 38, . . .) seems to be virtually impossible for the majority of pupils. In research involving mature adults seeking entry into the teaching profession (Orton, J. *et al.*, 1999), there were some successes and some notable failures on dot pattern tasks involving quadratic solutions. The triangle numbers (Figure 6.4) were just as difficult for the adults as they are for pupils, but other dot patterns which led to the sequences 1, 9, 25, 49, . . . and 1, 5, 11, 19, . . . were mastered more easily. In fact, some of the better candidates were able to find a general rule for these two sequences quite early, perhaps by trial and improvement, and then to use this to continue the sequence, which was the reverse of what was intended. At the same time, there were other candidates who engaged in the potentially never-ending task of extending the sequences term by term. Thus the triangle numbers warrant a special warning. A pattern-based approach to the general term $\frac{1}{2}n(n + 1)$ might not be impossible with some pupils, but the diagrammatic approach based on two staircases is likely to be more meaningful (see Figure 5.4). Any triangle number is the sum of consecutive natural numbers (for example, $u_5 = 15 = 1 + 2 + 3 + 4 + 5$). Each of the two staircases in Figure 5.4 illustrates this sum, and fitting the two staircases together makes a $5 \times 6$ rectangle. Thus we have an illustration of $2 \times 15 = 5 \times 6$, but more generally, we also have $2 \times u_n = n \times (n + 1)$, which implies that $u_n = \frac{1}{2}n(n + 1)$. In general, although a pattern approach to more advanced school mathematics such as quadratics may be helpful to some pupils, and is certainly possible in the sixth form, it would be unwise to expect too much from it with the majority of pupils.

Tasks in which number patterns are intended to lead to generalization are often set in pictorial or practical contexts, such as patterns of dots or tiles, or matchsticks, and two examples have arisen already (Figures 6.3 and 6.4). The reasons for this use of visual representations are often not clear, and it sometimes seems that the pictures just add another stage in answering the questions. Presmeg (1986) has claimed that both teachers and the curriculum tend to present visual reasoning as a first step, or as an accessory, in what is basically a number pattern situation. It may be that it is believed that picture tasks are simpler, or that pictures add meaning and purpose, or that they enliven a dull number sequence, or even add a real-life dimension. Whatever the reasons for using pictures, we need to know how pupils react. Do pictorially-based tasks produce new difficulties and complications, or do they provide additional support to the children?

An early research project was by Lee and Wheeler (1987), and they based a task on overlapping rectangles ('Dots in Rectangles'). Pupils used one of three strategies. Firstly, perhaps because the pictures appeared to suggest the L-shaped borders were significant, many students tried to use them, but this approach was not particularly helpful. Secondly, many students focused on counting the numbers of dots in successive rectangles, which the written tasks emphasized. However, the best approach was not to count dots at all, but to adopt a kind of area approach, and some students made rapid progress based on $1 \times 2, 2 \times 3, 3 \times 4, \ldots$ . Lee and Wheeler concluded that a

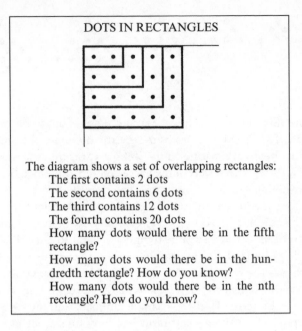

DOTS IN RECTANGLES

The diagram shows a set of overlapping rectangles:
The first contains 2 dots
The second contains 6 dots
The third contains 12 dots
The fourth contains 20 dots
How many dots would there be in the fifth rectangle?
How many dots would there be in the hundredth rectangle? How do you know?
How many dots would there be in the nth rectangle? How do you know?

borders perception of the problem was likely to hinder progress. There was also some evidence that the borders approach came first, but it eventually gave way to the rectangles perception. In retrospect, and from the point of view of generalizing the sequence (2, 6, 12, 20, . . .), separate rectangles with no borders might have provided better support, though as a research task it did bring certain issues to light.

Warren (1992, p. 253) discussed the possible complexities of using shapes in the context of a line of hexagonal flower beds and surrounding paving slabs (Figure 6.5). For Warren, the steps in obtaining a generalization are first to identify the component parts (flower beds, surrounding paving slabs), then identify the generalities, namely that each extra flower bed requires an additional four paving slabs, and finally to realize that the first flower bed has six paving slabs, two more than for the other flower beds. This task therefore requires 'sound visual skills [and] an array of specific thinking skills' (p. 253). Completing the task is not easy, and listing numbers does not appear to help, so it is best not to treat it as a number pattern question. Ursini (1991) used rather simpler shapes, and concluded that the children needed to understand (a) the pattern within both representations of the situation, the visual and the analytic, and (b) that both rules are the same rule. The underlying implication from both Warren and Ursini is that pictorial pattern questions can be more complex than we realize. In particular, it is questionable whether the curriculum provides experiences which would prepare pupils for visual thinking, and for thinking which requires taking both the visual and the analytic into account. Thus, picture questions need careful planning

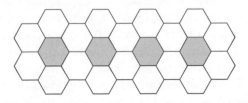

Figure 6.5

based on clear objectives, and also they do not have to lead to number sequences. Indeed, there are some grounds for thinking that well chosen pictorial questions could be used to wean children away from a number pattern approach to generalization and onto strategies which are based on understanding the structure of a situation.

A number of studies of children's patterning have been based on matchsticks, usually with the objective of obtaining a number pattern from the configurations. Pegg and Redden (1990) used pictures of matchsticks arranged into lines of triangles with eleven to twelve year olds (see Figure 6.6), and most pupils had no difficulty with

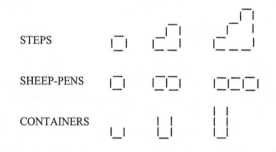

**Figure 6.6**

this pattern. What they did find 'challenging' was to try to work the other way round, that is to devise concrete representations from number patterns. Orton (1997) used matchstick tasks with children aged nine to thirteen, but the innovation here was that the pupils were able to handle the matchsticks and make their own shapes (Figure 6.7).

**Figure 6.7**

The pupils were interviewed as they attempted to construct additional shapes in the sequences begun by the interviewer. Most pupils were able to do this, but some ran into difficulties. It was also apparent that pupils perceived the configurations in various ways. For example, in the 'Steps' task some saw the next shape as requiring an extra match along each of four lines, others saw the need for an extra step at the top plus a match at the bottom, and a more unusual perception was as rearrangements of squares of matches of sizes $1 \times 1$, $2 \times 2$, $3 \times 3$, etc. Such a variety of perceptions shows how difficult it could be to talk about the configurations to a whole class. The match-stick patterns were used to derive number sequences, and some children quickly rejected the matches in favour of continuing their lists of numbers based on differences, leading to the typical misuses of differencing. Some children were slowed down by the matches, because they couldn't handle them efficiently or because they couldn't count them. The overall conclusion about using matchstick patterns must be that they might or might not provide the hoped for insight and support, but they could also introduce new complications.

All of this discussion of number patterns suggests a very mixed conclusion in terms of them leading to generalization and algebraic formulae, and also about using pictures to initiate a pattern approach. Certainly, this new route into algebra offers another alternative, and embraces features which are valuable mathematical experiences. However, there is no indication that algebra is suddenly made easier to learn, so there is no reason to assume that the pattern route should replace other routes.

## Pattern and proof

Any respectable mathematics curriculum must ultimately include proving, even if only for those pupils who develop most rapidly. In many school curricula around the world Euclidean geometry still provides the vehicle for teaching notions of proof, but in Britain the geometry is now as much based on transformations as on any other approach. However, there is little attempt to use the transformations which British pupils study to lead to proof, so the question arises as to whether ideas of proof might emerge from the study of algebra. In particular, we need to consider here whether the pattern approach to algebra might provide suitable opportunities. We also need to know the extent to which pupils have the capability to create proofs based on number patterns, and whether there are ways in which teachers might extend the study of patterns to a consideration of proof.

Proof in mathematics has been the subject of research in the past (see Bell *et al.*, 1983), but many studies have focused on proof as it arises within Euclidean geometry. In one study, however, Bell explained the development of the understanding of proof in pupils aged eleven to seventeen as passing through four stages. The second of these stages demands the recognition of pattern or relationship, but without any checking of the domain of applicability. Waring *et al.* (1999) have reported on a teaching study which was based exclusively on patterns which arise in mathematics lessons. The research involved attempting to introduce above average school students aged fourteen to sixteen to notions of proof based on the pattern route into algebra. In all of the tasks, pupils were encouraged to use the pattern to find a formula-based rule, and then to try to explain the formula. Individual exploration, group discussion and whole-class lessons were all used to support the production of a final written report for each task. There were genuine achievements, namely that pupils were able to come to an appreciation of the distinction between demonstration and proof, to understand the need for proof, and ultimately to produce a proof, though considerable 'piloting' was often required from the teacher. In general, however, the difficulties experienced by the pupils were greater than had been anticipated, and in particular a task based on the triangle numbers proved to be much more difficult than anticipated at first, though all the tasks were eventually completed with guidance. Task A, a matchstick task, is just one example of the large number used within the teaching and testing programmes.

At the end of the teaching sequence, post-tests enabled separate measures of capability in patterning and in proving, and also provided a comparison with scores on 'basic' mathematics (the remainder of the curriculum for the year). An end-of-year examination provided an opportunity to include what were in effect delayed post-test questions. Three normal school classes (about 25 pupils in each) were involved, comprising an experimental group (E) and two control groups, one of which had been taught without any reference to pattern (C1), but the other had included patterns within the traditional curriculum, though it had not included proof (C2). Some pupils were also later interviewed on an individual basis. The results on the 'basic' items confirmed the comparability of these three groups in terms of overall mathematical attainment. The outcomes of all the various assessments revealed that the success of the experiment was limited, though group E pupils did have more success on the proving tasks than the other two groups. In addition, C2 pupils were better than C1 pupils on pattern questions, but differences between the two control groups on proof

---

**TASK A**

For the above patterns of L-shapes, made from matches:

1. Copy and complete the following table down to n = 6.

| Side of large square (n) | Number of small squares (s) | Perimeter of L-shape (P) | Number of matches (m) |
|---|---|---|---|
| 2 | 3 | 8 | 10 |
| 3 | | | |
| 4 | | | |
| 5 | | | |
| 6 | | | |
| 10 | | | |
| 100 | | | |

2. Describe any patterns you see.

3. Find formulae for the following in terms of n:
   (a) the number of small squares (s);
   (b) the perimeter (number of matches round the outside) of the L-shape (P);
   (c) the number of matches used (m).

4. Prove that your formulae are correct by explaining how each one is connected to the diagrams. (*Remember – checking is not the same as proving.*)

5. Use your formula to calculate the values of s, P and m for n = 10 and n = 100 and put your answers in the table.

---

questions were not significant. Perhaps not surprisingly, the awareness of the need for proof had certainly been raised in the group E pupils, and they were more prepared to seek a proof than when the experiment began. It was also clear that these particular pattern questions had provided adequate motivation for the study of proof. Unfortunately, there was still a very strong tendency for pupils to rely too much on differencing, which sometimes inhibited progress towards finding a generalization because that really needed to be derived from structural considerations. Pupils often lost their way when they tried to proceed entirely algebraically, whilst there were many instances of pupils benefiting from the support of an appropriate diagram. It seemed (cf. Polya, 1957) that, if a task offered the opportunity to draw a diagram to support thinking, it is always sensible to do so. In general, when proofs were provided by the pupils, they were written informally, using sentences rather than mathematical symbols. In the interviews, pupils indicated very strongly that they found it difficult

> **TASK B**
>
> (a) Find $2^2 - 1^2, 3^2 - 2^2, 4^2 - 3^2$.
> (b) Continue up to $9^2 - 8^2$.
> (c) If $n$ is the smaller of the two consecutive numbers write down an expression for the larger.
> (d) Explain, using algebra and/or diagrams, why the above result will always happen for the difference between any two consecutive square numbers.

to explain in writing ('It's easier to talk'), and that the tasks weren't as clear as if a teacher had been available to explain ('I wasn't sure what I was doing').

Some of the test tasks were not based on the routine 'pattern → formula → proof' procedure, that is, they were unique, an example being Task B. It was very clear from the results that transfer of learning to unusual situations was extremely limited. Pupils were more likely to succeed with analysing new patterns if they were similar to patterns experienced earlier, and conversely were not likely to succeed with patterns arising from completely new contexts. We must therefore conclude that we have no evidence that the ability to produce a satisfactory proof in these pattern situations will extend to other areas of mathematics outside the narrow confines of this topic. The limited success of the experiment indicates that the search for strategies based on patterns which lead to greater success in understanding and producing mathematical proofs must continue. On the other hand, there is evidence that pattern situations can provide a legitimate approach to proof, can provide pupils with valuable pre-proof experiences, and might even enable some movement towards acceptable mathematical proofs.

## Pattern in relation to shape

It is in geometry that we realize how difficult it is to define what we mean by 'pattern'. Unfortunately, the term can take various meanings in the wider world. Grünbaum and Shephard (1986), in their classic book on tilings and patterns, confess that they could not find a satisfactory definition. For Sawyer (1955, p. 12), however, pattern is 'any kind of regularity that can be recognized by the mind'. Sawyer's regularity is basically achieved through symmetry and iteration, with symmetry being undoubtedly the key mathematical feature in the study of pattern in geometry. Tessellations, both those occurring naturally and those in manufactured designs, are fundamentally based on symmetry and iteration, but they also incorporate transformations. When we study wrapping paper and wallpaper from our own country, wall and ceiling designs from Islam, and textile patterns from around the world it is often tessellations which provide the first impact. Deeper analysis then reveals the symmetries and transformations, and it is therefore these two features which are singled out for discussion here.

Symmetry must be a basic element in any geometry curriculum, but symmetry may be reflective or rotational (or both), and the ideas of reflection and rotation are not of the same order of difficulty. Reflection is definitely understood before rotation, but other hierarchies of difficulty exist as well. Figure 6.8 (see Orton, 1999) illustrates some typical shapes on which explorations of reflective symmetry may be based.

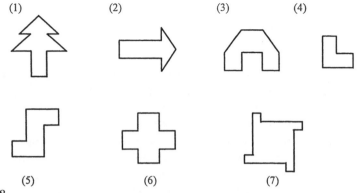

Figure 6.8

Here we have examples of vertical symmetry ('vertical' mirror line), horizontal symmetry ('horizontal' mirror line), and double symmetry (when both vertical and horizontal symmetry are present) – see Figure 6.9. Research studies have confirmed that there is a clear order of difficulty for such symmetrical designs. Chipman and Mendelson (1979), for example, working with children aged six to twelve years and with college students, concluded that:

> Sensitivity to double symmetry and vertical symmetry appeared quite early, whereas sensitivity to horizontal symmetry, diagonal symmetry, and checker-board organization appeared considerably later. Sensitivity to rotational organization . . . was not fully evident even in the oldest subjects. (p. 375)

**Types of symmetry**

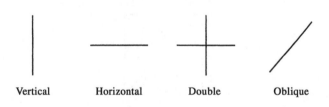

Figure 6.9

Similar conclusions have been drawn from other studies conducted in a variety of countries. Thus, the symmetries of shapes 1, 3 and 6 in Figure 6.8 should be identified most easily, shapes 2 and 4 can be expected to provide rather more difficulty, and shapes 5 and 7 are likely to prove the most difficult of all. Vertical symmetry exists in many objects in the world around us and seems to be easily recognizable, but this appears to lead to many children showing a tendency to impose vertical symmetry where none exists. However, research results indicate that this tendency does decrease with increasing age.

When it comes to transformations, Piaget suggested many years ago that the order in which children learn basic transformations is first translation, then reflection, and finally rotation. This is a very broad classification, however, and some curricula distinguish between different kinds of translations, reflections and rotations, rather along the lines of the different kinds of symmetry identified above. Dickson *et al.* (1984) quote results obtained separately by both Perham and Schultz which distinguish between horizontal, vertical and oblique transformations (see Figure 6.9) and which claim that the last is very difficult for children. Shultz, working with six to eight-year-olds, concluded that the image in an oblique translation was often given in the direction of the translation and also that the tendency with reflections and rotations was to turn the image so that it faced the direction of reflection or turn. These children might seem to be unusually young for such tasks, but there is even more evidence involving older pupils. The Assessment of Performance Unit (1980) concluded that only 14 per cent of eleven-year-olds could find the reflection of a shape in an oblique mirror line. Küchemann (1980) discovered that many fourteen-year-olds reflected vertically or horizontally across an oblique mirror, and they also had difficulty rotating a shape if the centre of rotation was not on the object. The distance and direction in which to reflect an object was helped if there was an underlying grid, but it neither prevented all errors nor helped significantly with rotation. Küchemann also provided descriptions of developmental levels of understanding in reflection and rotation. Bell *et al.* (1989) confirmed the common misconception that horizontal and vertical objects must always have horizontal or vertical images, whatever the orientation of the mirror line. He also found that many children believed that a line which divides a shape into two parts of equal area must be a line of symmetry (for example, the diagonal of a rectangle). Perham also found that children could select the correct image of a transformation from alternatives before they could construct the image, so this might suggest a good way to commence the study of transformations.

It might at first seem questionable whether shape recognition constitutes part of pattern awareness, but children have to be able to recognize the same shape in different positions and orientations in order to identify patterns. This ability is vital for other reasons too, for example, if children are to identify the shaded triangle in Figure 6.10 as one quarter of the whole square they must appreciate the congruency

**Figure 6.10**

of the four triangles. Orton (1999) conducted a major study in shape recognition with pupils aged nine to fifteen. In general, there was evidence of improvement with age, though if there was a relationship with general ability it was not a clear one. Three stages of development were identified, as follows:

*Stage 1:* copying a shape, simple pattern completion; detection of embedded figures; matching picture shapes; recognition of reflection in a 'vertical' axis; simple rotation and reflection completion with a frame of reference.
*Stage 2:* matching of embedded shapes; matching of simple shapes in different orientations; complex rotation and reflection with a frame of reference.
*Stage 3:* matching of complex shapes in different orientations; complex completion of patterns including rotation; recognition of most reflections and rotations.

The issue of whole or parts is also relevant to geometrical pattern recognition. Orton (1999) illustrated this issue with the diagram in Figure 6.11, and asked

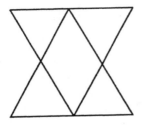

**Figure 6.11**

whether it is the whole or the parts which children see. There is obviously no mathematical name for the shape as a whole, so in breaking it down is it more helpful to treat it as two overlapping equilateral triangles, or as four separate equilateral triangles and a rhombus, or should the parallelograms be used in the analysis? This clearly should remind us of the discussion of Gestalt theory in the previous chapter, but more recent analysis and theory based on research projects can now provide greater detail about what children perceive. Ghent (1956), for example, who used overlapping figures with pupils aged four to thirteen, concluded that young children have difficulty in perceiving a given boundary as simultaneously belonging to more than one form. Reed (1973) found that the rhombus in Figure 6.11 was easier to identify than the parallelograms, and hypothesized that people mentally store the presented patterns as parts together with rules for linking them. Kolinsky *et al.* (1987, p. 399) concluded that 'the processes of post-perceptual analysis necessary to find a part in a figure are neither built-in nor the consequences of . . . cognitive growth, but depend on the instruction or experience usually found in school'. For more detail on theories of perception of mathematical shapes and pattern recognition see Orton (1999).

The conclusion drawn by Kolinsky is a reassuring one for teachers. It suggests that the pattern recognition experiences which children encounter in school, no doubt coupled with teacher-led class or group discussion of what shapes lie where within the overall configuration, are likely to contribute to pupils' growing ability to recognize and analyse patterns in shapes. Another practical suggestion for teachers comes from Bell *et al.* (1989), who has recommended the use of 'conflict' lessons to try to eradicate misconceptions about transformations. The idea is that pupils should first think about a problem on their own, then come together in small groups to discuss and debate in the expectation that suspect conclusions can be challenged in a less threatening atmosphere than the whole class. Once the small groups come to some agreement, whole-class discussion allows a wider debate leading to ultimate agreement. Such conflict lessons appeared to be very successful in dealing with the prevalent tendency to reflect incorrectly across an oblique mirror line, but they could undoubtedly be used more widely within mathematics teaching (see Chapter 11). The final word on symmetry and transformations should be given to Küchemann (1981). In reminding us of the reasons for the attempt to replace Euclidean geometry with a geometry based on transformations, he concludes that both are equally unsuitable, but that the study of the separate transformations can be a valuable mathematical experience in itself.

## Suggestions for further reading

Frobisher, L., Monaghan, J., Orton, A., Orton, J., Roper, T. and Threlfall, J. (1999) *Learning to Teach Number*. Cheltenham: Stanley Thornes.

Küchemann, D. (1981) 'Reflections and rotations' in K. M. Hart *Children's Understanding of Mathematics: 11–16*. London: John Murray.

Mason, J., Graham, A., Pimm, D. and Gowar, N. (1985) *Routes to/Roots of Algebra*. Milton Keynes: The Open University Press.

Orton, A. (ed.) (1999) *Pattern in the Teaching and Learning of Mathematics*. London: Cassell.

## Questions for discussion

1. To what extent is the appreciation of pattern innate and to what extent does it have to be learned?
2. What are the strengths and weaknesses of basing the introduction to algebra on pattern?
3. How can children best be taught proof in mathematics?
4. How can dynamic geometry software be used to support a pattern approach to geometry?

# Chapter 7

# Does What We Learn Depend on Where We Are?

## Applying mathematics

For mathematics teachers, there is nothing more galling than finding that non-mathematicians can be more competent in a mathematical activity than one is oneself. The pub darts team player has to be very quick at arithmetic, particularly at doubling and trebling, and at adding and subtracting. Many professional mathematicians must have marvelled at the speed with which a match commentator is able to complete the mental arithmetic and then deduce and describe the next throw(s), a speed which they themselves could not match. This everyday example indicates how numerical competence of a particular kind can be achieved by people whose earlier performance in the mathematics classroom might have been anything but exemplary. There are many such examples of mathematical competence in common everyday activities. Sensible betting, if there is such a thing, demands considerable mathematical capability, because it demands facility with odds in probability – and that involves fractions. Yet, in school, many pupils struggle with fractions, and probability is not a part of the curriculum which is always grasped. In both of these examples of popular adult activities the situation demands particular mathematical mastery. Teachers might claim that any expertise originated in the general arithmetic skills developed in primary school, but adults often assert that their school mathematics was of little or no help in achieving the very specific mastery which they display regularly.

For science teachers, it is very frustrating when pupils claim that they cannot cope with the mathematics required in analysing experimental results and discussing theory. Sometimes, mathematics teachers are blamed. They are accused of inadequate or unsupportive teaching, or for a curriculum which does not provide for the needs of other subjects. Outside of the mathematics classroom, many pupils seem to be unable to apply their mathematical knowledge as readily as teachers might have hoped. Indeed, usually the mathematics required is not difficult and has indeed been taught, but the situation is different and the children seem unable to transfer their learning. Yet one of the reasons given for teaching mathematics is that it is a very useful subject, and can be applied in so many different ways in other specialist areas of knowledge and in the world at large. Freudenthal (1968, p. 4) commented on this phenomenon when he wrote:

Very little, if anything, is known about how the individual manages to apply what he has learnt, though such . . . knowledge would be the key to understanding why most people never succeed in putting their theoretical knowledge to practical use.

For all teachers, it is a surprise when one finds that a child who struggled at school has gone on to achieve honour and acclaim in the very subject area in which the teacher laboured in vain to impart knowledge. An example of this was an overall better than average pupil whose weakest subject by a colossal margin was mathematics but who came top in mathematics in his first year as a naval cadet. It is easy to say that motivation was the key here. Motivation might well be important in attempting to maximize learning, but in this particular example it also required a change of situation, with the mathematics being seen to be directly relevant. There is a common view, frequently expressed by pupils who are not enjoying their mathematical studies, that school mathematics is not used in the world outside, at least in the world which they envisage for themselves. Yet particular occupations do require some mathematics, and people who aim to succeed in certain jobs must master the relevant mathematics, which they often seem to do within the activity having not impressed at school. Although mathematics is not the subject of television programmes very often (because planners and producers have to keep likely viewing figures in mind!), the mathematical content is often there if one looks carefully. A simple example lies in the gardening programmes, which appear so regularly on our screens. This practical, down-to-earth, area of mainly leisure activity demands particular facilities, such as the measurement and shaping of timber, and calculations concerning building materials in the design of garden features, some of which are quite intricate or complicated. It also sometimes requires a combination of art and geometry. On recent programmes, professional gardeners have marked out circles, for both flower beds and water features, and they have also constructed elliptical beds using two pegs and a loop of string, a method not always included in the school curriculum, and presumably passed on from one gardener to another. And then, of course, there is always the costing to be done. Such skills appear to be developed and committed to memory *in situ* and not in any school classroom.

All of the above illustrations suggest something of a separation or 'discontinuity' between school mathematics and 'real-world' mathematics. As mathematics teachers we need to recognize a number of truths: firstly, that many adults who use mathematics might not be aware that they are doing so; secondly that, when they are aware, they might not recognize the mathematics as being essentially the same as something they learned at school; thirdly that users of mathematics might find it more difficult to apply school-learned mathematics than we imagine, and finally that the mathematics classroom is not the only place where mathematics is learned. In our school lessons we often try to embed mathematical tasks within out-of-school contexts. One reason for doing this is surely because we hope we are forging links with mathematical usage outside the classroom. Other reasons include the belief that such tasks are altogether more meaningful and more interesting. However, just as there is lack of appreciation that the wider world might involve school mathematics, it also appears that children do not necessarily activate any knowledge they might have from the world at large in their attempts to solve a school problem. Often they arrive at solutions which we can only describe as defying common sense. Lester (1989) tried to explain these difficulties by stating that in mathematics classes the pupils are focused on symbols and rules, while in out-of-school situations we are focused on the meaning of the task in relation to the setting. In other words, the situation in which the mathematics is being used makes a difference.

## Everyday mathematics

The Cockcroft Report (1982) included a short discussion and analysis of the mathematics which is required by people in their daily lives. The purpose appears to have been to assess whether the mathematics which was being taught in school provided the mathematics which adults needed. Thus one assumption appears to have been that if we teach the right mathematics then adults will be able to tap into whatever is needed. In order to be able to include this section they commissioned a report, by Sewell (1981), which was based on surveys carried out in the street, and which was subsequently followed up in a larger survey by Gallup (which essentially produced identical findings). Many adults approached to take part in Sewell's research were very reluctant to involve themselves in anything to do with mathematics, and some refused point blank. Those participants who had good qualifications in other fields of study were inclined to express feelings of guilt about the weaknesses they felt they had in mathematics. It seems that there is a widespread lack of confidence amongst adults concerning ability in mathematics, not always justified on the basis of mathematical qualifications attained, and even present in people who need to use some mathematics in their lives. Particular feelings of inadequacy arose from participants believing on the one hand that they were not using the proper method, and on the other from being unable to obtain an exact answer, a phenomenon which appeared to persuade them that their answer could not be correct. Curious views were expressed about what were considered to be the innate characteristics of mathematics, such as accuracy, speed of working, and showing all working neatly. And there was widespread professed inability to understand some mathematical topics, such as percentages, graphs and timetables. Thus, some of the views of mathematics certainly indicated a discontinuity with the views of mathematicians. For the record, the basic mathematical needs of adult life emerged, perhaps not unexpectedly, as being quite modest. Counting, telling the time, handling money, measuring, facility with timetables, graphs and charts, and sensible estimation and approximation were all that most people needed.

The questions used by Sewell included best buys in the supermarket, interpreting charts and tables, adapting a recipe for other numbers of people than stated, and money calculations of many kinds. Such problems have been used in other research studies, the outcomes of which have tended to highlight the issues surrounding the relationship between school practice and life practice, and the differences between school learning and everyday learning. This distinction used to be referred to as the distinction between formal learning and informal learning. Formal school learning is principally de-contextualized, and pupils are often limited in the particular tools they may use, whereas everyday life activities are situated, and we all use whatever tools we need or have at hand. In other words, the calculations which we perform when shopping might be quite different from those used in comparable classroom problems. In school mathematics generalities and wide applicability are emphasized, whereas everyday situations are very specific. In school, an answer must be obtained, even if it is incorrect, but in shopping a particular comparison can be abandoned, a decision need not be made, and a product can be left on the shelves. Also, learning in school is primarily individual, whereas out-of-school activities are much more often carried out in groups.

One particular research study, the Adult Mathematics Project (Lave, 1988), included best buys in the supermarket as one source of problem situations. Participants were asked to choose the best value for money when the choice was from several articles of the same type and quality with varied weights and prices. The task was set both in the form of a test, like a school test and performed in the home, when the best buy was correctly identified in 59 per cent of the cases, and it was also carried out in the supermarket when the success rate was a remarkable 98 per cent. The obvious indication is that mathematical knowledge is linked to the situation in which it is used. Clearly, the calculation of a best buy in the supermarket matters a great deal to the purchaser, whereas a de-contextualized test question does not, and this might contribute towards the difference in the success rates.

In another kind of real-life situation, Lave (1997) reports on a study by de la Rocha of nine new members of Weight Watchers. The mathematical content of their activities revolved around the measurement required to prepare appropriate quantities of the right kinds of food in their diet. After a number of weeks in which the dieters were observed in their kitchens they then took part in a variety of arithmetic-testing activities. All of the participants were more successful on the practical food measurement tasks than they were on the isomorphic formal test questions. An interesting feature occurred because the daily measuring of food quantities takes time, so ways of short-cutting were devised. One example of this was always to pour the milk allowance into the same glass up to the mark on the pattern which previous careful measurement had revealed was the right level. This was just one of many examples of the dieters inventing their own units of measurement. In contrast to school mathematics problem situations, the dieting calculations also led to unexpected conflicts. For example, having followed the Weight Watchers guidelines to make a peanut butter sandwich, and having obtained the correct solutions (in nine uniquely different ways), the quantity of peanut butter turned out to be too great for the one slice of bread, so they scraped some off, despite knowing the amount was correct. Problem-solving in the abstract does not lead to such difficulties.

Formal and informal mathematics cannot always be distinguished easily, because the boundaries between them are inevitably not always clear. Nunes *et al.* (1993) adopted the working definition that informal mathematics is that practised outside school. They identified two forms of informal mathematics, namely one constructed outside school and one embedded in cultural practices. Their research included studies with Brazilian children working as street vendors, engaged in out-of-school selling activities in order to help supplement the family income. Thus, the term 'street mathematics' seemed appropriate, and this mathematics was compared with school mathematics. In one study, children were approached at their particular pitch (a street corner or market) and were engaged in both normal sales transactions and calculations based on other possible purchases. Subsequently, and no more than a week later, the children took a more formal test based on the kinds of calculation involved in the vending. Problems presented and addressed orally in the streets were more easily solved than those included in the more formal test in which pencil and paper were available. For example, one twelve-year-old street vendor calculated the cost of four coconuts at Cr$35 per coconut as: 'There will be one hundred five, plus thirty, that's one thirty-five . . . one coconut is thirty-five . . . that is . . . one forty'. The same child in the formal test calculated $35 \times 4$ as: 'Four times five is twenty, carry the two; two plus three is five, times four is twenty', and proceeded to write 200 as the answer (see Nunes *et al.*, 1993, p. 24). Several important questions demand attention on the basis of the results obtained. Firstly, how can it be that more correct answers were obtained in the street than in the formal test? Secondly, how is it that the children could not relate the formally presented questions to the comparable vending questions? Thirdly, what do results like these tell us about the commonly held assumption that we need to teach methods of calculation first, before the children can apply them outside the class? The facts that the vending involved familiar activity and orally-expressed calculation, whereas the formal test involved de-contextualized thinking and written arithmetic, have to be considered significant.

A further question concerns whether children construe their everyday problem-solving activities as involving mathematics at all. Abreu *et al.* (1997) described a study carried out with children in Madeira, where the life of the children outside school was claimed to have many similarities with the Brazilian children. These Madeiran children often found their school mathematics very difficult, it being 'prescribed from outside and based on a culture-free view of learning' (p. 238). Outside school, they helped in domestic activities such as shopping, some of the boys helped with the agriculture, and some of the girls helped with embroidery in the home. The study revolved around typical shopping and farming activities and attempted to ascertain whether the children believed particular situations involved mathematics. The outcome was that children expressed the view that people were using mathematics in some computational situations more than in others. Their reasoning appeared to be based on the belief that trading transactions were mathematical, but other situations were not. Thus, for the children, farming, carpentry and the fish market all involved the use of mathematics. The fact that carpentry also involved measurement was not considered as relevant as that it required computation. What is more, when children were asked to compare how problems were solved within a real-life activity and how similar problems were solved in school mathematics, they claimed there were differences – but the school methods were superior. Basically, the children's beliefs indicated that they did not see much connection between school mathematics and everyday mathematics. In school you do one kind of mathematics, out of school you do another and more inferior kind.

## Work mathematics

Most mathematical activity which adults and children engage in outside or beyond school is associated with work. The child street vendor studies could be classified as work mathematics rather than everyday mathematics, but work mathematics usually implies a more formally-organized and remunerated work or training situation. Again, the Cockcroft committee thought it important to investigate work mathematics, and indeed devoted quite a long section to the issues. This should not be surprising when one considers that a prime motivation for setting up the committee was reputed to be the many complaints from employers about inadequate mathematical knowledge amongst newly recruited employees. In other words, as with everyday mathematics, the major interest was with whether schools were providing adequate mathematical training for future employment, and it was again assumed that all we needed to do was teach the most appropriate mathematics curriculum and it would then be available for application at work. Not surprisingly, as with the every-day mathematics, the mathematical needs of employment were found to be quite modest. The study by Fitzgerald and Rich (1981), set up specifically to provide information for the Cockcroft Report (1982), found that many operatives used no mathematics, and that not many traditional school methods were in use. For example, fractions were certainly met, but school methods of combining them were not. The authors reported that many workers found it hard to recognize that they were using mathematics at all, the skills often being seen as common sense. Idiosyncratic job-specific methods applied in a purely instrumental way were frequently found, even though there were appropriate school algorithms available. These methods had been devised for a particular job situation, often by the workers themselves, illustrating the point already made that the mathematics classroom is not the only place where mathematics is learned.

One example of a unique method recounted by Fitzgerald and Rich was from a clothing factory, where the width of rolls of cloth was 60 inches, but the length (L) was measured in metres, a strange mixture of units but not untypical of practices in Britain at the time. The area in square inches was then obtained instrumentally by multiplying L × 2160 × 1.093614, and the workers had no idea why this procedure was appropriate. Readers might like to try to sort out why the method works! Another example from the wool industry involved the notoriously difficult algebraic formula:

$$\frac{1}{R} = \frac{1}{A} + \frac{1}{B} + \frac{1}{C}$$

and the algorithm being used for calculating R ran as follows:

1. Choose the highest number of A, B and C.
2. Divide it by itself and subsequently by each of the other two numbers.
3. Add the three answers together.
4. Divide their sum into the highest number of A, B and C. This gives R.

Numbers were frequently written in a more convenient form, when an employee could not handle the original. For example, the method shown here indicates considerable understanding of fractions, whilst at the same time it deviates from the school-taught algorithm for adding fractions.

$$\frac{3}{16} + \frac{5}{64} = \frac{3}{16} + \frac{1}{16} + \frac{1}{64}$$
$$= \frac{4}{16} + \frac{1}{64}$$
$$= \frac{16}{64} + \frac{1}{64}$$
$$= \frac{17}{64}$$

Other studies of the mathematics being used in employment have been carried out all around the world. Scribner (1984), for example, studied the work involved in 'pre-loaders' assembling containers of milk into cases in a dairy. The basic mathematical task involved the properties that a case held up to 16 containers, but naturally the retailers did not always order multiples of 16. The workers received computer-generated instructions for an order in the form of two numbers, the first referring to the number of full cases to be assembled initially. The second number was signed, and referred to extra containers (for example, +5), to be placed in another incomplete case, or containers to be removed from one of the full cases (for example, −3). This second number was numerically never greater than 8. In practice, however, there would frequently be incomplete cases left over from previous orders, and it was often much easier for the pre-loaders to create any additional part-case required for a new order by adding to or subtracting from one of the leftovers. In other words, the workers were not obeying the instructions but were using their own adaptation of the prescribed method. Their efficiency could be measured in terms of the number of units moved. In a comparison with drivers, clerks and students, the pre-loaders were the most efficient and the students the least.

In a comprehensive series of studies, Masingila *et al.* (1996) have researched the mathematical thinking of carpet layers, restaurant managers, dieticians and interior designers, comparing the approaches of these various professionals with the methods used by students solving the same practical problems. One example will suffice to illustrate that there were differences. The restaurant manager needed to adapt a recipe for fruit salad for six persons for a dinner party for 20 people. She decided to make enough for 24 portions, and divide the remaining four portions among the 20 fruit cups. The students were asked to use the recipe to make 10 portions. One pair of students started by using the proportional multiplying factor 10/6, and obtained quantities like 0.833, which they could not interpret in making up portions. They then excluded decimals and changed to working entirely with fractions, which again proved problematic and caused them to make up rules about what fractions to accept. Their orders included items such as $3\frac{2}{3}$ cups of apple and $1\frac{2}{3}$ tablespoons of butter. In other words, they saw the task as being to obtain quantities without regard to reasonableness in the work situation. Other students who started off trying to use exact proportions did eventually realize that things would be done less formally in an out-of-school context, and decided to make 12 portions and divide up the extra two between the other ten.

Fasheh (1991) contrasts his own mathematical knowledge, learned and subsequently taught in a Third World environment, with that of his illiterate mother. His teaching of mathematics in a school, he claimed, incorporated recognized good contemporary practice, with a revitalized curriculum, pupil involvement, discussion, clubs and magazines. His mother, on the other hand, was a dressmaker who used rectangles of cloth and fashioned them into well-fitting garments without the use of paper patterns, and with only the minimum of measurement. The mathematics involved in the manipulation of these oddment pieces was, he claimed, beyond his comprehension. She manipulated small pieces and made a new whole from them, whilst he manipulated symbols and concepts. Mistakes in her mathematics entailed serious practical consequences, mistakes in his did not. Her mathematics lacked the structure and theory of his, yet it was integrated into her work as it never was into his. Her work was valuable to the immediate needs and actions of her community, but it seemed no-one really needed his mathematics at all. These examples, and many others in the literature, illustrate that mathematical knowledge and application are frequently integrated with work situations, and the mathematics involved is often not the same as that taught in schools.

Much of the evidence relating to the mathematics of working practices concerns the use of relatively elementary mathematical skills and concepts, indeed they largely only involved simple measurement. Magajna (2001) set out to produce evidence relating to more advanced mathematics used in connection with computer-aided design in machining and in the relevant associated vocational schools in Slovenia. Three activities were considered: learning geometry in a vocational school for machine technicians, learning computer-drafting in a computer-aided design course in a vocational school for machine technicians, and the work setting of designing and manufacturing moulds for complex-shaped glass containers. The discontinuity between school and workplace mathematics was largely confirmed, but an encouraging finding was the importance of related school knowledge. There was evidence that school-learned advanced mathematical ideas can and did develop, and they became transformed into practice-related knowledge. The school-learned knowledge was, in these cases, an important basis for building the knowledge required in the profession. The mathematics in the workplace activities were, however, largely embedded within the technology, thus mathematical knowledge based on conceptual understanding was required to enable efficient use of the complex tools of practice. Magajna comments that since most workplaces are becoming more and more complex and mathematized, it is essential to learn, in schools, mathematical concepts on which to root the workplace knowledge. He further concludes that:

> As more and more mathematical knowledge is frozen in the technology used, it is important to realize that in making sense of technologized workplaces and in constructing representations and in using models in workplaces, [at least some] practitioners with vocational . . . training can and do build on, or at least significantly relate to, ideas from school mathematics. (p. 235)

An educationally relevant finding was the suggestion that an impediment to being able to use mathematics in another subject was inadequate knowledge of that other subject. Thus, in the observed setting, a very good mastery of the computer drafting program was a necessary condition for applying school mathematics. In this context Magajna also cites the work of Lagrange, who found that learning mathematics with a computer algebra system required a far better mastery of program technicalities than the teachers had imagined. Perhaps there is at least a hint here that, if pupils are to use their mathematical knowledge effectively in science classes, as referred to earlier, they must have a good mastery of the science as well as of the mathematics. Often, we expect pupils to apply mathematics in science lessons when their understanding of the content of either or both subjects is still very hazy.

## Transfer of learning and situated cognition

The evidence presented in the two previous sections, concerning everyday mathematics and work mathematics, respectively, is but a small sample from the huge number of research studies completed in recent years which illustrate the so-called discontinuity between the mathematics of classroom lessons and other mathematics encountered in everyday activities. If it is one of our intentions in teaching that we should equip our children with mathematics that will be needed for life after school then there is plenty of evidence that we do not succeed, at least certainly not in the straightforward way that we might hope. Our school mathematics curriculum is really based on the assumption that mathematics is a formal body of knowledge, a self-contained subject domain which contains mathematical objects with meanings which do not have to be applied outside the subject. This mathematics, it is assumed, can therefore be completely detached from the experiential world and can be studied purely for its own sake, although we do also intend our pupils to use them in later life. Bishop (1988b, p. 8) summed up the position as follows:

> The idea of the average person as a peripatetic problem-solver armed with a tool-bag of mathematical techniques and looking for a problem to solve is a myth. But it is a powerful myth. It dominates mathematical education at present, has done for a long time, and probably will continue to do so for a long time to come.

The fact that our pupils cannot use their knowledge in other domains is usually classified as being a problem of the transfer of learning. Transfer is, of course, a long-standing educational issue, and used to be referred to as transfer of training, which in itself indicates a shift in the way education is regarded. The evidence from the many investigations and research studies illustrated above, together with our own experiences of teaching, might often seem to suggest that very little learning, if any at all, is likely to transfer from one situation to another. Cormier and Hagman (1987), however, claim that it has been accepted for many years now that some transfer from one domain to another does occur, so the issue deserves deeper consideration. Two kinds of transfer have been discussed in the literature, namely horizontal (lateral) transfer and vertical transfer, with the latter being the less contentious of the two. Mathematics is generally considered to be a hierarchical subject, in which new ideas continually need to be constructed upon a base of earlier and more elementary ideas, and in this way vertical transfer should be occurring constantly. For individual pupils there might be frequent difficulties, yet gradual and steady progression from the less abstract to the more abstract is regularly assumed. However, this does not mean to say that there is agreement about the conditions under which vertical transfer optimally occurs, or indeed about the optimum sequence, or about the likely rate of progress. Lateral transfer, on the other hand, is recognized as being much more doubtful, and this is what is generally at issue when we hope that the mathematics which we have taught will be available in other subject areas, in daily life, and in future employment. And yet, without some lateral transfer, and in simplistic terms, the extent of everyone's knowledge would remain within what they have learned from direct teaching. If there is ever to be a solution to the transfer dilemma which is of help to educators it will surely only come with much better understanding of the conditions under which it might occur.

The problems of the apparent lack of transfer of school-learned concepts, methods and skills to other areas of activity, together with the propensity for individuals to invent or construct their own ways of solving the problems they encounter in life, have together led to the theoretical standpoint that all learning is essentially situated. In recent years, this theory of situated cognition has gathered many adherents, of varying levels of enthusiasm, and with varying views on the importance of the theory and the circumstances under which it might have justification. Kirshner and Whitson (1997, p. 4) explained the significance of the study of situated cognition as follows:

> One source of inspiration for situated cognitionists is the robust expertise that ordinary folks regularly display in ordinary situations. Against the backdrop of an educational enterprise that too often fails to engage students and develop their competencies are the multifaceted ways in which people succeed and learn in all sorts of out-of-school settings.

The theoretical foundations of the theory of situated cognition lie in both socio-cultural approaches to education and in anthropology – and, for some, in history as well. Often, proponents of the view that learning is basically situated have been influenced by the work of Vygotsky and Leont'ev. In recent years, one of the most influential proponents of a particularly strong form of situated cognition has been Jean Lave, and we need to consider her original standpoint in more detail.

According to Lave, we need to think of a situated mind, with cognition being 'distributed', or 'stretched over' mind, body, activity and setting. Lave has described many studies, some involving adults and some involving children. Those summarized earlier have revolved around adult learning behaviour, so it is appropriate to describe some of her findings based on work with children. In a study involving a high-performing mathematics class, Lave (1997, p. 29) tells of children who 'brought to a three-week unit on multiplication and division facts almost as much knowledge as when they finished'. Indeed, the performances of the less successful (on a pre-test) converged over time with those of the more adept. It seemed that during the three weeks the children gave no evidence of having adopted any of the specific methods or techniques which had been taught, rather they were able to use the methods which they had brought with them or invented, but they were able to use them in such a way as to make it appear that they had used the teacher's methods. In short, 'the teacher, text, and exercise books prescribed in detail how the children should act – what their everyday practice of math should be – while the children produced a different practice' (p. 30). Essentially, the pupils solved the problems using counting and regrouping strategies which had not been taught in the lessons and which were not supposed to be used. Lave further supports her case with other examples, including studies with Vai children in Liberia, where the local number system which tallies at 5, 10 and 20, together with the associated arithmetic processes, are different from those taught in school. Here, 'the children routinely develop a syncretic form of Vai and school-taught arithmetic, and become increasingly skilled in its use over time, although it is never taught' (p. 31). On the basis of results such as the above, together with her wider knowledge of schools in the USA, Lave claims that understanding in practice looks like a more powerful source of enculturation than the pedagogical efforts of teachers.

Another significant contributor to the situated cognition debate is Geoffrey Saxe. He particularly expressed concern that neither Piaget nor Vygotsky had been able to explain how the mathematical understandings of a cultural group that have emerged throughout history become the child's own, and are linked with the child's purposive problem-solving activities. In earlier studies (Saxe, 1991) he reported the use of body part counting among Oksapmin schoolchildren and unschooled adults engaged in selling goods on the streets in Papua New Guinea. Outside school, the subjects had learned a system of counting based on parts of the body which extended beyond simply using fingers. In this case, they also had to cope with a non-base counting system. In addition to his work among the Oksapmin peoples he also worked in a separate study with child candy sellers in Brazil. Saxe has expressed greater optimism about transfer than Lave, and has provided examples of candy sellers who were using school algorithms within their calculations. He has also claimed that sellers were witnessed using adaptations of candy-selling practices in attempts to solve school problems, thereby performing better on their school problems than non-sellers. His work suggests that successful transfer is unlikely to be immediate, but should perhaps be considered as a long process of repeated attempts at construction. Furthermore, he also emphasizes the importance of the depth of understanding of the relevant prior knowledge.

## Ethnomathematics

An obvious extension to the consideration of alternative mathematical practices within particular social contexts or situations is to consider the differences which exist across different cultural or ethnic groupings. This issue has already arisen, through the references to the Oksapmin and Vai cultures, which may be used to illustrate the potential for an enormous diversity of local practice. In accepting that such differences exist, however, we must also admit that mathematics might therefore not be the universally accepted body of infallible knowledge that we might have been educated to think it is. One consequence of an acceptance of variation is pressure for the school curriculum to respond and adapt to the nature of the society which it serves. In Britain, as in many countries, the claim is that our society is now more multicultural and multi-ethnic than ever before, and the response has been to try to develop a curriculum which draws from and relates to the cultural backgrounds of all pupils. In a broader historical sense, one might claim that the curriculum *has* continually responded and developed according to influences from around the world, for example, in our acceptance down the years of our current measures of time, angle, length, weight and capacity. Within the last one hundred years many standardized older systems of measurement have been phased out, particularly those relating to agricultural and other occupational practices. Given that linguists often emphasize the interdependence of language and culture one might even suggest that, if there are distinctive features of the mathematics of any cultural or subcultural group, they reflect the distinctive character of that group. We must also not overlook the fact that a curriculum is not just a list of topics and ideas to be taught, it also incorporates teaching methods, about which different cultures are likely to have very strong views, and in this we are moving into the realms of beliefs and values.

Ethnomathematics is the description now used for what Gerdes (1994) has referred to as the cultural anthropology of mathematics. The term was first coined by d'Ambrosio, who wrote (1991):

we will call ethnomathematics the mathematics which is practised among identifiable cultural groups, such as national-tribal societies, labour groups, children of a certain age bracket, professional classes, and so on. Its identity depends on focus of interests, on motivation, on certain codes and jargons, which do not belong to the realm of academic mathematics. (p. 18)

It has become clear that all societies and cultures around the world have developed mathematics in their own ways, but Bishop (1988b) has claimed that these can always be classified under the six headings of counting, locating, measuring, designing, playing and explaining. This also provides a way in which variations around the world may be classified and understood. *Counting* might involve fingers, but it might also involve other body parts; it can include using sticks, stones, bones, ropes or other objects for tallying. It is likely to involve number names, and these might incorporate some kind of linguistic structure. *Locating* involves mastering the spatial environment, and includes exploring, conceptualizing and mapping. Travel and navigation are dependent on mastering location, hence the link with astronomy. *Measuring* is essential for arranging in order and for comparing, and many everyday activities and transactions such as construction, and buying and selling depend on it. *Designing* is both creative and technical, but it also involves aesthetic appreciation or beauty. It should therefore be no surprise that, around the world, there is great variety of shapes and styles in dwellings and larger buildings for religious, administrative, military and political purposes. *Playing* is important to humans, and there are some universal games, but there are also many which are unique to particular cultures. *Explaining* is to do with putting all of our knowledge into perspective, and mathematical constructs and models can help with this. The enormous diversity of practice around the world is inevitable when one considers these six dimensions and the possibilities which might emerge, and have indeed developed throughout history. This should at least partly explain why Bishop (1991) was able to claim that there has been criticism from many regions of the world when there have been attempts to import a Western mathematics curriculum.

Magajna (2001) has used a three-way classification of ethnomathematics in order to help to expose its dimensions. Firstly, he asserts, there is the mathematics unique to various cultural groups, which is what raises doubts about the validity of claims that mathematics is a universally and objectively agreed subject area. Researchers in this first domain might attempt to bring to light the products and practices of any cultural group. Other studies might consider the historical development of mathematical ideas in different cultures. Yet others might investigate the practices of subgroups within a society, such as the child street vendors of Brazil. Secondly, there is ethnomathematics as an emancipatory movement, that is, an opposition to any claim to the superiority of Western mathematics. Significant examples of this, for Magajna, include the sociomathematics of Zaslavsky (1973, for example), and the frozen mathematics of colonized nations (see Gerdes, 1985) which would at first sight appear to have been lost or forgotten at an explicit level, but which still emerges in the technology of such activities as dwelling construction, basket making and weaving. Thirdly, there is ethnomathematics as an educational theory. The essence of this is the desire to base the teaching of mathematics on the cultural background of the pupils, thus using out-of-school experiences and practices, both extracting mathematical ideas from the environment and embedding them within it. Minorities within any society such as regional communities would come into the reckoning here. Many a teacher moving from a city school to an isolated rural village has gone through the learning experience of discovering that mathematical ideas can have different meanings, examples and implications in different locations which are not too distant from each other geographically. There is, however, a strong counter-argument to any simplistically conceived close association of school mathematics with local culture. Vithal and Skovsmose (1997) have highlighted the need to take account not only of a pupil's background, but also to acknowledge the need to prepare pupils to face their future, and for this, it can be argued, we need a curriculum with international credibility, which provides the tools for using and developing technology and thereby improving people's lives.

An important issue is therefore how best to promote learning in an ethnically-diverse mathematics classroom. How might we set about structuring a mathematics curriculum which caters for all children? One partial solution is to use mathematical ideas and constructs from the whole range of cultural backgrounds present in the class. In practice, however, the danger is that we shall still merely have a common Western curriculum, but one which allows the possibility of the occasional use of a variety of culturally-based activities to enlighten and perhaps enliven the statutory scheme. Perhaps because this limited acknowledgement of cultural diversity is often all that we have been able to achieve up to now, there has been pressure in Britain recently to allow the setting up of separate schools for children from particular ethnic and religious backgrounds. Or, alternatively, perhaps this pressure is more the result of differing beliefs and values which a national curriculum and associated teaching methods fail to acknowledge adequately. Bishop (1991, p. 38) has suggested that the six activities described earlier might provide a structural framework for curriculum construction, for, 'if those activities are universal, and if they are both necessary and sufficient for mathematical development, then a curriculum which is structured around [them] *would* allow the mathematical ideas from different cultural groups to be introduced sensibly'. Another approach, suggested and used by Harris (1997), is to base the development of mathematical understanding on the study of some major areas of human activity, and her main example is textiles. Her *Common Threads* exhibition, she claims, 'came at a time when research was confirming the significance of the context on learning mathematics, and when gender and cultural issues were high priorities' (p. 127). Bishop, however, also wonders whether it is even possible to create a 'culturally-fair mathematics curriculum', that is, 'a curriculum which would allow all cultural groups to involve their own ideas whilst also permitting the international mathematical ideas to be developed' (1991, p. 38).

Ginsburg *et al.* (1997) have considered another issue of cultural diversity, namely why it is that there are sometimes differences in examination performance between children from different ethnic backgrounds. This is the kind of problem which can persuade politicians that intervention on a large scale is necessary. Writing from the perspective of the USA, the problem Ginsburg *et al.* raise is that Asian-American children perform the best, African-American children and Hispanic children do poorly, and White children fall between the extremes. This kind of phenomenon has been noted in other countries too. The issue in the USA, as elsewhere, is compounded by issues of social class and relative affluence or poverty. The superior performance of Asian children has often, in the past, been ascribed to such factors as motivation, the high expectations of parents, and belief in the importance of effort rather than inherent ability. It has also been claimed that Asian teachers explain in more depth and place more emphasis on thinking and understanding than do other teachers. Ginsburg *et al.*, however, researched the possibility that the key might be differences in informal mathematical knowledge. They quote from recent studies from various countries which indicate that 'informal mathematical thinking develops in robust fashion before the onset of schooling', and that, 'much of this informal mathematics can develop in the absence of adult instruction' (see Chapter 11), and also that, 'many adults are quite surprised to learn how much their young children . . . know in this area' (p. 165). They further claim that informal mathematical development is vital for progress in school, because it provides a solid structure on which to build in a more formal way. However, their conclusion is that there is no convincing evidence that informal mathematical knowledge influences why some groups subsequently learn better than others. The problem appears to be more likely to result from differences in motivation and schooling. Also, in certain countries, some ethnic and other subgroups are subverted by a deep-seated anti-academic attitude. Ginsburg *et al.* do also point out, however, that:

> if [pupils] receive preschool instruction (like certain Chinese), or are born into a culture favouring quantitative activity (like the Japanese), or are privileged to be a member of a relatively affluent class . . . or a group with positive expectations about schooling . . . then their potential is more likely to be realized. (p. 201)

## The significance of the situation

It should now be clear that there are ways in which the situation can affect what is learned. Firstly, and at the most basic level, there are variations in mathematics curricula around the world, documented recently in, for example, Hoyles *et al.* (2003). Secondly, there are differing ways in which counting methods have developed in different societies, and these methods have often influenced subsequent mathematical development. Thirdly, there is the multitude of ways in which informal mathematics can develop according to the individual circumstances of both individual children and social groupings. Then there is the evidence of variations in examination performances among different ethnic groups within the same nation, which appear likely to be associated with home, society and culture. Then there are the individual ways in which small but highly motivated groups, and also teams of workers in particular occupations, solve their mathematical problems. So the main point at issue should really be the extent to which situations might affect learning. It should also now be clear that those who have, in recent years, contributed evidence to support a situational effect have themselves not all held identical views, some being much more extreme than others in their belief in the affect of the situation. One problem, not surprisingly, has been with the interpretation of situated cognition data, so we need to consider its robustness.

Evans (2000) has discussed some of the weaknesses of the conclusions drawn from the many studies on which Lave has based her earliest beliefs in situated cognition. Concerning the Adult Mathematics Project, he claims firstly that it was not clear that the categorization of the tasks as either school or everyday was straightforward, secondly that judgements of relative difficulty were suspect, thirdly that the results taken at face value did not justify a claim of discontinuity of performance, and fourthly that it was not justifiable to compare compulsory test results with non-compulsory behaviour in the supermarket. Indeed, one might also query whether the attitudes and motivations of these adult shoppers could ever have been exactly determined, let alone how their attitudes might have influenced their behaviour. Noss and Hoyles (1996) have similarly evaluated the supermarket research, summarizing it as follows:

> When shoppers *do* use mathematics in the supermarket, it is supermarket mathematics, . . . mathematics of this kind differs in substantial respects from the kinds of mathematics commonly taught in schools . . . situated cognition has no need for universal laws . . . it is concerned with getting the job done. (p. 33)

Evans (2000) acknowledges, however, that Lave's contribution to the situated cognition debate has been enormous, but he claims that the way ahead is a deeper analysis of the bases of observed differences in practice:

> [Lave] has shown how to look for, and to begin to describe, the ways that different contexts may be discontinuous, and may have effects on activity and thinking in them . . . however, it is important to avoid the cul-de-sac of the strong form of situated cognition. (p. 85)

Other major early contributors to the situated cognition debate are clearly Nunes, Schliemann and Carraher. Some of their seminal work concerning child street vendors in Brazil has already been discussed, but the question of whether like was being compared with like arises once again for Evans (2000), who claims that to attempt to draw conclusions about cognition across contexts based on an assumption that the same tasks were being used is highly questionable. Subsequently Nunes *et al.* (1993) have addressed further issues such as which aspects of different contexts could account for the observed differences in performance. They have suggested that one important difference concerns the social relations between researcher and subject, for example, whether the customer is known to be a researcher. In one study, keeping the context constant (testing in school), and comparing the three situations of simulated store problems, word problems and computation exercises, they were able to show that oral calculations were done correctly more often than written ones, and that when the procedure was controlled, the differences in performance across situations disappeared (Carraher *et al.*, 1987). Furthermore, Nunes *et al.* (1993) have separated out and researched different levels of transfer, namely application to problems with unfamiliar parameters, reversibility (use of a procedure in the opposite direction), and transfer across situations. Another significant conclusion (Schliemann, 1995) was that:

> Mathematical knowledge developed in everyday contexts is flexible and general. Strategies developed to solve problems in a specific context can be applied to other contexts, provided that the relations between the quantities in the target context are known by the subject as being related in the same manner as the quantities in the initial context are. (p. 49)

A similar conclusion expressed by Saxe (1991) has been stated earlier.

Bereiter (1997), in claiming that situated cognition has not provided a new educational vision, has set the debate within a much broader context than simply reviewing data and conclusions drawn from them. He accuses proponents of confusing process which is situated, and product which may not be situated. He claims that there are three ways in which humans may transcend their animal heritage. The first way is by transforming physical environments and creating new social structures and practices. The second is by acquiring expertise which enables us to function in a novel environment much as if we evolved within it. The third is by creating a world of immaterial knowledge objects and acquiring expertise in working with them. He then claims a direct mapping between these three ways and Popper's (1972) metaphoric schema of three worlds, the first level of which is the material world – both inanimate and animate, the second is the level of the subjective world of individual mental activity, and the third is the level of the world of immaterial knowledge objects. He claims that situated cognition might help us to understand the relationship between the first and second levels, but the third level represents the strongest sense in which humans may be said to have *overcome* situated cognition. The ability to work at the third level is what has enabled the human race to develop all the modern trappings of civilization, to continue to raise our standards of living year on year, and to perform incredible feats requiring great technological mastery. Mathematics beyond the early years of schooling, as it becomes increasingly more and more abstract, surely moves steadily further into the third level. Bereiter thus claims that formal education provides us with an escape route away from the confines of the situatedness of the lower levels. He admits that none of the three levels is likely to escape completely from the possibility of the effects of particular circumstances and environments, but the third level allows the best escape possibilities. Logical argument at the third level is extremely powerful, for when one works within the third level on premises which hold in the first level, then valid conclusions from the premises do as well. Also, and conversely, if valid conclusions turn out to be not true at the first level, then there must be something wrong with the premises. Disciplined movement between the levels thus gives us the hypothetico-deductive method and opens up the highest levels of thinking. Interestingly, Donaldson (1978), after discussing the logicality of the behaviour of young children, then suggested that during subsequent cognitive development this logicality becomes less and less dependent on the situation. Thus situated cognition has not provided a new and vital educational vision.

One benefit that has emerged from studies around and within the domain of situated cognition is a better understanding of many of the issues which affect the efficient transfer of learning. For Bereiter (1997), what mainly fails to transfer is learned intelligent behaviour. The technological advances referred to earlier suggest strongly that intelligent behaviour can transfer under the right conditions, and indeed it must transfer for society to continue to progress. Many of us will be familiar with the circumstances in which two friends who have previously succeeded at the highest level in external examinations at 16+ subsequently do not perform at the same level as each other in 'higher' examinations in later years. At this higher level it is possible for the first to pass with flying colours and the other to struggle and even fail. When this happens, we may conclude that the first has been successful in achieving transfer but the second has not. The second has very likely learned only how to pass the examination at 16+ and has not learned what is transferable. The first has engaged in intentional learning, which incorporates knowledge-building goals, the second has not progressed beyond task completion exercises and the successful passing of examinations. Knowledge-building, the continuous construction of understanding and knowledge, is the key, and it is only weakly connected to immediate situations. It requires learners to be looking all the time for connections and relationships based on structural or logical correspondences.

The situated cognition debate has produced other analyses concerning transfer. Evans (2000), for example, proposes seven guidelines for optimizing transfer. Particularly important suggestions include making the ability to transfer a specific and explicit goal, by establishing the links and inter-relationships between the contexts, by clarifying the similarities and differences, and by generalizing the methods used across the contexts. In other words, making every effort to set up transfer, rather than what has happened in the past – the all too common practice of just hoping transfer will happen. Transfer will never be automatic for any learner, and it will never be easy to understand for those who try to make more and more sense of how we might promote learning in others. But our knowledge of the conditions under which transfer can and hopefully should occur continues to develop, and the situated cognition debate has assisted us in moving our understanding forward.

## Suggestions for further reading

Boaler, J. (1997) *Experiencing School Mathematics*. Buckingham: Open University Press.

Harris, M. (1997) *Common Threads: Women, Mathematics and Work*. Stoke on Trent: Trentham Books.

Lave, J. (1988) *Cognition in Practice: Mind, Mathematics and Culture in Everyday Life*. Cambridge: Cambridge University Press.

Nunes, T., Schliemann, A. D. and Carraher, D. W. (1993) *Street Mathematics and School Mathematics*. Cambridge: Cambridge University Press.

Saxe, G. (1991) *Culture and Cognitive Development: Studies in Mathematical Understanding*. Hillsdale, NJ: Lawrence Erlbaum.

## Questions for discussion

1. What do you think the majority of adults have gained from their mathematical education?
2. To what extent does school mathematics equip pupils for the workplace?
3. What is the ethnomathematics of your country or home area?
4. What changes in school mathematics need to be adopted in order to enhance the transfer of learning to new situations?

Chapter 8

# Why Do Some Pupils Achieve More Than Others?

---

## Individual differences

A wide variety of differences between pupils will be observed when we ask them to do mathematics. How, for example, are pupils likely to react to this problem?

> *League fixtures*
>
> There are eight teams in a Junior League. How many league matches are required to complete all the fixtures in one season? If there were *n* teams, how many matches would be required?

Some children play in a local Junior League in some sport or other, so the context would be familiar. They might even have been motivated to have obtained the solution independent of mathematics lessons and long before the teacher posed the question. They, and some children who do not play in a local league, would find the problem interesting and worth attempting, but many other pupils would not. It might be found that more boys than girls are motivated by the problem, but it might not. Some contexts are more immediately appealing to a majority of girls and others to a majority of boys. Some children, despite finding the context interesting, might not be able to solve the problem. Amongst those who could solve the problem, a variety of different methods might be used. The fact that so much variety could emerge in response to one mathematical situation is another feature which needs to be taken into account in considering the learning process.

For those pupils who are unable to solve the problem the teacher might decide to demonstrate or discuss a solution. There are, however, so many different ways of setting about the problem that it is difficult to know which is to choose. Whichever method is chosen, it might not be the best for all pupils. A variety of methods of solution is outlined below, all based on numbering the teams one to eight.

*Method A*

The fixtures for Team 1 are:

| | |
|---|---|
| 1 v. 2 | 2 v. 1 |
| 1 v. 3 | 3 v. 1 |
| 1 v. 4 | 4 v. 1 |
| 1 v. 5 | 5 v. 1 |
| 1 v. 6 | 6 v. 1 |
| 1 v. 7 | 7 v. 1 |
| 1 v. 8 | 8 v. 1 |

so the total number of matches involving Team 1 is 14.

The fixtures for Team 2 are:

| | |
|---|---|
| 2 v. 1 | 1 v. 2 |
| 2 v. 3 | 3 v. 2 |
| 2 v. 4 | 4 v. 2 |
| 2 v. 5 | 5 v. 2 |
| 2 v. 6 | 6 v. 2 |
| 2 v. 7 | 7 v. 2 |
| 2 v. 8 | 8 v. 2 |

but two of these fixtures, 2 v. 1 and 1 v. 2, have already been counted amongst the fixtures for Team 1, so there are only 12 new matches.

Proceeding by listing might eventually lead to short-cutting, though it might not, but eventually the method results in this sum and total:

$$14 + 12 + 10 + 8 + 6 + 4 + 2 = 56$$

*Method B*

Each team plays all of the other seven teams twice, making 14 matches. But this approach counts each match twice, since 1 v. 2, for example, is counted both as a home match for Team 1 and an away match for Team 2. The total number of matches is therefore:

$$14 \times 8 \times \tfrac{1}{2} = 56$$

*Method C*

All we need to do is find how many home matches each team plays and total those. Each team plays seven home matches, so the total is:

$$7 \times 8 = 56$$

Mathematically, this might be considered the same as Method B, but pupils might not appreciate that.

*Method D*

There are eight numbers, 1, 2, 3, 4, 5, 6, 7 and 8, and we need to know how many pairs of numbers may be selected from these eight. This total is $8 \times 8 = 64$, but this includes 1 v. 1, 2 v. 2, etc. The number of matches is therefore:

$$8 \times 8 - 8 = 56$$

When the number of teams is allowed to vary, the generalization also permits variation of method.

### Method X

We know that a league of eight teams produces 56 matches. An extra team introduces another eight home matches and another eight away matches yielding this total number of fixtures:

$$56 + 2 \times 8 = 72$$

Then 10 teams would produce a total of:

$$72 + 2 \times 9 = 90$$

and so on.

### Method Y

Any of methods A to D applied to a different number of teams, to provide the same data as in Method X.

### Method Z

A tabulation of all numbers of fixtures for any number of teams, leading to a number pattern, which may be extended using, for example, the fact that the differences (see Chapter 6) are consecutive even numbers.

| Number of teams | Number of fixtures |
|:---:|:---:|
| 1 | 0 |
| 2 | 2 |
| 3 | 6 |
| 4 | 12 |
| 5 | 20 |
| 6 | 30 |
| 7 | 42 |
| 8 | 56 |
| 9 | 72 |
| 10 | 90 |

The tabulated data may now be used to generalize for $n$ teams. It might be clear to some pupils (but not necessarily to all), that the pattern reveals that the number of fixtures is always:

(number of teams) $\times$ (one less than the number of teams).

Other pupils might see things differently, in that the number of fixtures is:

(the square of the number of teams) $-$ (the number of teams).

Some pupils, who have successfully produced results like those in the table, will not be able to proceed with the use of letters, and will be mystified by $n\,(n-1)$.

This issue has been explored at length because the fact that different pupils will think their way through mathematical problems in a variety of different ways is a complication presented to all teachers. For two reasons, any taught method for solving a particular problem might not meet the requirements of all pupils. Firstly, it might not meet all of them where they are (Ausubel, 1968), in the sense that too many assumptions are made about prior knowledge. Secondly, it might not coincide with their preferred cognitive style. Discussion of a variety of different methods of solving the same problem could thus be considered much more beneficial. On the other hand such an approach might be rejected on a number of grounds, including boredom created by spending so long on the one problem, and lack of interest amongst those pupils who have decided that their method of solution is the only one that matters.

The issue of different methods favoured by different pupils on the same problem is only one within the complete range of issues associated with individual differences. Some pupils clearly do achieve more in their studies of mathematics than do others, hence there *are* differences. Abilities, preferences, attitudes and motivation all contribute to making some pupils more successful than others, and in the remainder of this chapter a variety of contributory factors are considered.

## Convergent and divergent thinking

It is necessary to consider the issue of convergent and divergent thinking first in order that reference can be made to it subsequently. The convergence/divergence dichotomy (or is it a spectrum?) is best introduced by means of examples.

Tests of intelligence are of many types but some, and particularly tests of non-verbal intelligence, include questions which are numerical, for example:

> 1, 5, 9, 13, 17 . . .
>
> What number comes next?

and

> 1, 2, 3, 4, 5, 6, 7, 8, 9
>
> Write down the difference between the largest and smallest of these numbers.

also

> Here are three figures:
>
> 5, 2, 7
>
> Add the largest two figures together and divide the total by the smallest.

Some general ability tests also involve diagrams, as in these further examples:

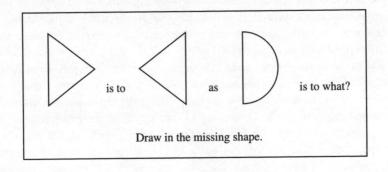

and

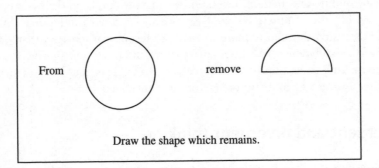

A good example of a test which includes items of the numerical and diagrammatic kinds represented here is that by Heim (1970).

All of these sample test items are basically mathematical. In addition, for all of the items, there is only one expected answer, that is, the questions are all convergent. To most people, mathematical thinking always seems to be convergent. In fact, there may be no evidence that divergent thinking skills are needed at all. In other curriculum areas it is very easy to produce questions which are divergent, that is, which provide the opportunity for a variety of acceptable responses, for example, the following:

Write down as many words as you can which end in

-ing

Test items in mathematics which are divergent are not much used. One which Guilford (1959) suggested was:

Make up as many equations as you can which follow from

$$B - C = D$$

and

$$Z = A + D$$

Even then, the opportunity for divergence is not as great as in the previous test item. In one sense, the recent trend to encourage the use of investigations in mathematics, many of which are 'open-ended', can be considered to be a reaction against the highly convergent nature of the majority of the usual school mathematics curriculum.

An early study of thinking skills was carried out by Bartlett (1958), who described and investigated several categories of 'thinking within closed systems', which he contrasted with 'adventurous thinking'. Getzels and Jackson (1962) researched into two types of child, those who were of 'high IQ' and those who were 'high creative', which appears to imply that high intelligence only depends on convergent thinking skills and that creativity is not related to intelligence. In fact it further tends to suggest that the typical IQ test often does not measure anything other than convergent abilities. Hudson (1966) used tests of convergent and divergent thinking with sixth form students in a fascinating research study into individual differences. In fact he used a battery of tests of both ability and personality, and concluded:

> Most arts specialists, weak at the IQ tests, were much better at the open-ended ones; most scientists were the reverse. Arts specialists are on the whole divergers, physical scientists convergers. Between three and four divergers go into arts subjects like history, English literature and modern languages for every one that goes into physical science. And, vice-versa, between three and four convergers do mathematics, physics and chemistry for every one that goes into the arts. (pp. 56–7)

Biology, geography and economics attracted convergers and divergers roughly equally, whilst classics went with the physical sciences and mathematics. Only a minority of students coped equally well with convergent and divergent items. Such results demand further reflection.

If most mathematics students are predominantly convergent thinkers, does this imply that few specialist mathematicians are capable of creativity or inventiveness? This surely cannot be the case, so do Hudson's results suggest that the only creative mathematics students are the minority who are either divergent thinkers or who are equally at home with both kinds of thinking? Furthermore, does the predominantly convergent nature of the thinking of the majority of mathematics sixth form students imply that this will remain the case throughout life? Does the typical school mathematics education produce the convergent thinkers which we find in the sixth form or is it the case that the pupils are already predisposed towards convergence and our mathematics curriculum both attracts them and also does little to counteract it? If we attempt radical changes to the mathematics curriculum so that it becomes much more based on open-ended situations will we deter those students whose preference is for convergent studies? What should we be doing, as mathematics teachers, to cater for both convergence and divergence in the preferences of our pupils?

In this particular domain of individual differences there may seem to be more questions than answers. Hudson pursued his research into the affective domain by looking for correlations between the convergence/divergence trait and personality traits. As a result, he suggested that convergent thinking is the preference of the pupil who likes to keep emotion apart from studies and that divergent thinking is the preference of those who like their studies to involve them emotionally. In short, the theory proposed by Hudson was that affective predispositions which reach right back into early childhood cause us to prefer either convergent- or divergent-related studies, so these are the kinds of studies in which we subsequently choose to specialize. Does this mean there is a connection with the introvert–extrovert spectrum? An interesting comparison here is between the typical behaviour patterns of mathematics teachers and, say, English and drama teachers. Of course, some of those who choose to specialize in mathematics are at ease with both convergent and divergent situations. Nevertheless, the theory cannot be dismissed lightly. A recent BBC television series entitled 'The Mind' chose to use a group of physics specialists as a typical collection of introverts. The following statements from two seventeen-year-old pupils were collected by the author and by Russell (1983, p. 79), respectively.

> I think the popularity of maths depends very much on the character of the person. Maths is an ideally suited subject to anyone who likes logic, clear-cut solutions, methods, definite right or wrong answers. Such people are bound to enjoy mathematics.
>
> English is very much you – far more of your personality comes through. Maths doesn't show your personality.

## Mathematical ability

The analysis of human abilities has been the subject of many studies which have taken a variety of different forms. At one extreme has been the method based on the statistical procedure of factor analysis applied to test scores. At the other extreme has been the anecdotal approach, often based on the reflections by famous mathematicians about their own ability. The outcome has been the clear indication that overall intellectual capacity is the most dominant influence on mathematical ability, and it is a matter of what other more specific abilities can be shown to exist. Some pupils, however, clearly do show more aptitude for mathematics than others, so the issue of mathematical ability is essential to a consideration of individual differences. Particular points of interest, apart from what it is that makes one pupil more able than another, include whether it is possible to identify pupils of high mathematical ability early in life, whether it is possible to foster such ability with a special study programme, and of course what should be done to make other pupils more able than they currently appear to be.

A major study of mathematical ability in pupils was carried out by Krutetskii (1976). The study was, in essence, based on observation of pupils and conversation with them, so it is not surprising that the research method used by Krutetskii has been compared with that of Piaget. The origins of mathematical ability were seen by Krutetskii to lie in the existence of 'inborn inclinations', as can be seen in the following statements:

> Mathematical abilities are not innate, but are properties acquired in life that are formed on the basis of certain inclinations . . . some persons have inborn characteristics in the structure and functional features of their brains which are extremely favourable to the development of mathematical abilities . . . anyone can become an ordinary mathematician; one must be born an outstandingly talented one. (p. 361)

This theory must be seen against the Soviet political background which did not accept that innate intellectual abilities existed. The resulting confusion between the relative contributions from innate inclinations and from environmental factors, contained in Krutetskii's book, therefore does not provide a secure foundation for explaining mathematical ability. In other ways, however, Krutetskii's work is helpful.

Krutetskii devoted considerable space to debating how mathematical ability might be defined. He referred to individual psychological characteristics that answer the requirements of school mathematical activity and that influence success in the creative mastery of mathematics as a school subject – in particular, a relatively rapid, easy, and thorough mastery of knowledge, skills, and habits in mathematics. His components of mathematical ability include the following:

1. An ability to extract the formal structure from the content of a mathematical problem and to operate with that formal structure.
2. An ability to generalize from mathematical results.
3. An ability to operate with symbols, including numbers.
4. An ability for spatial concepts, required in certain branches of mathematics.
5. A logical reasoning ability.
6. An ability to shorten ('curtail') the process of reasoning.
7. An ability to be flexible in switching from one approach to another, including both the avoidance of fixations (see Chapter 5) and the ability to reverse trains of thought.
8. An ability to achieve clarity, simplicity, economy and rationality in mathematical argument and proof.
9. A good memory for mathematical knowledge and ideas.

It is interesting to compare this analysis with that described by Suydam and Weaver (1977, p. 42), reflecting on characteristics of good problem-solvers in mathematics:

1. Ability to estimate and analyse.
2. Ability to visualize and interpret quantitative facts and relationships.
3. Ability to understand mathematical terms and concepts.
4. Ability to note likenesses, differences and analogies.
5. Ability to select correct procedures and data.
6. Ability to note irrelevant detail.
7. Ability to generalize on the basis of few examples.
8. Ability to switch methods readily
9. Higher scores for self-esteem and lower scores for text anxiety.

Suydam and Weaver also noted that 'more impulsive students are often poor problem-solvers, while more reflective students are likely to be good problem-solvers'.

It might be considered reasonable to assume that the existence or otherwise of mathematical ability stems from physiological sources, and Krutetskii discussed this in some detail. Mathematically-able pupils adopt a procedure in solving mathematical problems which suggests they can follow a plan which involves trying out ideas systematically and in which they appear to be able to see which ideas are worth pursuing and which are not. Less capable pupils, on the other hand, he claimed, show blind, unmotivated manipulations, and chaotic and unsystematic attempts. The physiological explanation provided by Krutetskii was that there is a control apparatus within the cortex of the brain, the acceptor of an operation, which evaluates results of any operation, comparing what has been tried with what could be tried and generally directing and regulating trials. Thus, 'when there is a pronounced inability for mathematics, a low level of functional maturity of the inferior parietal region of the cortex and of its connections with other sections of the brain is observed' (Krutetskii, 1976, p. 363).

Krutetskii also suggested that there were different kinds of mathematical ability. Some pupils had an 'analytic' mind and preferred to think in verbal, logical ways; other pupils had a 'geometric' mind and liked a visual or pictorial approach. A majority of students, however, had a 'harmonic' mind and were able to combine characteristics of both the analytic and the geometric, though they were likely to show some leaning towards either the analytic or the geometric approach. Pupils with a harmonic type of mind were most likely to show real mathematical aptitude. The suggestion that there are varieties of 'mathematical mind' has also been made by Hadamard (1945). Earlier attempts to describe mathematical ability provided by Hamley, Haecker and Ziehen, Oldham and Werdelin are also described by Krutetskii, but none of these studies has provided truly enlightening information about mathematical ability.

Hadamard (1945), in using evidence from studies of a number of famous mathematicians of his day and of earlier times, considered that mathematical ability was part of general ability. He justified this view in two ways. Firstly, he pointed out that few pupils who excelled in mathematics at school were useless in other areas of human knowledge. Secondly, he stated that many creative mathematicians had also been creative in other spheres of study, and he quoted Gauss, Newton, Descartes and Leibniz in support of this view. It must be admitted, however, that mathematicians who contributed in other fields usually did so in closely allied subject areas like physical science, and not in vastly different areas like literature. Others took their mathematical reasoning powers into logic and philosophy, though on the whole they adopted a mathematical approach. Nevertheless, Hadamard might be correct in general terms, and there certainly are some examples of eminent contributors to very varied fields of study, like Leonardo da Vinci and Lewis Carroll. The widely quoted correlation between mathematics and music is also of interest in this context, though evidence is sometimes anecdotal and the link is difficult to substantiate through research. Drawing conclusions from a few examples or from anecdotal evidence is always dangerous, but few teachers would disagree that the most mathematically-talented pupils usually have many other talents too.

Just as Krutetskii pointed out differences between mathematically able pupils, so too Hadamard cited differences between famous mathematicians. Riemann was said to have had an 'intuitive' mind, whilst Weierstrass was 'logical'. Hermite preferred analysis whilst Hadamard himself thought 'geometrically'. Poincaré is said to have claimed that he could not carry out an addition without making a mistake! Hadamard claimed to have experienced great difficulty in mastering certain mathematical ideas, like group theory, whilst being able to contribute original ideas in other branches of mathematics. Einstein, of course, has been described as having been useless at anything other than mathematics and physics, with even a suspicion that his analytical mathematical talents were limited.

The other phenomenon which needs to be taken into account is the 'prodigious calculator'. Hadamard suggested that this is a separate and distinct ability from mathematical ability because many prodigious calculators did not appear to be in any real sense mathematicians. Yet, in identifying pupils who are highly talented in mathematics, one of the signs to look for is said to be a fascination with numbers and high facility in handling them. The issue of the prodigious calculator has been considered more recently by Hope (1985). Many children become almost obsessed with one particular interest, such as sport, and are so motivated as to make themselves experts, possessing a wide knowledge of the statistics. In the same way, Hope suggested, some children's early fascination with number and number relationships motivates them to learn and memorize much more than is normal even for an able child, eventually resulting in the prodigious calculator. The characteristics of such a person, as described by Hope, are mastery of many number facts committed to long-term memory, excellent short-term memory with a capacity greater than the normal $7 \pm 2$ units (Miller, 1956), and mastery of methods of processing which make the best use of our limited short-term memory, for example, left to right calculation with replacement of running totals instead of the taught method of right to left calculation. There is also the likelihood that the prodigious calculator will make use of mathematical relationships which many pupils meet but which few value and use in calculations, for example $a^2 - b^2 = (a - b)(a + b)$ which assists in computations such as $63^2 - 37^2$. Expert calculators are frequently in the news, usually in the entertainment business but, of the many which history has recorded, only Gauss and Aitken have been considered to be mathematicians.

Throughout this century, many psychologists have attempted to investigate ability, both overall intelligence and also specific abilities. Many such psychological studies have been based on the statistical techniques of factor analysis (see for example, Vernon, 1950), though the basis of factor analysis has often been disputed. Generally, such studies have not produced evidence to contradict the well known theory of Spearman that a general intellectual factor (denoted by 'g') operates across all domains of human intellectual activity. In fact, factor analysis often suggests that the 'g' factor is dominant. Whether such separate abilities as mathematical ability, geographical ability, historical ability and the like exist has not been fully substantiated, yet we often describe people as having great musical or artistic aptitude or talent, and sometimes even great mathematical ability. Factor-analytic studies have been used to justify the existence of group factors, such as verbal ability, spatial ability and numerical ability, which are required over a whole range of school subjects. Thus mathematical ability might be a particular hybrid drawn from a number of group factors but, if so, would be difficult to identify. Vernon (1950) reported research that showed: common elements in attainments at different branches of mathematics, a small mathematical factor, and a tendency for verbal ability to correlate negatively with mathematical while spatial ability correlated only with geometry. Wrigley (1963) was more positive in claiming there was overwhelming evidence to support the existence of a group factor for mathematical ability, over and above the general factor (g). Nevertheless, g was found to be very significant, thus high intelligence must be a prime requisite for high mathematical ability. Bell *et al.*, (1983) used the work of Wrigley and others to claim that '. . . the relative independence of computational achievement is generally established', but also stated that '. . . not all factorial studies yield the same set of components [factors]' (p. 83). The latter statement reflects the real problem, namely that factor-analytic studies have not led us to a satisfactory understanding of mathematical ability. There have been some benefits, however, for example, the indication that verbal ability tends to correlate negatively with mathematical ability warns us of the danger of attempting to assess the potential of pupils on the basis of verbal tests alone – a practice still sometimes used.

Guilford (1959) used factor analysis to develop a unique approach to the study of human abilities. He proposed a cubical model of the intellect, with the three axes defining different kinds of classification (see Figure 8.1). One axis comprised the five

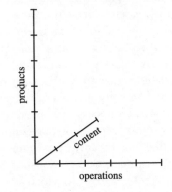

**Figure 8.1**

major groups of abilities which he claimed were suggested by factor-analytic studies, and these were cognition, memory, convergent thinking, divergent thinking and evaluation. These, Guilford termed 'operations'. A second axis was concerned with categories of content, namely figural (concrete material perceived through the senses), symbolic (symbols of all kinds including letters and digits) and semantic (verbal meanings or ideas). The third axis classified six kinds of products when a certain operation was applied to particular content, namely units, classes, relations, systems, transformations and implications, which he claimed factor analysis had suggested were the only fundamental kinds of products that we know. The outcome was a $5 \times 3 \times 6$ cubical arrangement, consisting of 90 smaller cubes or cells, each defining a particular ability in terms of a single operation on a single content type and a single product. Guilford was then able to demonstrate many of these particular abilities through sample test items. Examples of cognition/semantic/systems items in the mathematical domain can be provided, according to Guilford, by tests of 'necessary mathematical operations' such as the following multiple-choice arithmetic reasoning item from CSMS (Brown, 1981a, p. 25):

> A shop makes sandwiches. You can choose from 3 sorts of bread and 6 sorts of filling. How do you work out how many different sandwiches you could choose?
>
> $3 \times 6$  $6 - 3$  $6 + 3$  $3 - 6$
> $18 \div 3$  $6 \div 3$  $6 \times 3$  $3 + 3$

Examples of convergent and divergent items have been provided earlier in this chapter, though it is not easy to know which content and products these correspond to without careful reference to Guilford (1959). The divergent item concerned with making up equations from $B - C = D$ and $Z = A + D$, also quoted earlier, is an example of a divergent/symbolic/implications item.

The specificity of Guilford's 90 distinct abilities makes it very difficult to define an entity such as mathematical ability. It is not impossible to think of this in terms of assembling a collection of appropriate cells and grouping these together as 'mathematical ability', though it is doubtful if this is a practical proposition. Guilford's subsequent discussion of mathematical ability reverts to a broader suggestion that it involves largely symbolic abilities, except that some aspects, such as geometry, have strong figural involvement, and semantic abilities are important in all courses where the learning of facts and ideas is essential! Although Guilford's model of the 'three faces of intellect' is well known and is highly ingenious, it does not solve the problem of identifying mathematical ability.

Other studies of mathematical ability based on factor analysis have been carried out by Furneaux and Rees (1978). They claim strong support for the view that there is a mathematical ability factor independent of 'g'. Earlier work (Rees, 1974) had indicated that there was a core of mathematical test items which all groups of students found to be particularly difficult. Factor analysis techniques subsequently led to the isolation of two relatively distinct types of mathematical ability (Rees, 1981). One type, referred to as the 'g-factor', was found to be associated with more routine tasks and was dependent only on instrumental understanding (see Chapter 2). The other type of ability was found to be related to making valid inferences, and was more dependent on relational understanding. Tasks which involved inference were more difficult for students than those requiring only the 'g-factor'. In considering implications for teaching, Rees suggested, perhaps controversially, that very able pupils should be positively encouraged to develop inferential powers whilst average and less able pupils should concentrate on intellectual development via more instrumental approaches, with the possibility that relational understanding might develop in some domains. It was not possible to be certain to what extent the inferential factor represents a specific mathematical ability.

The existence of different forms of high mathematical ability (Hadamard, 1945) together with the elusiveness of a single mathematical ability as revealed by factor analysis suggests that mathematical ability can take many forms, each form derived from a different mix of other abilities. These other abilities presumably include numerical ability, spatial ability, verbal and non-verbal reasoning, convergent and divergent thinking abilities, and so on. One of these abilities which has attracted considerable research attention is spatial ability, and this is now considered separately.

## Spatial ability

Learning mathematics presents pupils with a wide variety of pictures, diagrams, graphs and visual presentations and representations. One specific problem is the two-dimensional representation of three-dimensional objects. Thinking about three-dimensional objects is not particularly easy, unless the object itself is present. A well known three-dimensional spatial problem involves a painted cube which is sliced across all three perpendicular directions so as to produce smaller, congruent cubes. Two equally-spaced slices across each dimension produces 27 smaller cubes. How many of these smaller cubes would have three painted faces, two painted faces, one painted face and no painted faces, respectively? What would be the numbers of cubes with different numbers of painted faces if the original cube was dissected into 64 smaller cubes, 125 smaller cubes, and so on? Try to think it out for yourself! Would all pupils of high mathematical ability and sufficient maturity be able to visualize the effects of this dissecting? The evidence of differing abilities amongst great mathematicians would suggest not. Would some pupils who were not noticeably of high mathematical ability be able to solve the problem? One would suspect they would, particularly if spatial ability is a distinct ability and not simply one facet of mathematical ability. Visual and pictorial applications are certainly not linked only with mathematics, as examination questions in other subjects indicate! The situation is even more complicated in that it might not be helpful to assume that spatial ability is the same as visualizing ability.

The anecdotal evidence of Hadamard exposed his own love of geometry and his ability to visualize, but it also cited Hermite's hatred of geometry. Krutetskii (1976), writing about school pupils who were mathematically very able, reported that some favoured spatial or geometrical thinking whilst others did not. Walkup (1965) provided further evidence of the capacity which certain people have to visualize in circumstances which do not at first sight appear to be conducive to visualization. He hypothesized that some creative people have developed the ability to visualize in the area in which they are innovative. Thus Faraday could 'see' the electrical and magnetic lines of force, Kekulé could visualize the benzene ring as like a snake biting its tail, and Einstein believed that thought was a matter of dealing with mechanical images and was not concerned with words at all.

Smith (1964) carried out extensive studies into spatial ability and concluded that it was a key component of mathematical ability. He also considered that the relationship between spatial ability and the cognitive trait which has become known as field-independence was very strong. The field-dependence/independence spectrum of cognitive style has been extensively researched, notably by Witkin *et al.* (1977). Such research has attempted to assess the extent to which the field which surrounds a situation influences perception. Examples of research studies include documenting both the reactions of people attempting to sit upright within a tilted room and also attempts to pick out a particular shape within a complex figure (see Figure 8.2).

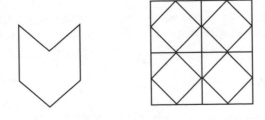

Figure 8.2

Towards one end of the spectrum, field-dependent individuals have difficulty in, for example, finding the shape within the complex figure or in finding true vertical in a tilted room. Those near the other end, the field-independent people, are able to ignore the confusion created by the surrounding field. Smith's perceived association between spatial ability and the field-dependence/independence spectrum is reflected in the inclusion of tests like the embedded figures tests in the catalogue of spatial ability tests (Eliot and Smith, 1983).

The existence of a measure which can place people on a spectrum of field independence (FI)–field dependence (FD) raises the question of whether the kind of teaching which pupils receive makes a difference. The evidence suggests that the characteristics of a strongly FI person include being: more interested in the abstract and theoretical, more likely to impose structure spontaneously on stimulus material, more inclined towards mathematics and science, comparatively insensitive to social undercurrents, better able to learn when no social cues are involved, and more appreciative of independent working opportunities. On the other hand, FD people learn better under guidance and with redundant social cues, and attend more to verbal messages which incorporate a social context. Naturally, if the FI–FD measure has real validity, there will be identifiable FI and FD teachers and teaching styles which affect a wider range of the curriculum than has been illustrated by the examples in the previous paragraph. Experiments in which FI and FD pupils have been deliberately matched or mismatched with FI and FD teaching styles have produced interesting results. Firstly, teachers and students who are matched view one another positively, whereas mismatch leads to negative regard. Secondly, teachers have higher expectations of matched pupils than of mismatched. Thirdly, pupils taught in a matched environment outperform mismatched pupils. Fourthly, being mismatched is much less important for FI pupils than for FD. In short, there is sufficient evidence of differences between pupils which, if substantiated over time, suggests that FD pupils would benefit considerably from the adoption of an FD teaching style. However, the relationship between the FI–FD distinction and other measures of cognitive style is still not clear.

Bruner (1973) suggested that, in education, we had hardly begun to scratch the surface of training in visualization, thus raising the issue of the extent to which spatial ability may be enhanced through teaching. Mitchelmore (1980) suggested that measured differences in three-dimensional drawing ability between American, English and West Indian children were the result of differences in teaching approach. English teachers, he claimed, tended to have a more informal approach to geometry, and to use more manipulative materials in teaching arithmetic at the elementary level and also to use diagrams more freely at both secondary and tertiary levels. The potential value of manipulative materials was also suggested by Bishop (1973) who found that children who have used such materials extensively tended to perform better on spatial ability tests than children from schools where such materials were hardly used. A recent issue concerning spatial ability relates to the widespread belief in mathematics learning that drawing a diagram assists thinking (c.f. Polya in Chapter 5). Perhaps such a tactic only assists those who possess a high enough level of spatial ability. Perhaps a diagram is a hindrance to those with limited spatial ability. A variety of issues concerned with spatial ability is discussed in Bishop (1980); this paper also includes a comprehensive review of the literature.

The possibility that there might be a spectrum rather than a dichotomy of abilities was raised in connection with field-dependence/independence. It is also possible, perhaps even likely, that all human abilities are similar. If there is a spectrum for every facet of ability and each one of us possesses a unique combination of levels of ability it should be no surprise that the study of abilities, such as mathematical and spatial, is so complex. There is certainly no evidence of one kind of mathematical ability which is the same for all mathematicians. Nor does research confirm that spatial ability is *the* most vital component of mathematical ability.

Additional insight into spatial ability has been obtained through medical research into the functions of different parts of the brain. In very simple terms, the brain consists of a left hemisphere, a right hemisphere and a region linking the two hemispheres, and the two hemispheres perform distinctly different functions. A great deal is now known about the functions of various regions of the brain in terms of motor and intellectual skills (see Springer and Deutsch, 1981, and Winston, 2003). The left hemisphere controls language and speech and excels in performing sequential tasks, logical reasoning and analysis. The right hemisphere processes stimuli as a whole structure (cf. Gestalt psychology in Chapter 5) and processes images rather than words. A complex shape is seen as a whole by the right hemisphere whilst the left hemisphere analyses the parts separately. This brief outline is an over-simplification for, as might be expected, we are not all exactly the same. In broad general terms, however, it is true to say that the right hemisphere generally controls spatial ability. There has been the suggestion that school education tends to concentrate on developing those abilities controlled by the left hemisphere, whilst the right hemisphere is comparatively neglected. At the moment, we do not appear to know how to act on the knowledge we have about the link between abilities and the hemispheres of the brain in terms of providing appropriate learning experiences.

## Gender-related differences

Changes in the comparative attainments of boys and girls in Britain in recent years have been profound, and many preconceived notions have had to be reconsidered. Girls are currently outperforming boys in many secondary school examinations at age sixteen, and where there have been major differences in attainment in the past, such as in mathematics and physical science, these are now virtually non-existent. Differences in attainment in mathematics, as measured by public examination scores, have been well documented throughout the recent past, both for Britain and for many other countries. In Britain, little difference has been reported at the primary school level over the years, though the Assessment of Performance Unit (1982a) recorded that what differences there were at age eleven appeared to foreshadow the main areas of mathematics where the differences are larger some five years later. Leder (1985) also found few consistent sex-related differences at the primary school level. Thus, what has happened is that the absence of a clear 'global' difference up to age eleven now extends at least to age sixteen. It might still be the case, however, that many more boys than girls choose mathematics as one of their specialist sixth form subjects, and comparatively few females have, up to now, taken up employment directly related to mathematics or dependent on high qualifications in mathematics. In Russia, and some other countries, it has been claimed fairly consistently over the years that there are no significant differences in overall mathematical attainment between boys and girls (see, for example, Krutetskii, 1976), though some might say that is no surprise. Suydam and Weaver (1977) reported that, in the USA, sex differences do not appear to exist in the ability to solve arithmetic word problems. None of this proves there are no differences in the detail, it merely suggests overall comparability.

In the years leading up to the end of the twentieth century, it was considered very important in Britain that the issue of the 'under-performance' of girls in mathematics was addressed. Reasons for observed differences in attainment were investigated from a variety of different standpoints including biological, psychological and socio-logical. The best documented conclusions emerged in relation to attitudes and the expectations of society. It was claimed that, in a variety of ways, girls were consistently being discriminated against in terms of mathematical education. This is clearly a serious issue whatever the relative performance levels of boys and girls, particularly since qualified mathematicians are permanently in short supply, and it was considered important enough to warrant a separate Appendix in the Cockcroft Report (Shuard, 1982a).

Whether there are measurable differences or not, the influences of society and from the environment which might result in differential performances between boys and girls still need to be clearly identified. There are countries in the world where boys still outperform girls in mathematics, and in Britain there is even a growing concern that girls might soon outperform boys, just as they do already in other school subjects. One major concern has involved differences in parental expectations and desires which may even have led to different pressures being exerted within the home. It may be that such pressures are not so prevalent in Britain nowadays, or that girls are able to ignore them. The usefulness and value of mathematics has always generally been considered to be in other school subjects also regarded as boys' subjects and in careers which have been viewed by society as male occupations. Russell (1983) has drawn attention to the fact that pressures might work equally unfairly against both sexes in that girls may not be encouraged to opt for mathematical studies whereas boys most certainly are, even when their ability and interest in the subject is, at best, indifferent. There is evidence that boys often opt for mathematics in the sixth form because it is expected of them and not because they enjoy the subject. Society appears to have conveyed the message that mathematics is a male subject and that certain other subjects are female subjects, but this may no longer be the case. Peer group pressures have in the past also added to the difficulties faced by girls when choosing subjects in a mixed school, but either these pressures are no longer so strong or they are being ignored. The current peer group pressures on British boys, under which it is not acceptable to study hard and education is not to be regarded seriously, are seemingly massive, and are now of much greater concern. Russell also drew attention to the ways boys and girls regarded themselves in relation to mathematical ability. Girls tended to underestimate their potential whereas boys tended to overestimate; boys displayed confidence about their ability in mathematics which was sometimes not justifiable whilst girls, perhaps with better test results, displayed unjustifiable anxiety. Such traits may still be prevalent in Britain, but if they are they are not as damaging to academic progress as it seems they might have been in the past.

There have also been many changes to the learning environment throughout recent years. If it is still the case that more mathematics teachers are male than female, the balance has certainly changed. In teacher training departments there are some-times more intending female mathematics teachers than male, particularly when the economy is booming and there are plenty of other career opportunities. Textbooks have changed too, and now there is a deliberate policy not to insinuate a male image into mathematics. Mathematics textbooks have in the past generally been written by men, so mathematical activities have tended to be set within contexts which were of much greater interest to males than to females, but there is a deliberate attempt to avoid bias now. Internal school organization has not always in the past allowed girls to combine the study of mathematics with their other choices, and in girls' schools pupils have sometimes been guided away from mathematics because of timetabling difficulties. Hopefully, that too has changed. Teachers have been shown to interact in the classroom much more with boys than with girls, have paid more attention to boys, have given more positive encouragement to boys, have allowed boys to gain their attention simply because they clamoured more than the girls. This is now well known, and needs to be addressed consistently. Some research has suggested that girls achieve more in mathematics in a single-sex school than they do in a mixed school. Boys, on the other hand, tend to perform better in a mixed school than in a single-sex school! Such is the range and variety of influences which might result in differences in performance in mathematics that it is easy to appreciate the summary by Leder (1985, p. 305): 'Sex differences possibly due to biological constraints are dwarfed by the far greater pressures imposed by social and cultural stereotypes about cognitive skills and occupations'. A more recent suggestion has been that girls have appreciated the change in examination styles, now that measures of attainment are no longer based entirely on a single timed written paper. Interestingly, if this has affected comparative performances, it would indicate that this *is* a difference between boys and girls – if only in their appreciation of different kinds of examinations. The literature has, however, also hinted at non-sociological factors, and publications over the years have attempted to clarify these.

In a discussion of differences in intelligence and special abilities between males and females Hutt (1972) clearly accepted that there were factors which originated from the biological and psychological domains. The main differences raised were as follows. First, scores obtained from applying general ability (intelligence) tests consistently produced different distributions for males and females. The scores for males tended to spread more widely whilst the scores for females were more clustered around the mean. The difference was not a large one, but there was a tendency for males to predominate in both extremes, the most able and the least able. Many other authors have referred to this phenomenon. Secondly, males were said to excel in spatial ability whilst females excelled in verbal ability. Thirdly, females were clearly superior in both manual dexterity and in rote learning ability whereas tests of divergent thinking tended to produce higher scores for males. In all cases the differences between the sexes were small. In such matters, differences between the extreme performances for either sex are always likely to be huge in comparison with any difference between the sexes.

An interesting feature of the measured differences in performance is that it is only in certain mathematical topics that boys have generally scored rather higher than girls, and vice versa. The Assessment of Performance Unit (1982b) recorded that the greatest differences were in the topics of mensuration, rate and ratio, descriptive geometry and unit measures. Wood (1977) observed similar differences. Drawing from the examination scripts of boys and girls educated in the same schools he discovered that the superiority of boys was most marked in items of two types, one concerned with ratio (scaling, moving between different orders of magnitude, moving between different units of measurement). Wood drew a parallel with the common core of difficulty discovered by Rees (1974) and claimed that the underlying difficulty was a 'comparison factor', which was basically the scaling up and down that is so important in coming to an understanding of metric proportionality. It was no surprise to him that fractions were found to be more difficult for girls than for boys. This is a difficult topic area for both sexes but Wood asked whether this was a major source of the difference between the sexes? Perhaps, he suggested, a concentration of effort on fractions, proportion and, more generally, comparison factors is what is required to compensate for the difference between girls and boys.

The other topic area observed by Wood as resulting in gender differences was geometry, also noted by the Assessment of Performance Unit (1982b). This alleged difference in spatial ability has been mentioned earlier, and was referred to by Wood in his claim that girls' weakness at spatial visualization and solid geometry problems was well documented. He further claimed that it was generally known that genetic causes are suspected. Spatial ability, as we have seen, is not required in all of mathematics, only in certain aspects, and many famous mathematicians have not felt themselves to be at all capable in geometry. However, if we accept that spatial ability is comparatively weaker in girls than in boys, this is a major handicap to a study of some parts of mathematics. The greatest gender difference in mathematical performance found by Wood was in answering a question which he described as an almost pure measure of ability to visualize in three dimensions. Fennema and Tartre (1985), in reporting on a longitudinal study, confirmed that there was a difference between girls and boys in respect of spatial visualization skills, but it was small. They did agree that low spatial visualization skill may be more debilitating to girls' mathematical problem-solving than to that of boys. It might also be debilitating in respect of attitude to mathematics. At the moment, whatever the changes in overall performance, there is still a view within the teaching profession that boys have something of a better spatial ability than girls, and that girls have a very much better verbal ability.

Suggestions from test results and classroom observation of comparatively poorer spatial ability in girls, and comparatively better verbal ability, have led to considerations of brain differences. We have already seen that the range of scores obtained from general ability tests is greater for boys than for girls, but there are other obvious differences too, for example, more boys than girls are colour-blind, and more boys than girls are autistic. Winston (2003) has now confirmed that such differences and many more are likely to stem from the fact that there are differences between the brains of males and females, and that from puberty the two hemispheres develop differently in girls and boys. Thus, the fact that girls have superior verbal abilities and boys have superior spatial and systemizing abilities he now claims is a direct outcome of brain differences. Boys prefer construction, rule-based and classification activities whereas girls prefer interaction with other people. In adult life, Winston claims, this shows up as a male preference for mathematics, science, engineering and construction – in other words an interest in how things work. Other genetically-based theories have also been proposed to explain the observable differences between girls and boys in terms of mathematical attainment, for example, the female x-chromosome leading directly to more skilled social interaction. It all adds to previous suggestions that boys and girls often reveal slightly different mathematical strengths and weaknesses. Overall mathematical performances, however, are comparable now in Britain, which may satisfy many people, but it is not the most important consideration. What is vital is whether we are managing to get the best out of both boys and girls, irrespective of whether there are differences or not.

# Preferences and attitudes

Hudson (1966) drew attention to the possibility that a liking for mathematics stemmed from preferred styles of study. Mathematics does not involve the learner in revealing emotions or opinions and hardly involves, of absolute necessity, any interaction with others. Private positive emotional reaction to the beauty or elegance of mathematical ideas and results is not ruled out, of course. But the fact that 'maths is just a matter of facts being hammered into you . . . it's not a subject you can humanize' (Russell, 1983, p. 81, quoting a sixth form student) is also a commonly held attitude. Russell also showed that pupils often perceive the mathematics classroom as being a place for competition, which is attractive to some and not to others; it can act as an incentive, particularly for successful pupils; for less successful pupils a negative attitude to mathematics can develop. The security of the traditional method of teaching mathematics via exposition and practice is attractive to some, and the fact that responses or solutions are categorically either right or wrong is very much appreciated by some pupils. Other pupils thrive on discussion, or wish to express their personality, and do not find that mathematics allows this. Preferences are part of the spectrum of individual differences and might exert a great impact on eventual achievement.

In terms of the totality of educational research, comparatively little work has been carried out in the domain of preferences and attitudes in learning mathematics. The Assessment of Performance Unit (1982a) found that the relationship between attitude and performance in mathematics at age eleven was surprisingly weak. Boys demonstrated greater confidence in their own mathematical ability than did girls, and this was also reflected at age fifteen (Assessment of Performance Unit, 1982b). Mathematics was believed to be important by a majority of fifteen-year-old pupils and there was correlation between ratings of usefulness and interest.

Major studies of cognitive preference include those concerned with the field-dependence/independence issue. Bruner *et al.* (1956) have suggested other preferences in problem-solving methods, between 'focusers' and 'scanners'. Thus, in looking for a relationship between items the 'focusers' would extract as much information as possible from the first item and then use the information as a basis for comparison and amendment in focusing on the other items in turn. 'Scanners', on the other hand, would select only one property and then scan all items, and would proceed by scanning all items for other properties. Under pressure of time, focusing was found to be the more effective method.

It is important to realize that a decision to study mathematics does not imply a positive liking for the subject. Russell (1983) found many sixth form boys studying mathematics who did not like the subject. They had opted for mathematics because they considered it useful, or perhaps it went with their other subjects. Girls, on the whole, did not perceive mathematics to be all that useful, and there was evidence that it was largely those girls who derived genuine enjoyment from it who pursued it into the sixth form. Mathematics was considered to be a high status subject, particularly by boys, but this does not of itself imply liking. The attitude of many girls to mathematics appeared to deteriorate steadily through the years of secondary schooling, alongside the growth of self-consciousness about errors and difficulties. There was some evidence from Russell's research that a good relationship with the teacher was more important for girls than it was for boys.

Mathematics teachers take for granted the acceptability of question and answer situations ('the recitation' in the USA). There is never any deliberate intention to expose weaknesses and inadequacies to peers but that is precisely what can happen, and there is evidence that pupils can find the situation embarrassing and unacceptable. Holt (1964) has provided anecdotal evidence of the strategies pupils use to cope with question and answer in class, and has also referred to cultures where such a situation – that is one in which individuals might be laid open to ridicule – would be completely unacceptable. Clearly, pupils who feel that they are being embarrassed in this way will develop a negative attitude to mathematics. They might become extremely anxious and hence, in Scheerer's sense of over-motivation (see Chapter 5), be unable to produce their best work. The whole subject of anxiety about mathematics has been comprehensively discussed by Buxton (1981).

## Suggestions for further reading

Buxton, L. (1981) *Do You Panic About Maths?* London: Heinemann.
Hadamard, J. (1945) *The Psychology of Invention in the Mathematical Field*. Princeton, NJ: Princeton University Press.
Hudson, L. (1966) *Contrary Imaginations*. Harmondsworth: Penguin Books.
Krutetskii, V. A. (1976) *The Psychology of Mathematical Abilities in Schoolchildren*. Chicago: The University of Chicago Press.
Springer, S. P. and Deutsch, G. (1981) *Left Brain, Right Brain*. San Francisco, CA: Freeman.

## Questions for discussion

1. What should mathematics teachers be doing to provide opportunities for divergent thinking?
2. How should we provide for the very able pupil in mathematics lessons?
3. How should we ensure that neither girls nor boys are disadvantaged in mathematics lessons?
4. How should mathematics be taught so as to foster a positive attitude and prevent anxiety?

# Chapter 9

# Does Language Interfere with Learning Mathematics?

## Issues of language

The fortnightly mental arithmetic test for a primary school class regularly included a question of the type:

> What is the difference between 47 and 23?

One child thought the question rather odd, but nevertheless answered it, as follows:

> One of the numbers is bigger than the other.

When the test papers were returned the answer was marked wrong. Such was the fear which the teacher generated in the pupils that there was no question of going to ask him why it was wrong. Better to try again next time and see what happened. Along came the next test, so our pupil tried a different answer:

> One number is about twice the other.

This also came back marked wrong. Next time, with growing desperation and anxiety, our pupil tried again:

> One number contains a 4 and a 7 but the other number doesn't.

This saga continued over many tests until the child found out from a friend what was the expected answer.

The story is in essence a true one, for the author was that child. Fear of the teacher and a misunderstanding of the language combined to create an unhappy and unfortunate situation. It illustrates a problem with language, which pupils experience in learning any subject. Problems of language are obviously not unique to children of any particular country; the following example appeared as a snippet in the May 1964 *Arithmetic Teacher*:

> A . . . kindergarten teacher drew a triangle, a square and a rectangle on the blackboard and explained each to her pupils. One little girl went home, drew the symbols and told her parents: 'This is a triangle . . . this is a square and this is a crashed angle'.

Such stories may be amusing to adults but they are often not the slightest bit funny for the pupil concerned. Obstacles can be placed in the path of children which have little to do with mathematics but which are created because of problems of language.

There are many aspects of the issue of language and mathematics which might affect learning (see, for example, Austin and Howson, 1979). Anecdotes about children experiencing difficulties because they do not understand the words are not hard to find, but they do introduce the importance of mathematical vocabulary. Even if the vocabulary is appropriate there might be problems because children do not always interpret statements literally, but sometimes appear to change the meaning into what they think the teacher intended to say. The special symbols of mathematics, as an extension to the language of the mathematics classroom, cause additional problems. Reading mathematics is different from reading literature, or even from reading texts in other subjects. Learning mathematics in a second language can present difficulties which first language learners do not experience. The place of talk in the classroom and the use of discussion between teacher and pupil, and between pupil and pupil, demands careful thought. The relationship between mathematics learning and language development is clearly crucial. The extent to which the acquisition or formation of concepts in the mind of the learner depends on the use of appropriate language is an important issue.

Barnes (1976) has argued that teachers are often aware of problems of form but are less likely to show concern about problems of use. It is not the particular terms used which are critical, it is whether the underlying concepts and processes are being communicated, whether meaning is being conveyed. In short, there is a danger of reducing to lists of difficult words and readability measures what is a more complex interplay. It is access to one another's meanings that matters in teaching. Skemp (1982) used the terms 'deep structures' and 'surface structures' to draw attention to the two levels, namely, the ideas of mathematics which we wish to communicate and the language and symbol systems which represent the ideas and which we use to transmit the meaning. It is important to be aware of potential problems of both form and use; we must know that problems might arise at the surface level of transmission and at the deeper level of meaning.

## The mathematics register

The following end-of-chapter summary was found in a textbook, though new names have been invented for the technical terms:

*Summary:*

A danding is a kambon if each trotick of the squidgment has only one ploud, for example the danding which dands each number onto its smallest lume tombage is a kambon.

To a child who did not grasp the terminology during the lessons in which the words were introduced, or perhaps revised, the summary does not help. To a child who missed the lessons through illness the summary is meaningless. The vocabulary of mathematics (the mathematics register) is more extensive than many teachers realize. Bell (1970) listed a basic vocabulary of some 365 words, in common use both within and without mathematics, which even our slowest learners need to comprehend just in dealing with the elementary topics of quantity, measurement, time, money, position and natural number. Beyond that basic vocabulary, most children might be expected to learn the meaning of one hundred or more new words in each year. This mathematical vocabulary ranges from simple words like 'find' and 'sort' to more specialized words like 'bilateral' and 'quadratic'.

Although there are serious problems in terms of the extent of the vocabulary of mathematics, there are additional problems when particular words carry a mathematical meaning which is different from the usual everyday meaning. One of the words in the summary above is a replacement for the word 'relation'. A mathematical relation is strictly a set of ordered pairs, but the ordinary use of the same word suggests a member of the extended family, and appears to bear no resemblance to the mathematical idea. It is possible to use the ordinary meaning of 'relation' to introduce the mathematical idea but, given what we are aiming at, is that a help or a hindrance? As we have seen, the word 'difference' has a mathematical usage which is very specific and which needs to be made clear to pupils. There are, of course, many words which are wholly specific to mathematics and about which there should be no confusion with an everyday meaning, for example, 'numerator', 'isosceles' and 'hypotenuse', but there must also be many other words which were in use in everyday speech before mathematicians adopted them and assigned special meanings, for example, 'field', 'group' and 'root'. Examples of confusion between everyday meaning and mathematical meaning must be numerous. Stories of children who think that 'volume' is merely a control on the television or radio set (set!) or who think 'axes' are only for chopping with, or who believe that a 'revolution' is what happens when a government is violently overthrown are too frequent for us not to pay attention to the problem.

Some words are particularly difficult for children. It is very questionable whether more than just a small minority of our pupils ever distinguish the mathematical meaning of 'similar' from its everyday meaning. The particular problem here is that the two meanings are not far apart, the distinction is quite a subtle one. Another interesting example is 'segment', which sometimes appears to be used in everyday speech when a better word would seem to be 'sector'. Some words are used with a different specialized meaning in other subjects, like 'chord'. Even the word 'circle' has two meanings, and only in mechanics are these two clearly distinguished as 'ring' and 'disc'. A few words might be very difficult for children to accept, like 'vulgar' and 'improper', and yet others are odd, like 'odd' and 'real'. Clearly, it is very important, when a word like 'root' is introduced in a mathematics lesson, that the pupils are given the opportunity to come to terms with the particular mathematical meaning. Many words in a language have a number of different meanings, for example, 'product', and that might be a problem for younger children. Older children may have realized this, but will still need time to get accustomed to any new usage. A salutary exercise for a teacher is to write down all of the many technical words used with a class through-out one year, and then classify them into categories: those which are uniquely math-ematical, those which are not unique and subtly different in meaning, those which are very different in meaning, and those which are odd or objectionable. Clearly, testing pupils, perhaps simply orally, will reveal at least some points of difficulty and will allow remediation. Otterburn and Nicholson (1976) and others have provided us with a clear indication of the kinds of difficulties which the technical terms of mathematics can present. One special difficulty for younger children revolves around the erratic structure of English number names, in which numbers between ten and twenty do not follow the pattern of other number names.

Apart from technical terms which represent mathematical concepts, some of the more general instructions are not understood as well as might be imagined. Children have been known to think that 'evaluate' means 'change the value of', and, even that 'tabulate' means 'take the tablets'. Frequently, the word 'simplify' does not really mean 'make simpler', it means 'carry out the mathematical process which has been demonstrated'. An unusual problem of language is one that we create ourselves when we make a careful definition and then misuse the word. The most obvious example of this is when we describe axes on a Cartesian graph as 'horizontal' and 'vertical'. It cannot help the many children who are still struggling to understand what we mean by 'vertical' when we carelessly use the word to refer to one of the horizontal lines on the graph paper on their desk. The word 'histogram' has a very precise meaning in mathematics, which distinguishes it from a 'bar chart', yet there are data collection situations in mathematics in which the boundary between the two ideas appears to be hazy and ill-defined (see Chapter 2), and this has perhaps led to misuse of the language. Another word which can create problems is 'chord'. There was a time when the word 'secant' was used to describe the line which was obtained when a chord was produced in both directions, but now we often attempt to use the word 'chord' for this extended line as well. We therefore have no idea what meaning is being registered in the mind of the student when we use the word 'chord', and this can be critical when it comes to introducing differentiation (Orton, 1983). It is interesting that even the word 'produced' can cause problems, and many pupils cannot understand why we do not use 'extended'.

It might be that problems of vocabulary are relatively superficial within the whole range of issues of language and learning mathematics, but it is nevertheless critical that such problems are not ignored in the hope that they will go away. In order to facilitate the learning of mathematical ideas it is important that children are given help with the language which they are going to be expected to use in discussing and generally processing those ideas. It is clearly necessary, when a new idea and its surface representation are introduced, that any new words and symbols are spoken, discussed and written down. Words like 'octagon' and 'quadrilateral' may become more meaningful when set alongside words with the same beginning (octopus, octave, octogenarian, octet, October) or ending (pentagon, hexagon, decagon). There are also specific vocabulary activities which are well known to children through work in other subjects and through puzzle books. A simple word search based on the mathematical topic just completed can help with consolidating words and their spellings. An elementary crossword can be used to attach the word to its meaning or to the way it might occur in mathematical text. Unscrambling words (for example, UARQES), matching a list of words with a list of meanings or a set of pictures, and a mixture of unscrambling and matching, all have some value. Selecting the best description for a word from a number of alternatives is another possibility. Using lesson time for such activities might be considered a nuisance until one realizes that coping with the vocabulary is vital to learning.

## Reading mathematics

Any mathematical textual material which is intended to be read by pupils must be readable. It is not easy to specify what we might mean by readability in completely explicit terms, but there is no doubt about what is intended; we want pupils to be able to learn without the language itself getting in the way. Thus, the lengths of words, the lengths of sentences, the particular words used and whether they form part of the vocabulary of the pupils may all be important. The readability of text has become of major concern in education in recent years, and a variety of different techniques have been proposed to enable teachers to carry out checks as to whether particular text is appropriate. The difficulty of defining readability seems to have been reflected in these proposals, however, because most of the techniques only incorporate a selection of the possible facets of readability. Thus the Dale-Chall formula is based only on the percentage of words not included in a set list of common words and the average number of words in a sentence. The FOG formula is based only on the average number of words in a sentence and the percentage of words with three or more syllables. The Flesch formula is based on the average number of syllables per 100 words and the average number of words per sentence. The Fry procedure is based on the number of syllables and the number of sentences in a one-hundred-word passage. And the 'cloze' procedure is based on the ability of the reader to fill in missing words in text. Such methods were clearly not developed with mathematical text in mind, nor are they necessarily applicable outside a particular country. Thus, for example, a formula devised for use in the USA would not necessarily be as applicable in Britain. The various readability formulas have been reviewed in more detail in Shuard (1982b) and in Shuard and Rothery (1984).

The readability formulas (formulae?) outlined above, and others not mentioned, are generally not applicable to mathematics because mathematical text is peculiar in comparison with text in other subject areas. One example of peculiarity is that the text does not necessarily flow left to right, line after line. It is sometimes necessary to move in unusual directions and even to move about the page in order to refer to tables, graphs or diagrams. The text is also likely to contain certain non-alphabetic symbols, which may or may not be numbers. This complexity of mathematical texts led Kane *et al.* (1974) to devise a readability formula for use specifically with mathematical text. Unfortunately, not only is the formula extremely complex to apply, it might not give appropriate results outside the USA. In general, apart from drawing the attention of mathematics teachers to the important issue of readability, specific formulas have not proved to be of much practical value. It is essential that teachers of mathematics should assess the appropriateness of text for their pupils, but the general recommendation at the moment is that this should be achieved by means of 'informed judgements'. Clearly, it is important to have the knowledge and insight on which to base such judgements.

It is possible to read a story or novel in a fairly superficial way, and yet still derive meaning, message and moral. It is even possible to use rapid reading techniques, perhaps skipping sentences or descriptive paragraphs which are not crucial. Non-fiction such as mathematics cannot generally be read in a superficial way without losing detail that might be essential. Mathematical text generally cannot be read quickly, for every word could be crucial and every symbol essential in the extraction of meaning. In order to ensure that attention is focused on all parts of the text, interaction might help. This issue arose in Chapter 3 in a consideration of programmed learning. Stimulus-response-based interactive texts are not currently popular for reasons which have nothing to do with the acknowledged importance of interaction. And many children learn mathematics today through the use of workcards which clearly necessitate interaction and which contain some explanatory text. An entire workcard scheme can be considered as a large-scale interactive text, similar in many ways to a programmed learning scheme. But however the material is presented, whether textbook or workcard, some parts will demand interaction.

Shuard and Rothery (1984) classified the main components of mathematical text as teaching, exercises, revision and testing. Revision and testing, however, could be considered as teaching and exercises but presented in a different, perhaps abbreviated, format, and included for a different purpose. For many pupils, and in the interests of readability, it is advisable that teaching sections are short, and that exercises and text are interwoven in order to achieve interaction. However, even if pupils interact, there is no guarantee that they will interact in the way intended. So how are pupils to be informed whether they reacted correctly or not? How do we ensure that pupils do not skip sections and resume reading at the next point where answers are provided? Many of the problems associated with interactive text are the same as some which were discussed under programmed learning (Chapter 3). The interactive task (Fibonacci Fractions) in Chapter 5 also illustrates many of the difficulties. It is not easy to provide an interactive, readable text which will be followed through rigorously by students, and which will guarantee learning.

Other features of mathematics not usually found in non-mathematical text are graphs, tables and diagrams. These offer the advantage of breaking up the text. However, it is essential that they are situated appropriately in relation to references to them within the text. It is also essential that pupils are compelled to interact with them and are assisted in extracting information from them. Worked examples are commonly found within mathematical text, and these can form an important reference for pupils when working alone, so they should not be ignored. Interaction may also be achieved through practical activities directed from within the text, and then it is helpful if the results of the activity are referred to in the subsequent development of ideas in the text. Before interaction of any kind can be achieved, however, the pupils must find the text sufficiently attractive. Variety in colour, type style, spacing and general layout all have a part to play. Pictures are valuable, in commanding attention, though it must be remembered that many adolescents are easily offended if they feel the attempts to brighten up the material are juvenile.

The correct and most appropriate forms and level of interaction are important in ensuring readability but so too is whether the meaning flows easily. Shuard and Rothery (1984) have discussed this issue and also the three types of meaning unit included within mathematical text. First, there are explicit statements, for example: 'The numbers in this sequence may be used to form Fibonacci fractions'. Secondly, there are statements or questions which demand activity from the pupil. This interaction ultimately provides information which is intended to be explicit, for example: 'Write down the next ten fractions'. Thirdly, there are gaps in meaning which the pupils must fill, either by inference from the text or by bringing knowledge from completely outside the text. An example of this from a primary school textbook is given here.

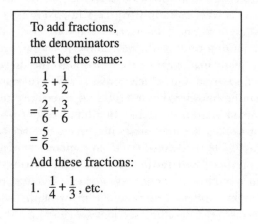

To add fractions,
the denominators
must be the same:

$$\frac{1}{3} + \frac{1}{2}$$

$$= \frac{2}{6} + \frac{3}{6}$$

$$= \frac{5}{6}$$

Add these fractions:

1. $\frac{1}{4} + \frac{1}{3}$, etc.

Clearly, in this example, there is more to deciding on this 'same denominator' than writing a number at random. The pupils must either infer that the required denominator is the product of the two given denominators or must bring knowledge about lowest common denominators or equivalent fractions from outside. Even then there is more for the pupils to fill in, for no mention has been made of numerators. In many cases, gaps have been 'filled' earlier in the course, but not always.

Shuard and Rothery (1984) proposed the use of a diagrammatic analysis of flow-of-meaning, using three different symbols for the three kinds of unit. The value of such an analysis to the teacher was summed up in:

> Pupils are not likely to notice many of the subtle points which the flow-of-meaning diagram brings out, but they may experience a feeling of general inability to follow the argument of the passage . . . Thus, a flow-of-meaning analysis may be useful in trying to understand the difficulties which pupils find in a particular passage, or in preparing a discussion lesson as an introduction to the work. (p. 74)

Unfortunately, the preparation of a flow-of-meaning diagram for even a short section of text may take considerable time.

In order to make an informed judgement about suitability for particular pupils it therefore appears that there are many facets of a text to take into account. At the most superficial level there is the general attractiveness and appeal of the text. Appropriate summaries can also be helpful in fostering retention. Then there is the relationship between text to be read and sections to provide active involvement. A more detailed scrutiny then needs to take in vocabulary, length of words, and length and structure of sentences. Particular features of mathematical text like tables, graphs, diagrams and special symbols need to be inspected. The flow-of-meaning requires detailed analysis if it is to provide useful information. Finally, the exercises themselves need to be considered, for they too must flow, from the relatively elementary to the more difficult; they must be correctly sequenced and appropriately paced. The issue of readability of examination questions has also been addressed by Mobley (1987).

## Mathematical symbols

The symbol '4' and the word 'four' convey the same idea, but the form differs. In reading mathematical text it is necessary to be able to read all forms, including those special mathematical symbols which are incorporated within the text. There are, however, peculiar difficulties with mathematical symbol structures. To the experienced student, the expression $(3 + 2) \times 4$ conveys a clear message but at the same time the parentheses make it awkward to dictate the expression to someone else. Some arrangements of symbols are not left to right, for example $\frac{3}{4}$. Sometimes it is necessary to read a collection of mathematical symbols before a clear message can be obtained, for example $\int_1^2 x^2 \, dx$. Sometimes different structures of symbols are intended to convey the same meaning, for example $3 \div 4$ and $4 \overline{)3}$, and at other times the same surface structure implies different meanings, for example 34 and $3x$.

Many problems occur for children in coming to terms with mathematical symbols and their corresponding words. In $5 + 3 = 8$, for example, it is common for the '+' to be read by young children as 'add'. Yet the instruction 'add 5 and 3' would hardly be written as '+ 5 and 3'. The symbolic representations '+' and 'add' are not exactly interchangeable. In the same example '=' might be read as 'makes' at first, but then eventually as 'equals'. Yet 'makes' would not be considered an acceptable replacement for '=' in

$$\frac{d^2y}{dx^2} + 3\frac{dy}{dx} = 7$$

The same '=' symbol might be read as 'leaves' in $5 - 3 = 2$. The instruction 'take 3 from 5', and even the more advanced equivalent 'subtract 3 from 5', requires reversal of order in conversion to $5 - 3$. The symbol '$\times$' in $3 \times 5$ is read as 'times' by many pupils and implies 3 lots of 5, but the secondary school teacher wants 'multiplied by' which conveys the idea of 5 lots of 3. The symbol '$\div$' is read by many pupils as 'shared by', despite the fact that $6 \div 3$ can represent the sharing of 6 items between 3 receivers and can also represent the number of groups of 3 items which can be obtained from 6.

Division also presents another problem in that $6 \div 3$, $6/3$, $\frac{6}{3}$, $3 \overline{)6}$ and $3 \underline{)6}$ are all found in mathematics texts as different ways of defining the same task. These five alternatives, it will be noticed, contain the two numbers, 6 and 3, in two different orders. The order does not matter when recording addition and multiplication because of commutativity, but it does matter in subtraction and division. We perhaps should not be surprised that $8\overline{\smash{\big)}4}$ frequently leads to the response, '2', as confused children often take the easy way out and divide the larger number by the smaller.

Discrimination between very similar symbols is vital in mathematics. The early symbols '+' and '×' are very similar, as are '−' and '÷'. In the secondary school the very different meanings of $2x$ and $x^2$ cause many problems. Skemp (1982) refers to the symbols of mathematics as surface structures, but it is the deep structures which they represent which are important – for example the symbols 23, $2\frac{1}{2}$ and $2a$ all have the same surface structure. Some pupils eventually have to be able to discriminate between a wide range of symbols with similar surface structures, for example $5C_2$, $^5C_2$, $5C^2$, $\Sigma C^2$ and $\Sigma C_2$. Most individual mathematical symbols have separate meanings, but a few do not. The fact that $\delta x$ is a single unit and not a product like $3x$ causes problems. In fact, in terms of elementary calculus, the situation is much worse (Orton, 1983), for $\dfrac{\delta y}{\delta x}$ is a quotient, $\delta y$ divided by $\delta x$, but $\dfrac{dy}{dx}$ is not quotient and needs to be regarded as a single entity. Once we have convinced students of this we can then feel free to start using $\dfrac{dy}{dx}$ as if it was a quotient. A discussion of the symbols of mathematics is also included in Shuard and Rothery (1984).

From the point of view of understanding symbols in mathematics, Skemp (1982) made a number of suggestions. He assumed that the critical problem was lack of understanding of the deep structures, thus the suggestions have similarities with those intended to encourage concept formation. First, the symbolism should only be introduced as the final stage of a learning sequence which is developed from physical or concrete embodiments of the concepts. Place value provides a good example of this, and many teachers have always provided a variety of forms of equipment from straws and bundles of straws to the more sophisticated Dienes Multi-base Arithmetic Blocks (see Chapter 10). Secondly, the mathematical ideas should be sequenced and presented so that assimilation to existing conceptual knowledge is eased, and should not be presented as a discrete unit of mathematics which bears no relationship to work which has gone before. Thirdly, spoken language needs to be used for an extended period of time, and pressure to convert quickly to abbreviated symbolism should be resisted. Finally, transitional notations could be used to form a bridge to the condensed symbolism, for example, children might be happy using 'area = length × breadth' when they are not yet ready to accept $A = lb$. The introduction of mathematical symbols too soon, without an adequate understanding of the deep structures, can be a major cause of alienation.

## Communicating meaning

Conveying meaning to pupils is the objective of teaching. This will not necessarily be achieved even when vocabulary is appropriate, symbols are understood and text is readable, for a whole variety of reasons including the fact that pupils will sometimes place their own interpretation on what we say. When we ask our own children at home to put the knives and forks on the table we do not expect to find that every single knife and fork in the house has been set out. We expect the children to know what we mean. The communication of meaning frequently involves interpretation on the part of the receiver, and this should warn us that messages could frequently be given incorrect interpretations by pupils. Donaldson (1978), who introduced the 'knives and forks' illustration, suggested:

> When a child interprets what we say to him his interpretation is influenced by at least three things . . . his knowledge of the language, his assessment of what we intend (as indicated by our non-linguistic behaviour), and the manner in which he would represent the physical situation to himself if we were not there at all. (p. 69)

The nature of young children's responses persuaded Piaget that the unexpected utterances were a consequence of stage of development (see Chapter 4). Donaldson and others have conducted experiments which, they have claimed, suggest that the difficulty is, in part at least, a problem of the interpretation of language. In one particular experiment four toy garages and a number of toy cars were used, and a toy panda then made judgements on the truth or falsity of certain statements. The children had to inform the panda whether the judgement was correct or not. The statements were: (1) all the cars are in the garages, (2) all the garages have cars in them. The numbers of cars present was: (a) 3 in the first experiment, (b) 5 in the second experiment. The expected responses were therefore: (a1) true, (a2) false, (b1) false, and (b2) true, but these expected answers were not provided by all the children. The conclusion drawn was that, irrespective of the actual words used, the children were concentrating on whether all the garages were full. There was also the suggestion from some responses that children were interpreting 'all the cars' to mean 'all the cars which ought to be there'.

(a)                    (b)

**Figure 9.1**

One of Piaget's conservation tasks involved two sticks arranged first in exact alignment (Figure 9.1(a)) and then secondly with the alignment destroyed but the sticks still parallel (Figure 9.1(b)). The fact that many younger children, answering the question, 'Are the sticks the same length?', said 'Yes' for (a) and 'No' for (b) was taken by Piaget to imply that such children did not accept conservation. If, however, these children were interpreting the situation as one in which the experimenter very deliberately draws attention to a change, and if they did not pay much attention to the exact words and their meaning, it is reasonable to assume something other than non-conservation. Rose and Blank have repeated this experiment without the first stage of exact alignment (reported by Donaldson, 1978), and fewer errors occurred. In the original experiment the children were not, perhaps, paying attention to the language so much as to other cues. It is important to note that alternative experiments have never produced correct answers from all children; they have produced a different balance of responses which has been taken to suggest that children have not interpreted language in the way that was expected.

Such results have drawn attention to the whole relationship between language and learning, for, '. . . behind words there is the independent grammar of thoughts'

(Vygotsky, 1962). The fact that children can interpret what we say in a way that is different from what we expected is but one part of the relationship between language and learning. The Cockcroft Report (1982) included the recommendation that mathematics teaching should include opportunities for discussion between pupil and teacher and between pupil and pupil. Bruner (1966) declared that language was not only the medium of exchange but the instrument the learner can use in bringing order into the environment. Language plays a vital role in learning in that it makes knowledge and thought processes readily available to introspection and revision (Barnes, 1976). Thus egocentric speech, talking for the benefit of oneself, is important for young children because it serves mental orientation and conscious understanding, it helps in overcoming difficulties, and it is intimately connected with thinking (Vygotsky, 1962).

The relationship between language and thought has been the subject of debate by psychologists over many years. To Piaget, language was important but it did not play a central role in the growth of thinking. Language helps the child to organize, experience and carry thoughts with precision but this can only be brought about by dialogue and discussion alongside action (Lovell, 1971b). To Vygotsky, language played a far greater role in the growth of thinking, for egocentric speech soon becomes an instrument of thought in the proper sense – in seeking and planning the solution of a problem. However, although there might be considerable difference in emphasis in these views, the relationship between language and learning clearly cannot be ignored in mathematics learning. One outcome of the language issue has been emphasis on the importance of allowing children to talk about their mathematics.

Talking offers advantages to the teacher in that some access is gained to the thinking of pupils. Traditionally, this access has been obtained through question and answer (or 'the recitation') but, although this is valuable, there is considerable doubt as to whether it allows sufficient pupil involvement. In any case, evidence provided by Holt (1964) and many others has suggested that teachers do not always obtain worthwhile feedback from such so-called classroom discussions, partly because children possess many strategies to deceive. Barnes (1976) refers to American research about the persistence of the recitation, all of which criticizes it as being unlikely to encourage the most valuable kinds of learning. Question and answer is basically a coping method – the teacher remains firmly in control, attention is maintained, content is 'covered', and limited demands are made on the energy of the teacher. Real contact with each individual child is only occasional in the recitation, and assumptions are often made by the teacher on the one hand from the responses of a few and on the other hand from non-linguistic cues. Flanders (1970) suggested that a 'rule of two-thirds' is in operation in most classrooms, that is, someone is talking for two-thirds of the time, two-thirds of the talk is teacher-talk, and two-thirds of the teacher-talk is direct influence. Direct influence was defined as exposition, giving instructions and exercising authority. Very little of most mathematics courses consists of genuine discussion, and even teachers who have believed that they were conducting a discussion lesson have been very surprised and even upset on hearing the transcript. If a teacher is to obtain the kind of access to a pupil's thinking which is desirable, a one-to-one situation is required for a much longer time than in the normal question and answer situation. Extended one-to-one interview situations are the norm in many research studies (see Chapter 1), but most teachers do not manage to find much time amongst all their other duties for this kind of interaction. Discussion between pupil and pupil in a small group situation is much easier to achieve, but it requires close monitoring and effective follow-up.

Other criticisms of teacher-led discussions have been reported by Sutton (1981). Firstly, such discussion often allows only the teacher to ask the questions, so the questions are not necessarily those to which the pupils feel they need an answer. The teacher's questions are almost inevitably carefully sequenced to lead towards a predefined objective not declared to the pupils. Secondly, even when pupils are allowed to ask questions, the teacher's response effectively annihilates the likelihood of contributions from other pupils, and so does not necessarily solve the pupils' difficulties. Those points which are raised by pupils are often reformulated in the teacher's own words, anyway. Thirdly, it is inevitable that the teacher will only take up some contributions, and the many pupils who are ignored are therefore not helped. Finally, it is also inevitable that some contributions from pupils will be received in a complimentary manner by the teacher, clearly indicating what the teacher wanted all along, thus preventing other pupils from suggesting alternatives which might have highlighted their particular difficulties.

The real objective of discussion is to foster learning. The growth of relational understanding requires constant appraisal and development of existing knowledge structures in the light of new knowledge. Concepts, as we have seen, are not formed and learned only to remain permanently fixed, they continue to change and develop as new contexts emerge and are studied. Talk allows appraisal and development of ideas to occur. Most of us are unwilling to concede that we talk to ourselves. Young children are not at all inhibited in this way, and engage constantly in egocentric speech. Older children, like adults, are not willing to be found talking aloud unless to others. Piaget believed that egocentric speech was a feature of a particular stage of growth and that it eventually disappeared, but Vygotsky believed that egocentric speech turned into inner speech, and in that form remained a feature of how ideas were manipulated. Inner speech, however, is not always sufficient, even for adults, and conversation often includes considerable periods of time when another adult is being used virtually as a sounding-board.

Until recent times the majority of mathematics teaching has been convergent, in that the objective has been to steer or pilot pupils towards attaining a specific objective. Only recently have more 'open-ended' situations been encouraged. Although discussion between pupils need not be thought of as necessarily leading to divergence, there is no doubt that discussion allows broad exploration and allows informal hypotheses to be formulated and debated. A number of minds attacking a problem in different ways ought to offer advantages. Gagné and Smith (1962) produced some evidence that pupils who were encouraged to talk about what they were doing were more successful than when talk played little part. Wall (1965) also pointed out that groups are more productive of hypotheses and therefore are likely to be more productive of solutions than individuals, the solutions reached also tend to have a higher quality, and there is a higher level of criticism of hypotheses and of suggested solutions in a group.

Barnes (1976) discusses group work in considerable detail, describing a number of ways in which the teacher can remain at a distance and yet still influence the activity and discussion. The first essential is that pupils should fully comprehend the purposes of a group activity, should be convinced that their contribution will be valued, and should not be constrained by formal language or by trying to guess what the teacher wants. If a task is not adequately focused the pupils are likely to flounder, but if it is too focused there will be too little scope for exploration. Targets and deadlines will be necessary, but pupils should not be pushed along too quickly and should be allowed sufficient time to try out their ideas and organize their thoughts. Pupils will also need help in reporting back, because this can be a daunting experience. Within a small group of friends there is little pressure, but the pressure increases with size of audience, and it can be very acute if the teacher is also present. Help will also be needed in organizing materials and ideas, and in preparing what needs to be said if pupils are expected to declare outcomes publicly.

Teachers are likely to be concerned that group methods might take up too much time. In the long run, however, if ideas are grasped more thoroughly, time could well be saved. So much of mathematics teaching seems to consist of teaching the same ideas again and again because pupils have not retained them. Clearly, for discussion to offer advantages to all concerned, every pupil must be actively involved in the sense of attending to the discussion in its entirety. Potential advantages of group discussion therefore might not materialize if the group is too large for all members to remain involved. Some pupils will 'sleep' if given the opportunity. Others will not be confident enough to make much contribution, particularly if there are dominant pupils in the group. However, all the evidence about using discussion between pupils to facilitate learning suggests that discussion is an important vehicle for sorting out ideas. Much more work still remains to be done to explore styles of mathematics teaching which will enable pupils to develop their mathematical understanding and thinking through varied use of language (Torbe and Shuard, 1982).

## Language, culture and mathematics

Communicating mathematical ideas so that the message is adequately understood is difficult enough when teacher and learner have a common first language, but the problem is more acute when their preferred languages differ. Many pupils, in most countries of the world, are expected to learn mathematics through the medium of a spoken and written language which is not the one used in the home. Mathematics is a very important subject in the primary curriculum, so the teaching of mathematics might have to commence in one language, only to change to another later (Morris, 1974). Whatever language is used for teaching purposes one would expect that pupils would have some knowledge of that language, but it might be a very restricted knowledge. As we have seen, language is important not only for communicating but also because it facilitates thinking. The language used for thinking is almost certainly the first language, thus mathematics communicated in one language might need to be translated into another to allow thinking, and then would need to be translated back in order to converse with the teacher. Errors and misunderstandings might arise at any stage of this two-way inner translation process. Berry (1985) contrasted the progress in mathematics of a group of university mathematics students in Botswana and a similar group of Chinese university students in Canada. The former group claimed they had to do all their thinking in English, because their own language did not facilitate mathematical proofs, and they did not find this easy. The Chinese students, on the other hand, claimed that they carried out their proofs in Chinese and then translated back to English, and that they were able to do this quite successfully. Berry concludes that the more severe problems would be likely to lie with students trying to learn mathematics through the medium of an unfamiliar language which is very different from their own.

There are many problems created by the interaction between language and mathematical education and these were the subject of a major international (UNESCO) conference (Morris, 1974). The variety of local languages in some countries necessitates that a national decision is made about the teaching language. Ethiopia, for example, has 70 different languages and many more dialects, and Tanzania has some 120 languages. A common experience for many children is that they use a local language at home, learn at primary school in a regional or national language, and finally follow more advanced studies in one of the international languages. Some countries have taken the decision to adopt a bilingual approach. There is a variety of reasons why it is not appropriate to attempt to educate children throughout their school life in their local language, and there can also be problems with regional and national languages.

The first problem which often needs attention is lack of vocabulary and symbolism. Despite a reputation for mental arithmetic, the Yoruba (of Nigeria) had no symbols for the numerals or for elementary mathematical operations, and despite the existence of symmetrical and octagonal constructions in Ethiopia there were no local words for 'symmetry' and 'octagon'. Sinhalese also lacked precise equivalents for words denoting mathematical operations. There was no word in Norwegian for 'power', so the same word as for 'force' was used. For such reasons, major programmes of language enrichment have been undertaken around the world – in, for example, Malaysia, Indonesia, Tanzania and many other African and Asian countries. Often, words adopted have been taken from another language, but differences in association of word-form with pronunciation have led to different spellings, thus 'cube' in Malay has become 'kiub'. Sesotho, the language of Lesotho, is also the language for many people in South Africa, but as a result of this separation of peoples, different words for the same concepts have been adopted in the two countries. (The same phenomenon is also present between English-speaking countries – for example, we tend not to use the word 'trapezoid' in Britain.) Problems of lack of vocabulary can, of course, eventually be solved, but a more difficult problem arises when ideas do not exist.

The Yoruba traditionally compared weights by lifting by hand and had no measures of weight, whilst in Amharic (Ethiopia) ideas of negative number and square root were foreign. The idea of a day in the Yoruba culture is that it lasts from dawn to dusk, not for 24 hours, and time is also measured from sunrise to sunset by those who speak Amharic. The ideas of zero and the empty set are very difficult to explain in Igbo (a Nigerian language) because of problems of the language representing slightly different ideas. Subsets are difficult to explain in Sinhalese and some kinds of mathematical questions are rendered ridiculous, for example, the translation of, 'Are roses flowers?' is, 'Are rose flowers flowers?' The Yoruba idea of direction is imprecise, being based on directions of sunrise and sunset. Inclusive calculations in Yoruba and in other cultures lead to the translation of 'the day before yesterday' as 'three days back'. There are cultures, like the Oksapmin of New Guinea, where there is no concept of number base and body parts are used for counting. Even where the idea of base is part of the number system the base might not be ten (see Saxe and Posner, 1983), and thus translation of mathematics into a second language might create problems because the mathematical constructions are different. The Yoruba are said to have an unusually complex system involving base 20, but other bases exist, for example, base four (the Huku of Uganda) and base fifteen (the Huli of New Guinea). The Dioulas (Ivory Coast) are able to identify commutativity in addition but not in multiplication because of asymmetry of linguistic construction, which hinders any concept that the multiplier and multiplicand may be exchanged. Morris (1974) has detailed many more examples of such difficulties across many cultures.

The problem may be even deeper than one of vocabulary and mathematical ideas, for there is also the suggestion that there is a problem caused by the 'distance' between the mother tongue and the language of instruction, which is also the language which has dictated the design of the curriculum. There is now the strong belief that the so-called Indo-European languages are 'close', but as a group they are far removed from, for example, the languages of many African countries. Berry (1985) has summarized these problems as:

> In general it is likely to be easier for a student to function effectively in a second language which is semantically and culturally close to his mother tongue than in one which is remote . . . [for] . . . the structure of the learner's mother tongue has a strong influence on his cognitive processes such as classification and recognition of equivalences – processes which are central to the understanding of mathematical concepts. (p. 19)

Clearly, if the problem is only that the language of instruction is not the learner's mother tongue, then it is necessary to provide remedial help of a linguistic nature. If, however, the problem is one of 'distance', and this problem can arise among unilinguals being taught in their own language, the appropriate remedial strategies are more likely to involve the mathematics rather than the language of instruction. There is apparently a great need to develop mathematics curricula which enable and encourage students to think in their mother tongue.

Berry (1985), in recounting the difficulties faced by two children, Mothibi and Lefa, in their school situations in Botswana, suggested that school is a threatening place because mysterious tasks are assigned for no apparently useful reason. The result is that disappointing progress is made in mathematics, and what progress is made is largely based on rote learning. Gay and Cole (1967), concluded from their research with the Kpelle (Liberia) that there were no inherent difficulties about learning mathematics, it was simply that the content imposed by the curriculum did not make any sense within the Kpelle culture. All over the developing world one hears of disappointing mathematics results and of great concern about the very small numbers of pupils who show the expected level of mathematical competence, despite curricula which, though derived from Western curricula, have been meticulously translated so as to reflect the world of the children who will use the learning materials. Is there more than a problem of language here? Anthropological and linguistic studies appear to indicate that language and culture are inseparable, so that no amount of translation will help many pupils around the world if the mathematics does not fit the culture. According to d'Ambrosio (1985), recent advances in theories of cognition show how strongly culture and cognition are related. Indeed, the growing body of knowledge about 'ethnomathematics' has already been considered (see Chapter 7). The conventional view that mathematics is 'culture-free' is in danger of concealing the complication of the cultural basis and derivation of knowledge. It is thus, clearly, also important to look at the relationship between ethnomathematics and cognition if one is attempting to improve the mathematical competence of pupils around the world. Perhaps this reinforces the view that curriculum change is necessary, and that it is necessary to consider more than just language. Gay and Cole, d'Ambrosio, and Gerdes (1988), all stress the importance of beginning with materials from the indigenous culture and utilizing them to extract the universal truths of mathematics. Which materials are used and in what ways will also have to take into account such issues as gender roles, if the mathematics is to be accepted by the community. Lancy (1983) has, in fact, gone so far as to propose an alternative stage theory for cognitive development, in which Piaget's sensori-motor and pre-operational stages are succeeded by a stage in which cognitive growth has much to do with culture and environment and little to do with genetics. Bishop (1988a) has suggested that it is at this stage that different cultures develop different mathematics.

It is only possible, in the space available, to provide a brief hint of the extent of problems of language and mathematical education, for a very considerable body of research has been documented (Wilson, 1981). Many questions still remain unanswered. Do bilingual children suffer academically when forced to learn in their weaker language? There is some evidence that mechanical arithmetic does not necessarily suffer but that, perhaps not surprisingly, arithmetic word problems do. Is it possible that learning mathematical concepts in two languages could help to free the concepts from dependence on language thus enhancing understanding, or would it depend which two languages? How does one teach mathematics in a language which lacks essential mathematical vocabulary? How does one teach mathematics when essential ideas or concepts are not present? How does one take account of ethnomathematics? These questions and the problems expressed earlier are not completely irrelevant for teachers who imagine they speak the same language as their pupils. Studies of problems of language and mathematical education might ultimately enlighten us all in terms of problems experienced by children, in particular those whose language is much more restricted than our own.

## Word problems

A word problem, or verbal problem, is simply a question which requires the application of mathematics in order to achieve a solution, but in which the required procedure has first to be extracted from within sentences. These sentences are often intended to provide a real-life setting for a simple task. Thus:

> Sarah had 5 sweets. Her father gave her another 3 sweets. How many sweets did Sarah have altogether?

is a simple word problem which only requires the use of the elementary procedure

$$5 + 3 = 8$$

In Chapters 2 and 5, problem-solving was described as what transpires when a learner strives to find the solution to a novel problem, in fact, when previously learned knowledge, rules, techniques, skills and concepts have to be combined in a new way. Word problems are often not particularly novel, being frequently simply another way of providing practice of simple algorithms. Indeed, they often only require the application of the 'four rules', that is, addition, subtraction, multiplication and division. Thus, word problems and problem-solving need to be differentiated, though there could obviously be overlap. Many teachers around the world express great concern about the difficulties which their children experience with word problems. Verschaffel and De Corte (1997, quoting Nesher) claim that pupils 'do not see the applicability of their formal mathematical knowledge to real-world situations; . . . they have only a weak understanding of arithmetic operations as models of situations; [and] they seem to dislike mathematics in general and word problems in particular' (p. 69).

One assumption made by mathematics teachers in the past has been that pupils first need to be confident in handling purely numerical tasks before they are ready to attempt the equivalent word problems. Carpenter and Moser (1982) have, however, repudiated both the suggestion that verbal problems are difficult for children of all ages, and that children must master addition and subtraction operations before they can solve word problems. It is interesting to compare this with the findings reported by Hughes (1986) which confirm that, with small-sized sets, young children could perform addition and subtraction as long as real-life situations were being described, in other words the question was not 'disembedded', to use the terminology of Donaldson (1978), who also has much to say on the issue. In the research reported by Carpenter and Moser the informal strategies used by children in addition problems were based on counting (variations on 'counting all' and 'counting on'), and subtraction was based on separating and matching together with counting techniques. The results indicated that children continued to use informal techniques based on counting well into the middle years of schooling, but that eventually most children began to use number facts and algorithms. The major problem which emerged was that:

> by the age of 9, many children mechanically add, subtract, multiply, or divide whatever numbers are given in a problem with little regard for the problem's content. Somehow in learning formal arithmetic procedures, many children stop analyzing the problems they attempt to solve. (p. 23)

It seems, therefore, that it is the transition from informal procedures which the child constructs to the procedures which the teacher teaches and expects the child to learn where one difficulty arises. This appears to be more a problem of learning than one of understanding language. It is certainly necessary to rethink the assumption that the numerical algorithms must come before the corresponding word problems. It is possible that the better way in some circumstances is to learn the algorithms through word problems.

All research into performance on word problems has revealed the enormous variety of sentence and overall problem structure which can arise. Carpenter and Moser describe seventeen different kinds of elementary word problem involving only addition and subtraction, and these are still not completely unambiguous. These seventeen incorporate three basic types known as 'Change', 'Combine' and 'Compare'. Verschaffel and De Corte (1997) claim that research indicates a clear order of difficulty for addition and subtraction word problems based on these three types and on what is the unknown. A more complete framework by Vergnaud (1982) extends these word problems to operations on integers. Laborde *et al.* (1990, p. 62) have also attempted to describe the main variables of word problems, as follows: (1) how relations between the given and the unknown quantities are expressed, and in particular the degree to which they are made explicit; (2) the order of items of information; (3) the degree of attraction of some words, such as the priority of numbers over words or the use of keywords like 'more', 'less' related to arithmetical operations, which may be distractors as well as cues; (4) the complexity of the syntax and of the vocabulary. This analysis appears to be particularly valuable when looking into whether changes in wording will lead to improvement in performance.

One of the seventeen examples provided by Carpenter and Moser is:

> Connie had some marbles. She won 8 more marbles. Now she has 13 marbles. How many marbles did Connie have to start with?

Verschaffel and De Corte (1997) emphasize how important the first sentence is, which could easily but mistakenly be omitted in attempting to economize. They believe that inexperienced pupils are more dependent on text-driven processing whereas more mature pupils have mastered complex semantic problem schemes. Thus rewording verbal problems so that the semantic relations are made more explicit facilitates the construction of a proper problem representation. It is now clear that the order of information, the relations between known and unknown and the transition from known to unknown all influence understanding of a word problem in younger learners. Thus, it should be possible to effect some improvement in performance on word problems by amending the wording. Verschaffel and De Corte have also claimed that pupils (and unschooled adults) may be inclined to produce bizarre responses to word problems because they just do not understand how to play the game of solving school-type word problems.

Research on multiplication and division word problems has focused particularly on the selection and execution of the appropriate arithmetic operation. A well-established finding is that one-step multiplication word problems are often answered by using addition. There is also an order of difficulty based on the nature of the numbers to be multiplied. Verschaffel and De Corte state:

> There is robust evidence that pupils are systematically better at choosing the correct operation for a multiplication word problem with an integer as multiplier, than when the multiplier is a decimal larger than 1; problems with a decimal multiplier smaller than 1 are still much more difficult. By contrast, the size of the multiplicand has no effect on problem difficulty. (p. 85)

The most frequently observed error in these questions is to divide rather than multiply. Two misunderstandings are at work here, both arising from the fact that the child's underlying intuitive model is repeated addition: firstly the multiplier must be an integer, and secondly the result must be larger than the multiplicand. Coping strategies include firstly using the given numbers and applying any well understood operation, secondly reacting to keywords ('more' means add; 'less' means subtract;

'each' means multiply, etc.), and thirdly using the operation which yields the 'nicest' answer. Children are also inclined to use informal solution strategies, like using objects which are to hand. Many informal strategies can yield the correct answer, and could be used as a starting point for teaching, but they often reveal that pupils have not internalized the formal strategy which they have been taught. When interpreting their result, some pupils are inclined to give meaningless answers (such as there were 6.5 children at a party). There are several possible reasons for this too: firstly they may not check their answer with the question at all, secondly any verification is often restricted only to the calculation, and thirdly pupils often do not detect an error even when they check.

All the available evidence suggests that it is not a simple matter to explain children's difficulties with word problems, so it not a simple matter to find ways of improving performance. Several obvious general points have emerged, but none are easy to convert into best practice. Apart from issues of wording, the most obvious improvement would be to take note of the comparative difficulty levels of the various categories of problem types described in the research literature, and ensure they are optimally matched to the level of progress of the children. Another way of trying to improve performance on word problems is to attempt to build better on the informal methods employed by children before formal instruction has modified and possibly confused their thought processes. This is even more difficult to implement because little is known about when is the optimum moment to attempt to introduce any new procedure, and also about possible detrimental effects of allowing children to continue to use informal methods for as long as they are inclined to do so.

## Suggestions for further reading

Austin, J. L. and Howson, A. G. (1979) 'Language and mathematical education', *Educational Studies in Mathematics*, 10, 161–97.
Durkin, K. and Shire, B. (eds) (1991) *Language in Mathematical Education*. Buckingham: Open University Press.
Harvey, R., Kerslake, D., Shuard, H. and Torbe, M. (1982) *Language Teaching and Learning 6: Mathematics*. London: Ward Lock.
Shuard, H. and Rothery, A. (1984) *Children Reading Mathematics*. London: John Murray.
UNESCO (1974) *Interactions Between Linguistics and Mathematical Education*. UNESCO/CEDO/ICMI.

## Questions for discussion

1. What methods might we adopt to try to ensure that pupils learn the vocabulary of mathematics?
2. How should the three facets of language (reading, writing and talking) all contribute to the learning of mathematics?
3. Discuss the suitability of a textbook you use from the points of view of vocabulary, readability, symbolism and the communication of meaning.
4. What lessons can we learn about the interference of language in mathematics learning from the experiences of countries around the world?

Chapter 10

# Is There a Theory of Mathematics Learning?

## Mathematics and theories of learning

The place of theory in supporting and enlightening the process of learning mathematics is a major theme of this book. Debate about how mathematics is learned has continued throughout the recorded history of mathematics teaching, yet the process is still not founded on a single universally accepted theory. Shulman (1970, p. 23) claimed that '. . . mathematics instruction has been quite sensitive to shifts in psychological theories', but also that, '. . . mathematics educators have shown themselves especially adept at taking hold of conveniently available psychological theories to buttress previously held instructional proclivities'. Some mathematics teachers and educationists have been very keen to look to learning theory for help in determining classroom practice, others have not been aware that there were theories, and yet others have reacted strongly against any suggestion that psychology could possibly have anything to offer. The concern of some teachers that there appears to be a variety of different theories and that it is difficult to know which is the correct one was part of the discussion in Chapter 1. The problem with a universally accepted theory would, of course, be that many teachers might then feel pressure to change teaching methods, and such pressure is not always welcome.

In searching for appropriate theoretical underpinning, two kinds of theory demand attention. There are theories which are specifically concerned with learning mathematics, and there are general learning theories which are clearly relevant. Given the complexity of the nature of human abilities and the fact that it is so difficult to isolate mathematical ability from other abilities and from overall ability (see Chapter 8), it seems reasonable to assume that a general theory of learning might have much to offer. General theories of learning certainly cannot be ignored. The theoretical approach to learning known as behaviourism is an example of a general learning theory which led to the specific application to mathematics (see Chapter 3). On the whole, behaviourism is out of favour with educationists in Britain, despite the widespread use of teaching methods which appear to be closely related to behaviourist beliefs. Dienes (1973, p. 5) certainly appeared to believe that behaviourism was out of favour, in saying that '. . . no one today doubts any more the fact that the stimulus-response relation leads to a training which most of the time induces mental blockages . . .'.

Stewart (1985, p. 1) endorsed the current view in declaring that '. . . behaviourism [is] essentially finished as a theory that could adequately explain the more complex aspects of human mental activity'. And yet experts on the functioning of the brain still emphasize the vital part that repetition plays in fixing knowledge in the mind. There is clearly an important distinction between thoughtful and necessary repetition and practice on the one hand, and mindless and potentially mind-numbing use of routine stimulus-response activities on the other.

The major alternatives to behaviourism are the cognitive learning theories. The work of Piaget (Chapter 4) was an important landmark in the development in the emphasis on cognition, though he did not attempt to present his ideas as a learning theory. Bruner's belief in the importance of cognition led to him promoting discovery learning (Chapter 5), and this has had a considerable effect on school curricula. Ausubel (1968) has also presented a comprehensive theory of meaningful verbal learning which demands careful consideration, incorporating results and concepts described by Piaget but also criticizing the wholehearted belief in the efficacy of discovery learning. The general theory of David Ausubel therefore demands consideration in this chapter. Before that, however, we consider two theories of mathematics learning, by Dienes, and by the van Hieles.

## The Dienes theory of mathematics-learning

Place value has been referred to earlier as being a difficult concept. It is therefore relevant to try to determine what the most appropriate sequence of learning situations might be, in order to help children to attain the necessary knowledge, understanding and skills. A behaviourist approach suggests the use of stimulus-response situations through which connections are practised, but it is difficult to see how the underlying structure of place value could be grasped in this way, and much might depend on the quality of subsequent reflection by the child. A cognitive approach suggests that children should be placed in a learning environment in which they might investigate, and perhaps discover, and in which understanding might be constructed through their own efforts. Piaget's work suggests that children learn by abstracting from concrete situations in which they have been actively involved. The Multi-base Arithmetic Blocks (MAB) of Zoltan Dienes provide an early-learning environment intended to promote the construction of an understanding of place value.

The MAB equipment consists of 'units', 'longs', 'flats' and 'blocks' in a wide variety of number bases (see also Chapter 5). The base ten Dienes MAB shapes are shown in Figure 10.1. If children experience handling this equipment we might hope that they will eventually notice and appreciate (with or without teacher intervention) that there are equivalences – ten units to a long, ten longs to a flat and ten flats to a block. This structure must become apparent if place value is to be learned through the use of this equipment. Furthermore, children might then be able to appreciate the foundations of simple arithmetical calculation through activities which involve exchanging shapes. Thus, for example, thirteen units could become one long and three units, and the paying of a forfeit of four units from a long would leave six units. Teachers of young children will know that teaching based on such activities can take quite a time. In fact, more equipment might be needed, for the structure of our number system is not dependent on the particular materials used, so matchsticks, bundles of

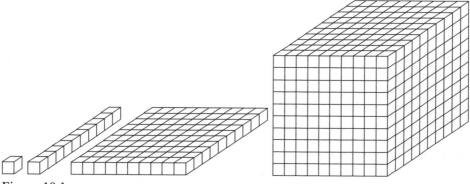

**Figure 10.1**

ten matchsticks, and boxes containing ten bundles could provide a parallel activity. An illustration of using the Dienes MAB equipment in this way is shown in Resnick and Ford (1984, p. 211). Some teachers would also want to divorce the place value concept from the base ten concept by providing activities which depend on other bases, like six 'eggs' to an egg box. Dienes provided MAB equipment in a wide variety of number bases for just this same reason. This outline of the teaching of place value introduces the practical application of the theory of mathematics-learning proposed by Dienes (1960).

Dienes began from the premise that mathematics could not be learned in a stimulus-response way because it was not content that caused the problem, it was the fact that mathematics-learning was so bound up with understanding structure. Although the equipment suggested by Dienes is comparatively well known to teachers (see Seaborne, 1975) it is not so widely appreciated that the apparatus was proposed, at least in part, as a way of putting the 'Dienes Theory of Mathematics-Learning' into practice. In addition to the MAB, Dienes commended the use of the Algebraic Experience Material (AEM), the Equaliser (Dienes' Balance) and the Logical Blocks, all of which encouraged the construction of understanding. Dienes drew his initial inspiration from the work of Piaget, Bruner and Bartlett, but his theory was also based on research of his own. The resulting theory of mathematics-learning comprised four principles:

1. The dynamic principle
2. The constructivity principle
3. The mathematical variability principle
4. The perceptual variability principle.

Dienes took Piaget's work to suggest that learning is an active process, and the *dynamic principle* was directly derived from the assumption that concept formation is promoted by providing suitable learning materials with which children can interact. In fact Dienes accepted 'Piaget's three stages in the formation of a concept', which he called the play stage, the structure stage, and the practice stage. The play stage was basically unstructured activity, so for place value it was playing with the MAB equipment, or with other suitable materials. Eventually, as the realization of structure grew, children's activities could be geared much more towards the structure, and teacher intervention could try to ensure that this structure was grasped. Practice of the structure could then lead to more overt use of practice exercises, leading to simple arithmetic and the written recording of calculations. The play–structure–practice sequence was to be seen only in relation to a single concept, and would thus feature over and over again as children learned other concepts, and the practice activities for one concept might be suitable as the play activities for a subsequent concept. It should also be pointed out that, for Dienes, the three dynamic stages subsequently became six (Dienes, 1973), and also that the play stage might not always seem, to older pupils, to be play.

It is appropriate, in the context of Dienes' three stages in learning mathematical concepts, to compare these with the three stages described by Bruner. In representing the world, or translating experience into a model of the world, Bruner (1966) suggested that the stages of learning were the *enactive*, the *iconic* and the *symbolic*. These stages were further elaborated in Bruner *et al.* (1966). Many forms of knowledge can only be learned in an active way, like riding a bicycle or playing tennis. According to Bruner (as with both Piaget and Dienes), the early phase of learning an abstract concept like place value might also require an enactive approach, with children engaged in manipulating concrete apparatus. A second approach to learning is, however, the use of visual images, so eventually the actual concrete objects might become iconic representations such as pictures of the objects. Textbooks, workcards and other written materials are heavily dependent on an iconic approach. Certain mathematical ideas might, however, be learned directly from pictures and without any prior dependence on enactive representation. The ultimate approach to learning is symbolic, through language and through other symbols of a specific mathematical nature. Naturally, for some pupils, some mathematical concepts might be learned directly through the manipulation of symbols and without prior dependence on either enactive or iconic approaches. The three stages may be regarded as a sequential approach to learning a concept or structure like place value, with concrete equipment followed by pictures, followed by pencil-and-paper tasks. Alternatively, the three forms of representation might be regarded as three different approaches to learning, with their appropriateness related to characteristics of the particular learner such as prior experience and knowledge, and to the characteristics of the concept or structure being studied. Bruner did not suggest that there was any direct connection between the enactive, iconic and symbolic stages of learning new concepts and the stages of intellectual development suggested by Piaget. Certainly, any feeling that the appropriateness of a particular form of representation is related to the age of the learner would indicate a developmental aspect to the theory which was not intended by Bruner. Thus Piaget, Bruner and Dienes have all introduced the notion of stages to explain learning, and though these stages were distinctly different, they can all claim to be relevant to trying to understand how children learn.

Dienes also believed that mathematics must be a constructive activity for children, rather than an analytic one. Formal logical thinking, dependent on analysis, may well be something which adults can engage in, but the *constructivity principle* is based on his conviction that children need to construct their own knowledge. In the case of place value, this is accomplished by using a variety of forms of concrete activity, possibly in a variety of number bases. It is interesting to speculate on the relationship between Piaget's concrete operational stage and Dienes' views on the construction of knowledge, and on the relationship between Piaget's formal operational stage and the ability to think analytically. Dienes did not refer to Piagetian stage theory directly in the exposition of his theory. This conviction that children need to construct their understanding, and indeed can only construct, is an example of views which would now be classed as constructivist (see Chapter 11).

The issue of how to accelerate mathematics learning was answered by Dienes in terms of providing varied learning experiences. Earlier discussion of concepts in this book (Chapter 2) has drawn attention to the fact that concepts describe some regularity or relationship within a group of facts (Novak, 1977), and that concepts are learned from examples and counter-examples (Skemp, 1971). Dienes concluded that a mathematical concept usually contains a certain number of variables and it is the constancy of the relationship between these, while the variables themselves vary, that constitutes the mathematical concept. This led Dienes to the *mathematical variability principle*. In place value, it was important to Dienes that children should work with a wide variety of number bases. When learning about parallelograms, another example considered by Dienes, it was essential that lengths, angles and orientation should all vary. In fact, orientation has often not been varied in the experience of many children, and the belief that a square in certain orientations was not a square but was a 'diamond' was mentioned in Chapter 2. Teachers of less able children are often unconvinced by the suggestion that a variety of number bases is essential, believing that such an approach can confuse. The exhortation to apply the mathematical variability principle in teaching about geometrical shapes, however, cannot be ignored.

Another issue considered by Dienes was that of individual differences (see Chapter 8). This led to two recommendations, one being to organize learning on an individual or small group basis, perhaps using workcards, and the other being the *perceptual variability principle*. He considered it important that the perceptual representation of a concept should be varied, thus, in place value, the specifically provided wooden or plastic blocks of the MAB would not be sufficient. The idea of matches or straws and bundles of matches or straws has already been mentioned. Some writers have suggested different coloured counters (5 yellow = 1 green, 5 green = 1 red, etc.) but there are disadvantages with this equipment because, perceptually, one counter of one colour does not look equivalent to five of another colour. Dienes also suggested that some of the AEM material, based on shapes other than cuboids, was appropriate for place value. In the case of parallelograms, these may be represented on paper and chalkboard, may be made out of wood, metal and plastic, may be outlined with pegs on a pegboard or elastic bands on a nailboard, be made by putting two congruent triangles together or by dissecting a rectangle, and be seen in shapes in the real world, for example in windows and other features of buildings and floors, and in patterns on wallpaper and many other designs. The need for 'variability', in both mathematics and materials, is often referred to as the principle of *multiple embodiment*.

The four principles of Dienes' Theory of Mathematics-Learning were not intended to apply only to concepts of elementary mathematics. One of the most difficult aspects of more advanced and abstract mathematics is algebra. Attention has already been drawn to the use of certain Dienes AEM wooden blocks to promote an early understanding of $(x + a)^2 = x^2 + 2ax + a^2$ (see Chapter 4). Whether earlier understanding than normal is sought or not, there can be no doubt that equipment can be used to approach quadratic expansions constructively rather than abstractly. The constructive approach might involve either using wooden or plastic squares and rectangles, as in

```
O  O  x        O  O  O  x        O  O  O  O  x        O  O  O  O  O  x
O  O  x        O  O  O  x        O  O  O  O  x        O  O  O  O  O  x
x  x  ■        O  O  O  x        O  O  O  O  x        O  O  O  O  O  x
               x  x  x  ■        O  O  O  O  x        O  O  O  O  O  x
                                 x  x  x  x  ■        O  O  O  O  O  x
                                                      x  x  x  x  x  ■
```

Figure 10.2

the illustration in Chapter 4, or placing patterns of pegs in a pegboard, as in Figure 10.2. The patterns obtained can then reveal the following relationships:

$$3^2 = 2^2 + 2 \times 2 + 1$$
$$4^2 = 3^2 + 2 \times 3 + 1$$
$$5^2 = 4^2 + 2 \times 4 + 1$$
and
$$6^2 = 5^2 + 2 \times 5 + 1$$

Thus we might deduce that, in general,

$$(x + 1)^2 = x^2 + 2x + 1$$

The formula has thus been constructed, but it has not been proved. The numbers have been varied, but the structure remains the same, so mathematical variability has been applied. The same result can be approached using square regions on a nailboard, coloured regions on ordinary squared paper, or Dienes MAB equipment, so perceptual variability can be applied. The result can be extended, by a process of construction, to

$$(x + a)^2 = x^2 + 2ax + a^2$$

and to

$$(ax + 1)^2 = a^2x^2 + 2ax + 1$$

and so on, until the whole range of possible quadratic expansions has been explored, and appropriate generalizations constructed.

The Dienes Theory of Mathematics-Learning is very satisfying in a number of ways. It is clearly a cognitive approach, and builds on the work of Piaget, Bruner, Bartlett and Wertheimer. Certain other important issues like how to accelerate learning and how to cope with individual differences are incorporated. Current views on learning are placing considerable emphasis on the belief that knowledge is constructed by each individual and often cannot be simply transferred ready-made from teacher to learner. But Dienes' theory has limitations. The constructivity principle relates to learning individual concepts, and the relationship between the learning of a new concept and the existing knowledge structure already held in the mind is not considered. Mathematics is, after all, a very hierarchical subject in which new knowledge generally must be secured onto existing knowledge; if prerequisites have not been mastered the new knowledge just cannot be learned. Nor was the issue of readiness explicitly tackled by Dienes; it was tacitly assumed that adopting the four principles would lead to learning, and likewise that forgetting would not occur. Certainly, it is clear that the community of mathematics teachers and educators has not accepted the theory as the ultimate answer to anything. Dienes proposed it as a feasible skeleton theory of learning mathematics, and not necessarily as an ultimate answer. It should therefore be interpreted as a useful contribution to debate, from an educator to whom the essence of mathematics was structure. What must also be gratefully acknowledged, however, is that Dienes has given us a wealth of teaching ideas. In particular, many teachers believe that the manipulatives which he promoted are very valuable.

## The van Hiele theory of learning geometry

Anyone who has tried to teach Euclidean geometry to teenagers must have been frustrated by their seeming inability to comprehend the nature of proof. In the first place, some pupils seem not to see any need for a proof, particularly if it is related to a result that looks obviously true. In the second place, having been shown a proof by the teacher, some pupils clearly reveal that they do not truly comprehend precisely what had been achieved. The outcome of setting riders as class or homework tasks then very likely results in the teacher having to provide all or nearly all of the solutions the next day. The theory of Pierre van Hiele and Dina van Hiele-Geldof was the eventual outcome of their concern over these and other issues. After studying the work of Piaget, they thought that pupils might well develop geometrical competence by progressing over a period of time through successive levels of thinking. Thus, if a pupil was not able to cope with a particular geometry task it was likely to be because completion demanded a higher level of thinking than the pupil had so far attained. In other words, the van Hieles postulated sequential levels of geometrical thought but, in addition, suggested phases of instruction intended to enhance the learning of geometrical ideas.

For older British teachers, all this might bring to mind the long-standing recommendations of the Mathematical Association (1923, 1939). In Britain, the study of geometry was basically Euclidean until around 1970, when the introduction of what was loosely termed 'modern mathematics' introduced ideas of transformations, matrices and vectors. At the moment, it is difficult to describe the British geometry curriculum simply, but it certainly is not Euclidean. In many other countries around the world, however, Euclidean geometry is still taught. Concern about the difficulties which the Euclidean approach to geometry presented even for clever pupils was expressed by many educators in Britain throughout the second half of the nineteenth century and into the twentieth (see, for example, Ministry of Education, 1958). This concern led to the formation of the Association for the Improvement of Geometrical Teaching in 1871 (later renamed the Mathematical Association), whose two reports on the teaching of geometry contained recommendations about the teaching of geometry in five stages.

The stages advocated by the Association addressed the issue of the intrinsic difficulty of Euclidean geometry, and provided practical recommendations concerning how pupils might be taught at the various stages. The descriptions of the stages with their curriculum suggestions remained major guidelines for the teaching of geometry in Britain until the late twentieth century. Stage A was known as the Experimental Stage, in which work was to be based on real problems such as land measuring, and illustrated by the use of drawing instruments and other simple apparatus. In due course, it was claimed, fundamental facts would emerge, relating to angles, lines and triangles (Mathematical Association, 1923). Deduction was to be phased in gently, and usually conducted orally. Stage B, the Deductive Stage, was when theorems were studied, and proofs were learned. The main interest here was in the systematic process, but it was accepted that the systematizing instinct was not strongly developed even up to age 15 (for selective pupils!). It was also considered better to experiment and investigate rather than to attempt the proof of properties that appear obviously true. Stage C was the Systematizing Stage, and it was not anticipated that all pupils would reach this level before they were entitled to leave school. There were two other stages (D: Modern Geometry; and E: the Philosophy of Geometry) to be pursued later, but very few pupils ever reached them because the geometry of the sixth form was based on coordinates.

Although the stages of the Mathematical Association represented an early attempt to phase the teaching of geometry in line with developmental considerations, the fact that even the best pupils only reached Stage B was the inevitable outcome of what were very broad divisions of subject matter and approach. The van Hieles' belief in somewhat narrower stages is clear from their claim to have discovered that there were times when it appeared that learning had stopped, and the teacher was unable to take pupils further until it seemed that the children had matured (or reached a higher level of thinking). They analysed the nature of their postulated levels of geometrical thinking in much finer detail than the Mathematical Association, and although the work of Piaget (see Chapter 4) formed one of their bases, they clearly did not accept all that Piaget stated. The four principles of Gestalt theory and Gestalt views on the importance of insight (see Chapter 5) provided additional theoretical background, for example, to explain why Level 1 pupils could not easily distinguish components in a geometrical configuration. They also believed that the pupils needed particular teaching and learning experiences to assist them to progress from one level to the next. Burger and Shaughnessy (1986) have used the terms visualization, analysis, informal deduction, formal deduction and rigour to sum up briefly what was the nature of each of the five levels. In more detail, some of the characteristics of the levels are as follows (developed from Fuys *et al.*, 1988 and Zachos, 1994).

Level 1: The pupil can only recognize shapes as wholes and cannot analyse them according to component parts; visual impression and appearance exert a strong influence, thus a square cannot also be a rectangle; drawings of shapes are based on holistic impressions and not on component parts; names may be invented for shapes according to their appearance, for example, 'slanty rectangle' for parallelogram.

Level 2: The pupil can see components such as sides and angles but cannot relate properties logically; properties and rules of a class of shapes may be discovered empirically (for example, by folding, measuring, or by using a grid or diagram); a figure can be identified from its properties; generalizations become possible, for example, all squares have four sides, the angles of triangles total 180°.

Level 3: The pupil can relate properties and can make simple deductions, though the intrinsic meaning of deduction is not understood; a shape may be defined using the minimum number of properties; reasoning can be used to establish that a square is a rectangle; a statement cannot be separated from its converse.

Level 4: The pupil can appreciate the need for definitions and assumptions, and can give proofs within a postulational system; the meanings of deduction, converse, axiom, necessary and sufficient conditions can be understood; proof as the final authority is accepted; inter-relationships among networks of theorems can be established.

Level 5: The pupil can work abstractly and can compare systems, can examine the consistency and independence of axioms and can generalize a principle or theorem to find the broadest context.

Fuys *et al.* (1988, p. 8) have summarized the most important features of the system of levels as:

(a) the levels are sequential;
(b) each level has its own language, symbols and network of relations;
(c) what is implicit at one level becomes explicit at the next level;
(d) material taught to students above their level is subject to reduction of level;
(e) progress from one level to the next is more dependent on instructional experience than on age or maturation;
(f) one goes through various 'phases' in proceeding from one level to the next.

The phases of (f) were described as information, guided orientation, explicitation, free orientation and integration. The significance of the van Hiele theory in comparison with other theories of learning is its dependence on the role of instruction.

Evaluation of the van Hiele theory includes the following comments. Bell *et al.* (1983) have suggested that Level 2 closely resembles Stage A of the Mathematical Association, which makes Level 1 even more elementary; also that school geometry is likely to have to focus largely on Levels 1 to 3. Zachos (1994) suggested that there is little chance of finding any pupils who have reached Level 5, and so there is little evidence to support the existence of Level 5, as it is described above. It almost seems as if Level 5 is hypothetical, and merely consists of those geometrical notions which were not attained in the lower levels. Subsequent research, largely carried out in the USA, has studied the basic thesis (that levels can be identified, are discrete and form a hierarchy), the pattern of levels in given populations, and the possibility of basing instruction and learning materials on the model. One interesting outcome is serious doubt about both the discreteness and the globality of the levels, because a child can seem to act at different levels in different contexts and can even change level within the same task (Hershkowitz, 1990). This is, of course, reminiscent of the problem of 'décalage' within Piagetian theory. Usiskin (reported in Zachos, 1994) was able to assign around 90 per cent of a large sample of American students to a van Hiele level with considerable confidence. It was those students who were in transition who were difficult to classify. Senk (in Zachos, 1994) suggested that a measure of knowledge of content would have the same predictive powers as the van Hiele levels, i.e. would be just as good. Nevertheless, whatever the doubts, the literature reveals genuine enthusiasm about the likelihood of finding ways of improving the learning of geometry by building on knowledge obtained from research into the van Hiele levels. In fact, the theory has affected and changed the teaching of geometry in various countries around the world, for example, the Soviet Union in the 1960s.

## Ausubel's theory of meaningful learning

### Meaningful learning

Any theory of learning mathematics must take into account the structure of the subject. It is not possible to learn about integers and about rational numbers before natural numbers are understood meaningfully. Meaningful learning implies more than knowledge of the number system which allows counting and simple accounting. It implies an understanding of constraints, for example, that subtractions and divisions cannot always be carried out within the set of natural numbers. When the existing knowledge structure is sufficiently rich and varied, and better still when the child is asking questions which require new input, the time is right for injecting these new concepts. If an attempt is made to force children to assimilate and accommodate new ideas that cannot be related to knowledge which is already in the knowledge structure the ideas can only be learned by rote. A range of examples should illustrate this point.

The algorithm for calculating the arithmetic mean is a simple one. It is so simple that it is all too easy to teach without paying due attention to linking the algorithm in a meaningful way to existing knowledge. Without such links the algorithm will be learned by rote and will likely be forgotten. It will also not promote flexibility of thinking, such as is required to cope with increasing the numbers of numbers being averaged. Basically, the arithmetic mean is one of several measures associated with the idea of a representative value. Children writing to pen-friends might wish to include some information about their class. In terms of height they could say, 'we are all about 150 cm in height', or 'a lot of us are exactly 148 cm in height (to the nearest cm)', or 'we range in height from 140 cm to 157 cm'. The ideas of mean, median, mode and range can be seen as attempts to convey information about a population, and the comparative value, particularly of the three forms of average, would need discussion. Another situation familiar to children concerns sharing out sweets. If the teacher leaves a tin of sweets for the children to help themselves, different children would take different numbers of sweets, and that would not be considered fair. Instead of Adam having eight, Stephanie having seven, Inder having three and Darren having two they should all really have the same number of sweets, which we could calculate by putting all the sweets together and sharing them out. The abstract equivalent is to add up the numbers of sweets held by all children and then divide by the number of children. In other words, it is possible to link the idea of arithmetic mean to previously held knowledge, thus conveying ideas in a meaningful way.

The introduction of the sine and cosine ratios to secondary school pupils needs to be linked to several ideas, including similarity (or enlargement) and ratio, triangles, right-angles, other angles and lengths. The real meaning and purpose of sines and cosines will not be absorbed if these two ratios are not linked with previous knowledge and with some kind of motivation like the need to be able to perform calculations in triangles. Often either the motivation or the previous knowledge is not there. In terms of prior knowledge, both similarity and ratio are difficult ideas, and may not be adequately formed. One must, however, acknowledge that they might become better formed through a study of elementary trigonometry, but if there is no relevant knowledge there at all, sines and cosines would once again have to be learned by rote. The problem of motivation is not easily solved either, for different real-life situations may be meaningful to different pupils. A link with prior knowledge, however, is important.

Certain mathematical knowledge is so basic that there is unlikely to be any relevant knowledge already in the mind to which new ideas can be linked. Very young children usually enjoy trying to slot odd-shaped wooden or plastic objects through holes in the top of a box, designed in such a way that only one shape will fit into any one hole, and then only with one particular orientation. It is a process of discovery for children to solve this problem, but eventually they become quite proficient and their interest wanes. This particular game has, however, taught them a great deal of basic spatial knowledge. At a later stage in life pupils might be given Cuisenaire (or other) rods to play with, and will discover that 'red' + 'pale green' = 'yellow, and 'orange' − 'pink' = 'dark green'. Without such a period of discovery using coloured rods, or using beads or counters, or using other equipment, it is difficult to see how children could learn the basis of number combinations. The only alternative would appear to be by rote. Certain mathematical knowledge is so basic that there might not be any part of the existing knowledge structure with which it could be connected.

The theory of meaningful learning proposed by David Ausubel (1968) was a general theory and was not specific to mathematics. It incorporated the ideas presented above and so, to Ausubel, meaningful learning was a process through which new knowledge was absorbed by connecting it to some existing relevant aspect of the individual's pre-existing knowledge structure. If there were no relevant concepts already in the mind to which new knowledge could be linked, the new knowledge would have to be learned by rote and stored in an arbitrary and disconnected manner. If new knowledge was assimilated within the existing knowledge structure as a related unit, and if appropriate modification of prior knowledge (accommodation) took place, the result was meaningful learning. It was therefore not necessary for all, or perhaps even much, knowledge to be acquired by a process of discovery. Good expository teaching could ensure that new knowledge was linked to relevant existing ideas, and this might not only be more economical (in terms of time taken) than was discovery, it might be more efficient in terms of quality and breadth of learning. If you really could ascertain what the learner already knew, you would then know what and how to teach. Some discovery learning would be necessary with very young children, and at this stage of life the emphasis would need to be on encouraging concept formation rather than teaching for concept acquisition. But once a rich structure of knowledge has been learned the most efficient way to proceed would be by exposition. Discovery methods might occasionally be appropriate, but only rarely with older pupils − meaningful verbal learning could, in most circumstances, be at least as effective and in some ways better than any other method.

Clearly this theoretical stance can only become reality if one can find out in sufficient detail, and in a reliable way, what the learner already knows, and if one can then ensure good, as opposed to indifferent or bad, expository teaching. Given good teaching, if subject matter was inadequately learned the reason would then be that pupils did not have the required foundation of relevant knowledge on which to anchor new ideas. It would, of course, also be necessary for *all* members of a class to have the required foundation of knowledge, something which is not easy to obtain in the normal school situation. Such difficulties would not invalidate the theory, but would raise problems for the teacher.

Ausubel's theory of meaningful learning contained a number of other ideas which will require discussion in due course, but first, the relationship between the ideas of Ausubel and Piaget demands attention. Ausubel used data collected by Piaget, accepted the ideas of assimilation and accommodation, and from time to time referred to 'concrete' and 'formal' or 'abstract' stages, without accepting the full implications of Piagetian stage theory. Novak (1977), whose own work ably explained, clarified and expanded Ausubelian theory, claimed no operational conflict exists between the ideas of Piaget and Ausubel. In terms of readiness, Ausubel's view was closer to that of Gagné than to that of Piaget. The existing parts of the knowledge structure to which new learning needed to be linked were referred to by Ausubel as *subsumers* or 'subsuming concepts'; subsequently they became known also as 'anchoring' ideas or concepts. So, if the subsumers were there, the pupil was effectively ready. Readiness was only related to stage of development in its most open interpretation as dependent on having more and better developed subsumers. Shulman (1970) certainly expressed the view that Ausubel was in fundamental agreement with Gagné in that the key to readiness was prerequisite knowledge. Novak (1977), however, indicated that he thought Ausubel's view on readiness was close to that of Bruner. Perhaps this can be taken as an indication of the reconciling power of Ausubelian theory! To Ausubel, even if the child was not ready in the sense of having appropriate subsumers, all was not lost. There was then the possibility of using an *advance organizer* to bridge the gap.

Matrix multiplication can appear very arbitrary, complex and meaningless to pupils, and therein lies a recipe for disaster in terms of meaningful learning. Despite attempts to motivate the idea through using shopping bills and the like, despite attempts to base the introduction on transformation geometry or on simultaneous equations, there are arbitrary aspects to the procedure. Matrix multiplication is, however, essential to the long-term development of an understanding of modern algebra, and it may be applied, as a technique, in a number of different topics in school mathematics (though it has seemed to jump in and out of the prescribed syllabus like a yo-yo). Different authors have used a variety of different ways of introducing matrix multiplication but Matthews (1964) used a very ingenious method. Secret messages were to be coded for transmission by: (a) representing each letter by a number; (b) changing the messages to strings of numbers; (c) grouping consecutive numbers in fours as $2 \times 2$ matrices and (d) applying an encoding $2 \times 2$ matrix to each matrix of the message to convert the original string of numbers into another string, thus completely hiding the original message. The messages were then despatched as strings of numbers which could not be decoded without applying the decoding matrix, the inverse of the encoding matrix. For many children the whole activity was at best fun, at worst different. The object of the whole exercise was, naturally, not to teach how to send coded messages, but was to persuade children to master an arbitrary rule. Ultimately, this rule would be needed in more mainstream curriculum mathematics, but pupils might not be so motivated to learn about matrix multiplication in contexts which did not readily enable them to see where the unusual procedures were leading. Having implanted this arbitrary and disconnected knowledge in the mind of the learner there was then an anchoring concept onto which to latch more important applications of matrix multiplication. In a sense, the use of matrices to send and decode messages was an advance organizer.

To Ausubel (1960), advance organizers were more general, more abstract, and more inclusive than the ideas and knowledge which were to follow. It is therefore doubtful whether sending coded messages would satisfy strict Ausubelian criteria for an advance organizer. The use of less rigorously-defined advance organizers is probably quite a common teaching technique, but finding advance organizers which satisfy the criteria of being more general, more abstract and more inclusive is not so easy. Scandura and Wells (1967, p. 295) translated the idea of an advance organizer into: '. . . a general, non-technical overview or outline in which the non-essentials of the to-be-learned material are ignored'. The idea of an advance organizer is certainly too useful to be rejected for technical reasons, so perhaps any idea which we can put into the minds of learners which will act as a bridge for subsequent, more detailed knowledge should be accepted. Novak (1977, p. 220) claimed that, '. . . research studies that focus on the use of various forms of advance organizers . . . are not profitable'. The hierarchical nature of mathematics would also appear to suggest that there should not be many occasions when new knowledge cannot be linked to existing knowledge, but the idea of the advance organizer is still valuable.

Concept maps were introduced in Chapter 2. The psychological justification for using them can now be seen in relation to meaningful learning and the relating of new knowledge to an existing knowledge structure. Ausubelian theory must be regarded as an original source for the idea of concept maps, though it has been Novak (1977 and 1980), Novak and Gowin (1984) and many others, who have advocated their use in recent years. Novak and Gowin (p. 15) state that a concept map is '. . . a schematic device for representing a set of concept meanings embedded in a framework of propositions [which] work to make clear to both students and teachers the . . . key ideas they must focus on for any specific learning task'; when the learning sequence is completed they '. . . provide a schematic summary of what has been learned'.

## Superordinate and subordinate learning

The organization of knowledge in the mind demands constant review and rearrangement. It involves the realization that a particular conceptual structure may be differentiated into concepts which might, in one sense, be considered *subordinate*. It involves the realization that certain ideas are all part of a more inclusive or *superordinate* concept structure. Skemp (1971) discussed the ideas of primary concepts which were derived from our sensory and motor experiences of the outside world, and secondary concepts which were abstracted from other concepts. He expressed the view that certain concepts were of a higher order than others, which implied they were abstracted from others. Ausubel (1968) wrote of *progressive differentiation* in learning, in which the most inclusive elements of a concept are introduced first and then the concept is dissected or progressively differentiated in terms of detail and specificity. He also wrote of superordinate learning, when previously learned concepts are seen to be elements of a larger, more inclusive, concept structure. The kind of reorganization of knowledge involved in learning mathematics is certainly likely to involve the two-way process of relating concepts both to subordinate and to superordinate concepts, as in the following examples.

Early learning experiences in mathematics are largely concerned with developing competence and understanding in numbers and the 'four rules', and considerable time is spent on addition, subtraction, multiplication and division. Over the years, these same operations are applied to fractions and to decimals and eventually their application to all real numbers should be mastered. Some students proceed to apply the same four operations to complex numbers, and a wider perception of, for example, multiplication is achieved. In some curricula, children study sets, and operations are introduced here, too, with union and intersection being the most likely, though not the only ones possible. Many pupils learn about vectors, and the operations of addition, subtraction, and scalar product (for some pupils), and perhaps eventually vector product, are introduced. Operations are applied to matrices, through addition, subtraction and multiplication. Some students learn propositional calculus and use operations such as conjunction and disjunction. Eventually, and perhaps at some stage within the learning sequence above, the concept of 'binary operation' might be introduced. The only sensible way to approach the idea of binary operation with pupils is to have many examples of such operations on which to define the more inclusive concept (cf. the idea of multiple embodiments from Dienes). In this sense, the idea of 'binary operation' might be considered to be superordinate to 'multiplication'. In just the same way the concept of 'commutativity' would make little sense without examples of commutative operations and non-commutative operations (defined on particular sets) on which to build the more abstract idea. Superordinate learning appears to be very much a part of learning mathematics.

In contrast, the important concept of 'symmetry' is usually studied rather differently. On the basis of a few examples like human and animal faces, butterflies, inkblots, mirror reflections, and the like, the idea of symmetry as a kind of repeated regularity is introduced. Having introduced what is, in essence, bilateral symmetry in two-dimensions, the possibility of other repeated regularities in familiar objects and in mathematical entities is investigated. In some shapes the regularity is seen to be a rotational one, which leads to a differentiation into bilateral and rotational symmetry. Rotational symmetry itself, when analysed, leads to the idea of order. Both bilateral and rotational symmetry involve the idea of axes of symmetry. Further differentiation between two-dimensional and three-dimensional objects introduces another idea, that of planes of symmetry. Having developed the idea of symmetry by progressively differentiating a general idea of regularity, the learner is then able to look at symmetry in mathematics, and perhaps even in the natural world and the man-made world, with much greater insight. The distinction is that with symmetry, the overall notion of regularity comes first, but with binary operation it comes last.

Ausubel expressed the view that concept development proceeds best when the most general, most inclusive elements of a concept are introduced first and then the concept is progressively differentiated. A much quoted example is that, to many young children, four-legged animals are all 'dogs', and it takes progressive differentiation to sort out which of these 'dogs' are cats, cows, horses, sheep, and so on. The same is variously true about fish, about ducks in the park duck-pond, and about cars. Yet, either there are exceptions, or learning works both ways, from the superordinate to the subordinate and vice versa. Children learn what are apples, what are oranges, what are bananas and only subsequently come to know them collectively as fruit. In mathematics, they learn about squares and rectangles (and perhaps parallelograms, kites and even rhombuses) before being able to fully comprehend quadrilaterals. It is, in essence, a matter of whether all four-sided shapes are seen by the child as squares, the idea then being progressively differentiated, or whether squares, rectangles and other particular four-sided shapes are seen to be different and quadrilaterals are then perceived as a superordinate idea.

In fact, learning mathematics must involve both progressive differentiation and superordinate learning working together; treating the two ideas separately is merely a convenience to enable analysis of their meaning. The various different number sets and the relationships between them have already been used as illustrations several times in this book. It could be legitimately considered that learning about numbers involves progressive differentiation, but, equally, it could be said that a variety of different kinds of numbers is introduced over a period of time until eventually the superordinate concept of real numbers is introduced. Although learning about quadrilaterals appears to be an illustration of superordinate learning, it is possible they could be studied the other way round, and the study of triangles certainly appears to take place by progressive differentiation. At a higher level, the factorization of quadratic expressions has usually been tackled systematically, by gradually introducing more and more complicated collections of coefficients, and this appears to be progressive differentiation. Readers will probably have their own views on illustrations of progressive differentiation and superordinate learning. Novak (1977) admitted that the determination of what in a body of knowledge are the most general, most inclusive concepts and what are subordinate concepts is not easy, so complete agreement about progressive differentiation and superordinate learning is unlikely. It is important, however, to consider relationships between concepts for: 'One reason school instruction has been so ineffective is that curriculum planners rarely sort out the concepts they hope to teach and even more rarely do they try to search for possible hierarchical relationships among these concepts' (Novak, 1977, p. 86). Clearly, concept maps could play a part in curriculum planning which attempted to analyse the relationships between concepts.

## Conflicts and failures in learning

There are times when conflict occurs in learning, and also when learning either does not take place or is quickly forgotten. All of these issues require consideration, and Ausubel has again provided us with a theoretical model. Conflict of meaning, termed *cognitive dissonance* by Ausubel, might occur for many reasons. It might arise when our use of the word 'vertical' in graph drawing suggests a meaning which is in conflict with the previously understood idea. It might arise when one teacher implies that a triangle is a polygon and the textbook claims it is not. It might arise when one mathematical text provides a definition of natural numbers which includes zero and another book excludes zero. It might arise when the mathematical definition of gradient is seen to be different from the meaning of the concept in the real world. There are many ways in which cognitive dissonance can occur. Essentially, this is a problem of accommodation, though rather different from most accommodation problems. Conflicting ideas create disequilibrium and somehow they must be reconciled, and this is achieved by the process of *integrative reconciliation*. Without integrative reconciliation it is possible that learners might compartmentalize the conflicting ideas thus, for example, accepting that force and acceleration are in proportion in mathematics lessons but acting as if they think otherwise outside the school. In the case of gradient it is necessary to compartmentalize, with the attendant danger of legitimizing the holding of two different definitions for the same entity. It is not easy to prescribe for integrative reconciliation, but cognitive dissonance is a common feature of school learning. It is especially difficult to achieve reconciliation when the cause of the conflict crosses subject boundaries, as in the case of there being one definition for histogram in mathematics with perhaps a rather different one in biology.

Reasons why learning does not take place include the non-cognitive, such as not paying attention at the critical time, and the cognitive, like not being ready in the sense of having adequate subsumers. The issue of forgetting is equally complex. In the first place there appear to be degrees of forgetting, for it is possible to forget but then recall everything when appropriate cues are presented, and it also seems to be possible to forget irretrievably. Novak (1977) claimed that most information we learn cannot be recalled at some time in the future, thus suggesting that forgetting is the norm and that it is remembering that requires explanation. Ausubel's theory explained variation in rates of forgetting in terms of the degree of meaningfulness of the learned material. In the case of material learned by rote, the expectation would be that it would be forgotten, probably sooner rather than later, because such knowledge must be stored in a part of the knowledge base which is unconnected to major integrated knowledge structures. The learning of the vocabulary of a foreign language is almost inevitably at least partly by rote, but words are remembered better under certain conditions such as regular use in sentences (which introduces a degree of meaningfulness). Ausubel described 'overlearning', meaning repetition, revision, and perhaps some extension, and in this way rote-learned material might be retained for considerably longer than without overlearning. When knowledge has been acquired meaningfully the expectation would be that retention would be for very much longer. Forgetting can, however, still occur because of *obliterative subsumption*.

When a new idea is introduced and becomes connected to relevant subsumers accommodation might lead to changes in the way both the new idea and the subsumers are understood. This is how we learn – by assimilating and accommodating at the same time. Subsequent new knowledge might then also produce change, both in the previous new knowledge and in the subsumers. This process continues throughout life so that, with successive modification and amendment, a body of knowledge or a conceptual structure might become so modified that it cannot be brought back to mind in its original form – the earlier notions have been obliterated through subsumption. This is a very neat theory which it is difficult to confirm or deny, after all, its verification requires examples of knowledge which have been forgotten! It is certainly possible that we have learned techniques and methods of solution which were valuable when introduced but which have been forgotten because subsequent techniques have, in subsuming them, effectively obliterated earlier ones. Most pupils who learn about quadratic factorization are provided with tips, rules, or processes to help with the difficult early stages. Eventually, the elementary techniques fall into disuse and can easily be forgotten altogether once greater experience and expertise creates a state in which factorization is no longer found to be difficult. For example, one factorization technique applied to $10x^2 + 23x + 12$ is as follows:

We require two numbers A and B with product equal to $10 \times 12$ and sum equal to 23, that is,

$$A \times B = 120 \quad \text{and} \quad A + B = 23$$

The two numbers, found by a mixture of trialling and insight, are 15 and 8, so:

$$10x^2 + 23x + 12$$
$$= 10x^2 + 15x + 8x + 12$$
$$= 5x(2x + 3) + 4(2x + 3)$$
$$= (5x + 4)(2x + 3)$$

Eventually, however, it becomes possible for many pupils to short-cut this procedure and factorize very quickly by inspection, so the above method falls into disuse and may ultimately be forgotten. This illustration may not be ideal as an example of obliterative subsumption but it does show how knowledge which is temporarily valuable may subsequently fade into oblivion without the learner becoming deprived.

The phenomenon of obliterative subsumption appears to suggest that meaningfully-learned material often cannot be recalled in the exact form in which it was originally stored, whereas rote-learned material can only be recalled precisely as the original form, since it cannot be subjected to obliterative subsumption. If that is true it indicates one advantage of rote-learned material, but all other advantages appear to be in favour of meaningful learning. Knowledge which is acquired in a meaningful way is retained longer than if acquired by rote and it contributes to the growth and development of more subsumers and therefore facilitates further meaningful learning. However, teaching experience suggests that rote-learned material is *not* always recalled, by children, in the form in which it was learned, but this can then be explained by forgetting (Novak, 1977).

The learning theory proposed by Ausubel (1968) must be seen as extremely comprehensive, and space has allowed the consideration of only a selection of the issues. For the most part, mathematics educators have not paid much attention to Ausubelian theory, so the relationship to learning mathematics has not been sufficiently widely applied and debated, and few authors have provided a variety of mathematical examples in connection with the theory. But contemporary views on learning frequently draw from the work of Ausubel, as well as from Piaget and Bruner, so it is helpful to know something of the views of all three if one is to be able to place current views in context. Science educators have paid rather more attention to Ausubel, but frequently their interpretations have filtered through to the classroom level only in terms of practical suggestions like the commendation of the use of concept maps (sometimes given other names). The very comprehensiveness of the theory of meaningful learning proposed by Ausubel suggests that it is a useful model with which any future learning theory might be compared in order to help assess its value. There have, of course, been critics of Ausubelian theory, for example, some mathematics educators would react strongly against any suggestion that verbal or expository learning is as effective and as efficient as Ausubel claimed. This is difficult to determine anyway, because the key to the theory is that one must first ascertain what the learner already knows and then apply not only appropriate, but good quality, expository teaching. At the risk of being repetitive, it is not only difficult to ascertain in real detail what a learner already knows, it is also difficult to define what we mean by consistently good expository teaching, and therefore to apply it. It is certainly the case that the strongest supporters of Ausubelian theory have always accused critics of not studying the theory in sufficient detail.

# A brief note on information processing

It seems that any study which attempts to investigate and understand how information is processed in the mind can claim to be a part of that approach to the study of learning commonly known as information processing. The wide variety of studies which have been carried out, however, makes it impossible to define simply a theory of information processing. Cobb (1987) has claimed that information-processing psychology developed as an alternative to behaviourism, by attempting to study what happens between stimulus and response, but his own paper is principally concerned with considering information processing from a constructivist perspective (see Chapter 11). As for links with Piaget, Sternberg (1989, p. 454) declared:

> That Piagetian theory is compatible with information-processing theory is shown by the fact that Rumelhart and Norman . . . have proposed two modes of knowledge acquisition in information-processing language that correspond almost exactly to assimilation and accommodation [called 'accretion' and 'restructuring'].

The work of Newell and Simon (1972) is often cited as being seminal in information-processing approaches to learning theory, and some of this has already been considered in Chapter 5. Other significant research is documented in Stewart and Atkin (1982) and Stewart (1985). Krutetskii (1976) included a discussion of the characteristics of information processing during problem-solving. Lindsay and Norman (1977) have considered how knowledge is commited to long-term memory. More recently, many studies have been carried out into the methods which pupils use in solving elementary problems using the basic operations of addition, subtraction, multiplication and division, and in the errors which are made. Other work has focused on elementary algebra. A physiological equivalent to the psychological study of information processing is described in Esler (1982).

An important feature of much information-processing research has been the comparison of the performances of experts and novices. One major weakness of such research lies in how to define an 'expert' and a 'novice', and many different definitions have been used by different researchers. A further weakness results from the range of the chosen expert–novice spectrum. The more the researcher departs from the extremes of the expert–novice scale, the harder it is to distinguish their respective mental processes. The closer to the ends of the expert–novice spectrum the two groups are, the less is the information gained, for easy tasks do not result in any information about experts, and difficult tasks do not provide knowledge relating to novices. Furthermore, because the information-processing paradigm deals with performance at a microscopic level, it has been suggested that it is impossible for it to provide information which is valuable in the macroscopic level of teaching an instructional programme.

That part of computer-assisted learning which has become known as artificial intelligence has become very much associated with the information-processing approach but it has many critics as well as advocates. One impact of the electronic computer on education is that contemporary theorists of human learning have frequently considered the computer as a model of the human mind. Memory is seen to be the key to learning, for the objective is storage within, and ready recall from, long-term memory.

Thus the computer components of input, control, processing, store and output is seen as a simple interpretation of long-term memory The analogy with the computer has been taken further, in suggesting that the human mind has a built-in ready-for-action ROM (read only memory) from the moment of birth.

There have been many criticisms of information processing, however, for example, this from Vergnaud (1990, p. 22):

> information-processing models . . . do not provide any theory of what a concept is, and especially of its operational character, . . . [do] not offer any plausible theory of the part that language and symbols play in thinking . . . [and do] not offer any plausible view of the long-term development of students' competencies and conceptions.

## Suggestions for further reading

Dienes, Z. P. (1960) *Building Up Mathematics*. London: Hutchinson Educational.

Fuys, D., Geddes, D. and Tischler, R. (1988) *The Van Hiele Model of Thinking in Geometry among Adolescents*. Reston, VA: National Council of Teachers of Mathematics.

Lindsay, P. H. and Norman, D. A. (1977) *Human Information Processing* (Chapters 8–10). New York: Academic Press.

Novak, J. D. (1977) *A Theory of Education*. Ithaca, NY: Cornell University Press.

## Questions for discussion

1. How valuable is Ausubel's theory in preparation and planning, both macroscopically and microscopically, for teaching mathematics?
2. To what extent must the logical structure of mathematics be subordinated to psychological issues in any theory of learning mathematics?
3. Is there any place for behaviourist as well as cognitive views within a theory of mathematics learning?
4. How would an acceptable theory of mathematics-learning influence your teaching?

Chapter 11

# Can Pupils Construct Mathematical Knowledge for Themselves?

## Constructivism

Hughes (1986) has provided evidence that pre-school children are able to invent their own symbols and symbol systems to represent quantities. His research did incorporate a modicum of interaction with teachers, but the evidence of the ability of children to invent appropriate notation is convincing, and Hughes is also able to claim that the children even invented a suitable symbol for zero. Yet the same children experienced great difficulty in coming to terms with conventional symbolism. Hughes also drew attention to the similarities between many of the children's own invented systems and number systems used by earlier cultures. Formal arithmetic presents children with symbol systems and methods of manipulation which are the products of hundreds of years of development and refinement. How is it that children can devise their own symbols but find difficulty in coming to terms with the systems and methods which teachers try to impose?

Askew and Wiliam (1995, p. 6) have reported evidence that, before beginning formal schooling, 'many young children can count meaningfully, use terms like "more" and "less" appropriately, have some understanding of addition and subtraction with small numbers, [and] invent strategies for solving problems'. Unfortunately, this so-called informal knowledge is often ignored by teachers when the children start school. Carpenter and Moser (1982) and MacNamara (1990) have suggested that strategies for operating with numbers introduced by teachers may run counter to the knowledge brought to school by the children, and this may cause regrettable and unnecessary disequilibrium. Children generally base their informal arithmetic on counting strategies, but school mathematics programmes are based on combining and separating sets. MacNamara has also claimed that the ability of young children to 'subitize' is often completely ignored by teachers. Subitizing is the ability to recognize how many objects there are in a group without counting them, and it seems that most children commencing school have this capability for groups of up to five. At school, the children would very likely be taught techniques which do not acknowledge subitizing, and which therefore run counter to their natural inclinations.

We have already seen in Chapter 6 that children in the middle primary years often spontaneously begin to derive new addition facts from known facts, particularly from ties and from bridging 10, for example, in $8 + 6 = (8 + 2) + (6 - 2)$. Later, when faced with a multiplication task like $23 \times 7$, many children will decline to use the taught algorithm and will construct their own methods. Some of the weaker pupils, even in the later secondary years, will add 23 seven times. Others, still dependent on addition but with slightly more confidence might use an alternative addition method, such as $46 + 46 + 46 + 23$, or $46 + 46 + 69$, or $69 + 69 + 23$. The really knowledgeable pupils might use $20 \times 7 + 3 \times 7$, or $23 \times 10 - 23 \times 3$, or $13 \times 7 + 10 \times 7$, or even $12 \times 7 + 11 \times 7$ or $42 + 42 + 77$. Children could use a very wide variety of alternative procedures which have not been specifically taught, all of which should produce the correct answer. Indeed, children should be encouraged to be creative in this way, but the point here is that many pupils become capable of exercising a certain amount of creativity in constructing their own methods. Resnick and Ford (1984) have also reported convincing evidence of the ability of some children to invent their own more efficient methods of solving simple addition and subtraction tasks, methods which seemingly could not be taught:

> [So] why not teach the more efficient routines directly? Why rely on children's inventions? In the present cases, the answer lies in the sheer difficulty of explaining the efficient routines to children. Groen and Resnick tried this informally; they found themselves bogged down in awkward, incomprehensible explanations and found the children bored or frustrated. (pp. 81–3)

Nunes *et al.* (1993) have shown that Brazilian children with little or no formal education can, on their own or as a community of street vendors, invent their own methods of carrying out calculations in order to earn a living in the 'informal sector' of the economy (see Chapter 7). These mainly mental calculations make sense to the child, being based on real transactions in which goods or services are sold for cash. The evidence appears to indicate that problems which make sense in this way are more easily solved than the de-contextualized ones of formal arithmetic. Schliemann (1984) has also compared the problem-solving capabilities of professional carpenters and their apprentices. These unschooled professionals sought realistic solutions to real problems and were comparatively successful. On the other hand, schooled apprentices were inclined to treat the problems as school assignments and were often wrong; what is more they were unable to appreciate when they had produced an absurd answer.

These examples expose the dilemma that children often seem capable of constructing at least some mathematical knowledge for themselves when school-taught knowledge might be misunderstood, misapplied and even rejected. A considerable amount, some might say the majority, of the teaching that takes place in mathematics lessons seems to be based on the view that it is easy to transmit knowledge from teacher to learner, and that what is received is an exact copy of what was transmitted. Yet we know that this is not the case. A major reason why children fail to achieve lasting learning is that the transmitted knowledge was never comprehensively grasped in the first place. Transmission learning often only achieves limited success, and the severity of the limitations may not be discovered until much later, or indeed may never be discovered. Each individual child is likely only to internalize a unique subset, and possibly quite a small subset, of what was transmitted. An important alternative view that, if placed in a suitable environment, children can discover mathematics for themselves has been considered in Chapter 5. Guided discovery, in particular, has many advocates but this involves teacher input, it being in a way merely a combination of discovery and transmission. The issue here is that we cannot ignore one of the fundamental assumptions of cognitive learning psychology which is that new knowledge is in large part constructed by the learner (Resnick and Ford, 1984). This assumption is the fundamental basis of what has become known as constructivism.

The view that knowledge must be constructed, or reconstructed, by each and every learner has attracted a great deal of interest in recent years. Lochhead (1985, p. 4) outlined the basis of constructivism as follows:

> What I see as critical ... is the recognition that knowledge is not an entity which can simply be transferred from those who have to those who don't ... Knowledge is something which each individual learner must construct for and by himself. This view of knowledge as an individual construction ... is usually referred to as constructivism.

This is reiterated in the claim by von Glasersfeld (1987, p. 16) that, 'knowledge is not a transferable commodity and communication not a conveyance'. In fact, not only does constructivism attempt to explain the process of learning, it has implications for motivation too, according to von Glasersfeld (pp. 16–17):

> if students are to taste something of the mathematician's satisfaction in doing mathematics, they cannot be expected to find it in whatever rewards they might be given for their performance but only through becoming aware of the neatness of fit they have achieved in their own conceptual construction.

Clearly, the origins of constructivism would be difficult to trace, since the so-called Socratic method seems to have been based on the notions that questions should be countered with questions, and that the students themselves should ultimately provide their own answers. In fact, around fifty years ago, Dienes (1960) revealed his own brand of constructivism in his constructivity principle. He suggested that mathematical learning is pre-eminently one of construction – followed only afterwards by a critical examination of what has been constructed. He also speculated that exceptions to the otherwise gloomy picture regarding the learning of mathematics seem to occur when self-motivating learning situations are created, where the information reaches the child in such a way that he can formulate it in his own language. It is Piaget, however, who must be regarded as the most significant mid-twentieth century contributor to the early development of contemporary constructivist views (see Chapter 4). Kamii, in the titles of two books (1985, 1989), has described her work with children inventing or reinventing arithmetic as 'implications of Piaget's theory'. Thus constructivism seems to be a simple but profound expression of contemporary cognitive views of learning, having evolved naturally from earlier attempts to explain learning.

Constructivism is therefore based on the view that, in the last resort, we all have to make sense of the world ourselves; we develop our understandings throughout life continuously, and through our own efforts and insights. Such a straightforward claim may appear to some readers to be a truism, but the claim conceals contentious and potentially difficult issues such as which version of constructivism is the truest (for there are alternatives), what are the implications of a belief in constructivism for classroom practice, and what are the major difficulties when teachers attempt to use methods which they believe are the best for enabling the construction of meaning. It is particularly important to scotch, at this point, any attempt to equate constructivism with 'free-for-all activity', 'child-centred education', 'progressive education' and even 'discovery learning'. In any case, many of these terms, in addition to being used frequently in recent years in pejorative ways, themselves mean different things to different people. The following statement about constructivism from Cobb *et al.* (1991, p. 165) is quite categorical: 'constructivist teaching does not mean that "anything goes" or that the teacher gives up her authority and abrogates her wider societal obligations'. At a time when educational methods are under scrutiny from wider society and require careful justification, it is important to define precisely what is meant and what is not meant by constructivism. And if there are different versions of constructivism we need to understand them all.

## Versions of constructivism

Lerman (1989, p. 211) described constructivism in the following hypotheses:

1. Knowledge is actively constructed by the learner, not passively received from the environment.
2. Coming to know is an adaptive process that organizes one's experiential world; it does not discover an independent, pre-existing world outside the mind of the knower.

The first hypothesis is essentially another summary of our earlier discussion, but the second is much more radical. Those who accept only the first hypothesis are sometimes known as 'weak constructivists', but those who accept both are 'radical constructivists'. According to Lochhead (1991), constructivism is a statement about the nature of knowledge and its functional value to us. For the most radical constructivist there is no possibility of any certain knowledge about the world. The most radical form of constructivism would, in fact, claim that 'we can never have access to a world of reality, only to what we ourselves construct from experience; all knowledge is . . . necessarily constructed' (Goldin, 1989, p. 17). Therefore it could be claimed that it is impossible to ensure that any two learners have acquired the same knowledge, because each learner has constructed a unique model.

The concept of 'understanding' thus once again emerges as problematic. In the words of Lerman (1989, p. 220):

> if all understandings are private and individual constructions, no student behaviour will allow me to do anything other than make my own private construction about what the student 'understands' of my 'understanding' of the concept or idea in question.

In other words, there is a problem if we try to tie the notion of 'understanding' to the idea of certain and absolute mathematical concepts, for none of us can be sure what the absolutes are, if they exist, never mind whether our understanding incorporates any of the proposed absolutes. There is not only a problem in knowing whether the understanding achieved by another is the same as ours, there is also the problem as to whether it is the same as anything which could be considered objective. Indeed, in relation to the use of language as the only way we have of comparing our notions, we might therefore also be led to wonder whether it is ever possible to grasp what anyone else is saying! This radical view of knowledge is naturally in opposition to more objectivist views which do support the notion of the existence of agreed objective knowledge. It is also relevant here to introduce the concept of a 'consensual domain', which von Glasersfeld (1991, pp. xv–xvi) explains in this way:

> If . . . people . . . look through distorting lenses and agree on what they see, this does not make what they see any more *real* – it merely means that on the basis of such agreements they can build up a consensus in certain areas of their subjective experiential worlds . . . one of the oldest [such areas] is the consensual domain of numbers.

The distinction between weak constructivism and radical constructivism is a vital one, but there is at least one other important interpretation of constructivism, namely social constructivism or socio-constructivism. Here, an important feature is the role of social interaction and communication in assisting individuals to construct their own understanding. Cockcroft (1982) drew attention to the desirability of discussion between teacher and pupils and between pupils themselves without saying a great deal about the purposes of such discussion in relation to how it helps learning, particularly between pupils. The Department of Education and Science (1985) claimed that the quality of pupils' mathematical thinking as well as their ability to express themselves are considerably enhanced by discussion. Discussion has already been considered within the context of the issue of language and mathematics (Chapter 9). Cobb *et al.* (1991, pp. 173–4) wrote, 'social interactions between partners influence their mathematical activity and give rise to learning opportunities'. These are standard claims about the value of discussion, but the claims of socio-constructivism are that meaning, or understanding, is being actively *negotiated* through such discussion. In terms of radical views, if there is no absolute knowledge, only our own interpretation of the world, discussion at least allows the possibility of some mutual agreement within a group, the development of a consensual domain. Indeed, Solomon (1989) described it as encouraging the development of an essentially social being for whom knowing number involves entering into the social practices of its use. For Balacheff (1991, p. 89):

> Students have to learn mathematics as social knowledge; they are not free to choose the meanings they construct. These meanings must not only be efficient in solving problems, but they must also be coherent with those socially recognized. This condition is necessary for the future participation of students as adults in social activities.

In the value it places on social interaction and the negotiation of meaning, the socio-constructivist perspective thus perhaps owes more to the work of Vygotsky than to Piaget's view of the solitary knower who must construct meaning alone. The role of the teacher within a socio-constructivist approach is a sensitive one. According to Lochhead (1991, p. 82):

The primary goal ... is to help students develop skills of constructing, evaluating and modifying concepts ... The teacher's role therefore is to work to improve the quality of the discussions rather than to focus from the beginning on the 'correct' ... answer.

The evidence available suggests that many of us have great difficulty in not focusing on the correct answer when 'guiding' discussion; indeed, we often have great difficulty in holding back from direct interference and telling. Basically, we wish pupils to construct what we think they should construct, because we have a prescribed curriculum to teach!

Yet another alternative contemporary version of constructivism, which also depends on interaction and debate within groups, is the sociocultural view. Sociocultural theories are related to the transmission of meaning from one generation to the next as part of the process of acculturation. The view expressed by Solomon (1989) and quoted above might appear to be more sociocultural than socio-constructivist. The same conclusion might even be drawn from the statement by Balacheff (1991), though it was written in relation to constructivism. There is undoubtedly some common ground between socio-constructivism and sociocultural views in that both accept the importance of collective activities in which agreement comes about through discussion, but the literature suggests there could also be important differences in relation to the negotiation of meaning.

As a postscript to this consideration of different forms of constructivism Johnson-Laird (1983, p. 156), in his discussion of mental models, states:

Human beings ... do not apprehend the world directly; they possess only internal representation of it, because perception is the construction of a model of the world. They are unable to compare this perceptual representation directly with the world — it is their world.

The suggestion is that we all form mental models of the environment and new experiences are then subsequently interpreted in relation to the models we have constructed. Newell and Simon (1972), writing about problem-solving, claimed that the solver first constructs a representation of the 'problem space' and this then governs the way the encoding of information is carried out. So how we set about solving problems is less likely to involve logical thinking and is more likely to be based on our model of the situation, and this in itself is context dependent. What happens after that may well be a form of hypothesis testing. The last word on versions of constructivism should be given to von Glasersfeld (1987, pp. 15–16):

teachers tend to assume that there exists in every particular case an objective problem and an objectively 'true' solution ... students of any age are therefore expected somehow to come to 'see' the problem, its solution, and the *necessity* that links the two. But ... logical or mathematical necessity does not reside in any independent world — to see it and gain satisfaction from it, one must reflect on one's own constructs and the way in which one has put them together.

## Some constructivist teaching experiments

Constance Kamii has supervised an interesting programme of innovative classroom activities with young children. For her, the beginnings of arithmetic lie in learning about numbers and number combinations through playing dice games, leading to the memorization of number combinations without any direct teaching or reinforcement. This may be regarded as a form of rote learning, but here the method works well, the use of games providing essential motivation. Subsequently, numerical questions posed by the teacher form the focus for class discussion of answers suggested by individual children, usually privately to the teacher, but sometimes openly to the whole class. Thus the teacher remains very firmly in control and, as opposed to many group methods, the questions and suggested answers are presented on the chalkboard to the whole class. Drill and worksheets do not play any part at this stage, and pencil and paper are not available, so the emphasis is on 'mental' rather than on 'mechanical' or written arithmetic. Number tasks are not invented by the children but are part of a carefully devised sequence of the teacher's making which is intended to provide for and enable progression in capability and knowledge. The teacher plays a critical role. When errors are committed, it is said, these arise because the children are thinking and not because they are careless. Thus the task of the teacher is not to correct from the outside, but to create a situation in which the children will inevitably correct themselves. Kamii claims that children construct knowledge more solidly when they are encouraged to defend their ideas within a group or even a whole class. When answers are offered by individual pupils, others declare whether they agree or disagree. Lack of unanimous agreement among children about a particular answer leads to other suggested answers. When there is consensus, a pupil who provided the accepted answer is encouraged to explain how the answer was obtained. This is a very revealing aspect of the method, for there is normally variety in how the children have constructed their solutions, so children have the opportunity to reflect on alternative approaches. For example, the task:

$$27$$
$$-18$$

might lead to some children thinking of it in terms of $28 - 18 - 1$, others as $27 - 17 - 1$, others as $20 - 10 + 7 - 8$, others as $20 - 10 - (8 - 7)$, and so on. In terms of generalities, allowing children to construct reveals that most children deal with the tens before the units, this perhaps going some way to explaining why attempts to teach the algorithm can be difficult, because it runs counter to what at this stage seems to be a natural tendency. It also confirms that some number combinations are remembered more easily than others, for example doubles like $6 + 6$ are remembered more easily than $5 + 6$, which explains why, when dealing with $26 + 7$ many children will deal with the units as $(6 + 6) + 1$ (see Chapter 6). At a much later stage, Kamii has also produced evidence which shows quite young children not only constructing methods of multiplying two two-digit numbers, but eventually arriving at a form of the usual multiplication algorithm on their own. The sceptic might want to suggest that particularly sensitive or introvert children would find such teaching approaches disagreeable. Nevertheless, this deliberate application of what seems to qualify as a socio-constructivist approach to teaching needs to be taken seriously.

Another interesting set of experiments which appear to have at least some similarities to the work of Kamii has been reported by Bell *et al.* (1989). The experiments were based on identifying and then eliminating particular misconceptions using a diagnosis–conflict–discussion procedure. The method demands good diagnostic test questions which it is known will reveal difficulties and misunderstandings, such as many of the tasks used by the CSMS project (see Hart, 1981). According to Bell, subsequent direct instruction focused on such known misconceptions has been shown to be comparatively unsuccessful, in the respect that there was very little transfer to points not so strongly focused upon. Conflict-discussion teaching has proved much more successful. The procedure is that a lesson in which pupils might record their own responses to diagnostic questions is followed by discussion in small groups. Finally, group conclusions are placed before the whole class for further discussion and amendment, as thought necessary. The assumption is that the small group work helps to ensure that pupils' wrong ideas are actually brought out and expressed, and that these can be subjected to challenge and criticism in an unthreatening situation. The small group work is also more likely to expose the extent of any misconceptions from a wider range of pupils, because pupils are more prepared to talk and are more prepared to be put under pressure to talk in a small group. Clearly, the intended unthreatening nature of the situations might be difficult to achieve for all individual pupils, and indeed in certain cultural environments. Although Bell does not claim that the method is based on constructivist principles, and in fact claims no support from any particular theory or epistemology, the constructivist underpinning of this technique is captured in the statement 'the aim is that pupils should reach well-founded convictions based on their own perceptions, not take over superficially-understood ideas from the teacher'. Cognitive conflict has, in fact, been claimed by Underhill (1991) to be one of the two major mechanisms which motivate learning and induce reflective activity, which itself stimulates the cognitive restructuring required within the process of constructing knowledge and understanding. Early reports of the success of this technique are very encouraging. A very significant common feature between the methods described by both Kamii and Bell seems to be the emphasis on social interaction through discussion, debate and even argument. There is clearly a connection between the use of cognitive conflict here and the idea of cognitive dissonance from Ausubel.

A further experiment of great interest has been the Calculator Aware Number (CAN) Project, directed by Hilary Shuard. This project was really set up as a part of the PrIME Project, which operated with the wider brief of providing a much more exploratory and investigative approach to mathematics in the primary school. The basic intention of the CAN Project was to teach mathematics with a calculator always available, and not to deprive children of what is a very powerful, useful and ubiquitous aid to calculation. In the English context this was a radical move and, quite naturally, advocates of proficiency in pencil-and-paper mathematics (many of whom are not teachers) have viewed what they would regard as a revolutionary development with suspicion. It is curious that there should be this lingering firm belief in the value of pencil-and-paper methods when there has not been the same emphasis on them in many other countries. Not all developing countries have the resources to provide regular pencil-and-paper facilities, and yet others have depended on regular use of primitive technology like the abacus. The calculator can, of course, be used in an exploratory and investigative way, so CAN pupils could use their calculator in constructing their own understanding. If calculators are not built into the mathematics curriculum the chances are that the pupils will still use them at home, and will learn ahead of the teacher, and will also come to regard school mathematics as antiquated. The progress made by children taught within this scheme has been described by Shuard *et al.* (1991, pp. 56–7):

> Not only had the children become more enthusiastic, but their work also showed much greater mathematical understanding . . . the children were willing to 'have a go' at any problem and persist with it far beyond the teacher's normal expectations . . . [they] developed a wide variety of methods of non-calculator calculation [which] often made an intuitive use of basic mathematical principles.

Elsewhere, through newsletters, the CAN project drew attention to the new confidence of the children, to the fact that routine algorithms were not taught at all, and that the children had learned that in mathematics one learned to think things out for oneself.

Several criticisms might come to the sceptic at this point. The first is the usual one that such methods as described in these three examples are all very well, but they take too much time, and there is a syllabus to get through. It does take considerable time when children are allowed to think things out and debate among themselves, and the only possible rejoinder is to suggest that time might be saved in the long run. So much time in mathematics lessons is currently spent on re-teaching and providing routine practice of ideas which do not seem to have been mastered however many times they are re-taught in the 'traditional' manner. If the extra time leads to genuine progression and mastery of mathematics, if ideas are understood more firmly and lastingly by encouraging the construction of knowledge by the pupils themselves, this is a more worthwhile gain than the teacher 'covering' a syllabus more quickly.

The second potential criticism relates to the unfortunate outcomes which might result from pressure being placed on pupils to conform to a particular view. The non-threatening climate of a small group discussion situation is frequently emphasized in descriptions of socio-constructivist practice. However, it is possible that meaning is only negotiated to the extent that some pupils finally have to accept a majority view without understanding the reasons. For the sake of survival alongside peers, pupils might say they accept the group view, but at the same time their confidence might have been undermined if they believe they are the only member of the class who still does not understand. They may consequently become further convinced that they are weak at mathematics, and their attitude might deteriorate even more. Such a situation is hardly non-threatening, for silent but no less worrying threats are likely to be experienced within the minds of such pupils. Teachers might need to guard against survival acceptance of class views by very careful monitoring of individuals.

A third criticism of all experimental teaching situations is that they are invariably better resourced than in an ordinary classroom in an ordinary school. The implication is that whatever is being tested would not work without the extra provision. Ongoing research projects often do have more equipment and might sometimes have more than one teacher in the room. But those who teach in developing countries look askance at the resources of 'ordinary' classrooms in the Western world in any case, never mind special projects, so it is an issue of relativity. In other words, there are really no such things as ordinary classrooms and ordinary schools, for they are all different.

Nevertheless, the underlying issue is an important one. It is possible that there are limits to what can be attempted according to class size, general resource provision and the quality and experience of the teachers.

The three major 'projects' described above are certainly revealing, but teachers are not always convinced by results from teaching situations which may be regarded as different from their own. And yet, even prior to the development and clear exposition of constructivism as a concept in the final decades of the twentieth century, mathematics teaching, in many countries, had begun to change. The shift in teaching methods in some countries and by some teachers has normally been to move away from a reliance only on the 'traditional' transmission mode. Investigational methods, problem-solving and extended projects are now clearly built into the curriculum in some countries. There may be reasons for these developments in the minds of curriculum planners which have nothing to do with constructivism, but constructivism could provide a clearer rationale for such methods, and also provide teachers with clearer guidelines as to procedures to adopt when practising the methods. If the major intention becomes that of providing pupils with opportunities to construct their own understanding of mathematics, and if this is to be carried out at least partly on a social rather than an entirely individual basis, then teaching needs to be structured in such ways as to attain these ends optimally. Lochhead (1991, p. 75) has admitted that: 'To date constructivist thinking has been more effective in describing what sorts of teaching will not work than in specifying what will'. Unfortunately, it is true that constructivism does not directly dictate to us what teaching methods to use, so it is appropriate to look in rather more detail at which of the methods in widespread use in mathematics classrooms are legitimate to a contemporary constructivist. We must note, however, that there are various interpretations of constructivism and it does not appear to be clear how classroom practice might be guided by any particular version.

## Constructivism in our classrooms

First, we must clarify that the evolution of constructivism does not imply a rejection of earlier attempts to facilitate more effective learning within a cognitive learning environment. It is a misunderstanding of constructivism to suggest that there is little the teacher can do to facilitate learning simply because the construction must be carried out by the learner. The American literature contains many references to 'inquiry' learning, as being best for the construction of understanding, but the teacher still has to organize it. The literature also regularly dismisses transmission as being inappropriate to a constructivist approach to teaching. Instead, the emphasis is placed on situations where pupils explore and discuss in an active and creative way. According to Cobb *et al.* (1991, p. 158) 'at a risk of over-simplification, an immediate implication is that mathematics ... should be taught through problem-solving'. Constructivism most of all appears to suggest that the teacher needs to provide the 'scaffolding' which allows the child to progress, and it requires great skill to provide the best scaffolding for each pupil. A consistent policy of complete non-intervention by the teacher is therefore certainly not likely to be the best way to promote the construction of knowledge. However, a policy of non-intervention with a certain child at a particular point in time or with a particular group might be appropriate, especially when the responsibility for learning has been fully accepted by the child or group, as might occur in the ideal 'open learning' or 'supported self-study' scheme. Whether learning is basically active or passive is not really the critical issue. What matters is whether the approach used has enabled the construction of meaning. In particular:

> it makes no sense to assume that any powerful cognitive satisfaction springs from . . . being told that one has done something right . . . the 'rightness' must be seen to fit with an order one has established *oneself* . . . the teacher's role [is not] to dispense 'truth' but rather to help and guide the student in the conceptual organization of certain areas of experience. (von Glasersfeld, 1987, pp. 15–16)

As a generalization, active methods do seem to be preferable for many younger children and for much of the time, but we certainly need much more knowledge about what methods best promote construction. Such knowledge, of course, may well be both topic-specific and child-specific! It must also be acknowledged that any interpretation of constructivism is itself a construction of the interpreter.

Activity is clearly important to many constructivists, but what is meant by mathematical activity and how is it to be encouraged? Richards (1991) has claimed that students will not become active learners by accident, but by design – in other words it is up to us, the teachers, to arrange the environment. It might well be true that pupils frequently seem to appreciate a classroom buzzing with activity and in which they are engaged in practical tasks. It might well seem to us that learning through physical activity with concrete objects is often a good way of trying to promote the learning of particular ideas. However, what is most important is creative mental activity, and if there is no reflection and no thinking the practical activity might be a waste of time. This is a misunderstanding which it is easy to hold, for example, about the use of apparatus (see Chapter 5). On the other hand, we must accept that our minds can be very active even when listening to a teacher or when reading a book, or in other occupations which at first sight might appear passive. In other words, any interpretation of constructivism as activity-based learning is too simplistic because, for many people, this would certainly carry a notion of physical manipulation or movement. Also, for a constructivist, interaction might be considered an important component of whatever is thought of as action. The optimum balances between concrete manipulation and mental activity, and between individual study and cooperative discussion and debate within the mathematics curriculum are likely to vary according to age and capability of pupil, to nature and type of content, and to the resources available anyway.

Many examples of pupils learning through the use of apparatus come from the approaches to number work in the early primary years. It is therefore very satisfying when examples which fit with notions of constructivism can be found from the teaching of older students. Williams (1985) found that the use of apparatus in learning mechanics helped a great deal. It should perhaps be clarified that there is a difference between structural apparatus which sets out to provide concrete support for the extraction of ideas which are modelled by the structure and other apparatus which contains no such exact match with ideas. The mechanics apparatus used by Williams was not 'structural' but it did provide practical experience. It mostly helped the students because it revealed data which challenged preconceptions about motion in dynamics, it revealed beliefs which were not borne out when the apparatus was used (and which were also, of course, contrary to those which the teacher hoped to promote). It therefore fostered discussion, further controlled experiment and the exchange of opinions which ultimately led to change of belief. The whole process from the revelation of alternative conceptions to the coming to an agreed view had to run its course, and this took time.

Often, the use of apparatus is curtailed by the teacher when it is judged either that enough time has been spent or that the majority of pupils ought by now to have learned the knowledge or skill in question. Of course, it is always difficult for a teacher to know when there is no longer any need to provide apparatus, but some pupils might be deprived of learning opportunities too soon. From a constructivist perspective this is very regrettable. And then there is a danger that the use of particular apparatus leads to worksheets too soon, so becoming almost behaviouristic in its implementation. Often the use of apparatus does not demand that pupils think, discuss, argue and conclude. The success in the mechanics context was not solely due to the apparatus; it was due to allowing students the time as well as the opportunity to construct their own understanding. It perhaps also involved the resolution of cognitive conflict within a social context. There can be no guarantee that larger groups of younger pupils would eventually ever be able to use their experiences with Multibase Arithmetic Blocks, say, to come to a better understanding of place value in the same way that the mechanics students eventually constructed their understanding. That surely is compatible with, rather than a failure of, the notion of constructivism.

Sometimes, when using equipment, too much is expected. The equipment is merely a vehicle which can provide both analogous concrete experience and opportunity for group discussion and the construction of meaning. Naturally, it might not have the desired effect. In many cases of reported failure, the focus has perhaps been too much on the provision of appropriate equipment and not enough on what goes on in the minds of the pupils. Indeed, some people would claim that the concrete embodiments of abstract ideas only directly convey the ideas to those who already understand them, so failure will be frequent. Nevertheless, we ought to persevere with a whole variety of teaching methods, for no method is guaranteed to work. With apparatus, it is important not to lose sight of the Piagetian view that it is the activity which is to be mathematized, not the equipment itself, nor to lose sight of the importance of discussion and argument, both between teacher and pupils and between pupils themselves. As regards discovery learning, similar conclusions are legitimate. Setting up what is intended to be a discovery learning situation is naturally not automatically going to guarantee learning, and may be an abysmal failure. Discovery learning can only succeed when it is reconstituted as providing opportunities for construction. Situations which introduce cognitive conflict and the opportunities for the negotiation of meaning within a group are important when one sets out to implement constructivism. Unfortunately, some teachers might feel that an over-full curriculum and lack of encouragement to look for better ways of teaching do not encourage thoughtful constructivist strategies.

As we have already seen, the traditional and ubiquitous whole-class teaching method which has become known as transmission teaching has been fairly categorically rejected by many constructivists as being ineffective for most of the time for most of the class. However, we must also recognize that individual children often need only the transmission of a quick answer to a question to promote their cognitive development, and a further question from the teacher may not only be unnecessary, it might be a frustration. As a result of being told something, another mental cog might fit into place. It therefore does not seem legitimate to assume that constructivism suggests you should never tell any child anything. Also, even if the child cannot totally integrate a notion with ideas already in the mind, subsequent reflection can sometimes fill in the gaps. Ideally, the teacher should accept there may still be uncertainties in the child's mind, and should continue to provide experiences over a period of time which will help to consolidate a notion which is proving difficult to accommodate. The best kind of verbal interaction between teacher and pupil is not one of telling anyway, it is one in which the two minds are interlocked for a time whilst a notion is explored together, in the same way as it is hoped that pupils will operate in discussion groups.

Behaviourism has influenced teaching methods around the world since the nineteenth century. It led to emphasis on drill and practice in mathematics in the belief that 'practice makes perfect', and the classroom experience of many teachers will perhaps lead them to believe that there should still be a place for practice, both mental and written. The belief that children sometimes need practice in their mental activities just as they need to practise motor skills such as riding a bicycle or swimming is supported by Winston (2003), though not as any direct support for behaviourism. This very recent discussion of the place of repetition comes from our growing understanding of how our brain works, and the belief that neural connections are forged by repeating the same mental activity until it becomes firmly attached and related to existing structures. This belief also incorporates the converse, namely that deterioration of the physical link will occur when practice ceases (see Chapter 3). Once the link is fully established, however, one must assume that the risk of deterioration is less, for strong networks have been created, and so we do not lose the ability to swim, ride a bicycle, multiply numbers or solve a simple linear equation. Perhaps it explains why even intelligent adults can forget so much of the mathematics they supposedly learned at school, because skills have ceased to be practised before they fit into a network of knowledge which is going to be consciously preserved. One must suspect than many adults never really forged firm enough connections and so did not absorb much of their mathematics education in the first place. We must allow a place for relevant practice within any approach to teaching and learning mathematics, but if it is used it surely must be practice which engages the minds of the pupils and is not mere mindless repetition.

It is interesting that practice is said to be excluded from Kamii's innovative approaches to early number work. Rote learning (learning by heart and without meaning) has often been associated with behaviourism, perhaps unfairly, and has certainly been a traditional method of school teaching. However, rote learning is accepted as a necessary feature of the approach to learning mathematics associated with Kamii, but it is not forced, it takes place in a natural and enjoyable way. Ausubel, too, has suggested that some forms of learning by rote might be necessary with younger pupils, up to the time when notions start to become associated into networks of knowledge. Many people have successfully and happily learned aspects of mathematics without fully understanding at the time. Many able pupils seem to be able to preserve some knowledge in a kind of holding bay in the mind, awaiting the time when it can either be stored meaningfully, rejected, or discarded. On the other hand, many others have come to reject mathematics as a subject because they did not understand enough – there was too little in the way of connections between networks in the mind. Rote learning does not feature in most descriptions of constructivist teaching.

The exploration of teaching methods which might be used by constructivists has led to interesting novelties which could become valuable common practice. The idea of concept mapping (see also Chapters 2 and 10) is one that can assist pupils in both checking and consolidating in a constructivist way what it is that they have learned. At the nodes of a concept map (network) might be items of knowledge, or concepts, or anything which a child remembers from lessons. Linking the nodes, lines can be drawn to show connections or relationships of any kind which the child believes exists. Figure 2.2 shows a pupil's own representation of what had been learned about triangles, together with the perceived connections. The constructivist point of view would be that it is better for children to construct such representations of their own, showing what they understand of what they have learned rather than for the teacher to tell them what they ought to have learned. The diagram is then available for others to challenge and perhaps improve. Figure 11.1 is an example of a map

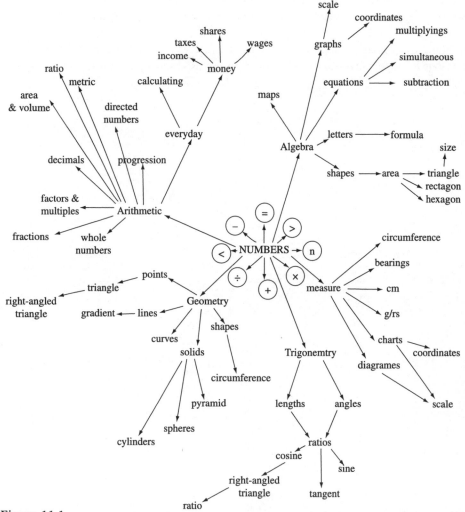

**Figure 11.1**

constructed by two secondary school pupils working cooperatively (original spellings retained).

Another variation on concept mapping has recently been suggested by Entrekin (1992), and this she calls 'mathematical mind mapping'. The basic idea is to begin a teaching sequence by asking for a word or phrase which best described what a recent lesson had been about. This word or phrase might then be recorded on the chalkboard. Subsequent questions could include, 'And what did we discover about it?', or possibly, 'And what else do you remember about it?' The aim here is to build up a map of what is in the minds of pupils in the class. This can clearly lead to discussion, debate and argument, with the ultimate stage being either an agreed best map, or each pupil's own individual best map, of a subject area, showing how separate nodes are related to a main node and to each other. Maps completed individually after some early discussion can then lead to consideration of who has the best, and why, perhaps in a small group situation. An example of what might be produced is shown in Figure 11.2. Although not produced by pupils, a more complicated map of the algebra curriculum, incorporating the three different dimensions of tools, themes and concepts, is to be found in Picciotto and Wah (1993). Exploring sections of the algebra curriculum and attempting to build up parts of this kind of map might be a very helpful constructive class activity.

Some mathematical topics might lend themselves to students writing their own sections for a personal 'textbook'. One example used by the author is from statistics,

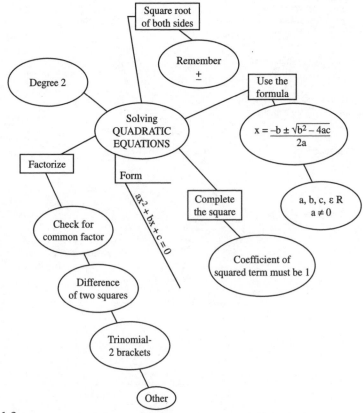

**Figure 11.2**

and concerns the theorem that distributions based on sums and differences of two given distributions have mean equal to the sum (or difference) of the two means and variance equal to the sum of the two variances. This can be 'proved' by students, thus providing greater satisfaction than a proof transmitted by the teacher. Initial group investigation with suitable simple numbers will suggest what the results are, and the students can then be set to work to produce algebraic proofs. The draft proofs produced in this way may then be debated and discussed and ultimately written out in a format which is as good as is found in any textbook. In this way a new theorem has been constructed and not delivered, with the likelihood that it will not only be better remembered, but will always be used correctly (not always the outcome of transmission teaching of this theorem). Here, however, we are clearly talking of able pupils. At the other extreme we have to acknowledge that there are academically weaker pupils who may have very different needs. Not enough is known about the extent to which weaker pupils can construct their own understanding. The first reaction of many teachers is that such pupils need very clear instructions and a great deal of help, and that even then the quality of learning is often still poor. Other teachers, however, hold the view that constructivist approaches must be tried out with weak pupils as well, because the success rate can hardly be worse than it is with traditional transmission and practice. Underhill (1991) has described several more teaching techniques which can assist teachers to move towards styles of teaching which better promote construction. Some of the difficulties which teachers might experience in adopting constructivist teaching approaches are discussed in Orton (1994).

## Cognitive obstacles

The issue of cognitive obstacles is one that must be taken into account in connection with any theory of how mathematics is learned. In Chapter 1, reference was made to the existence of notable stumbling blocks in learning mathematics, and the examples provided in that chapter included place value, ratio and algebra. The last of these, algebra, is different from the others in that it is a potentially huge subject area, so it probably contains many stumbling blocks – often referred to as cognitive obstacles. One example of such an obstacle in algebra was described in work by Collis (1975) and is known as 'lack of closure'. Young children come to expect that the addition of two numbers should produce a single number as the answer, for example $2 + 3 = 5$. In algebra, however, additions like $x + 3$, $2x - 1$ and $3x^2 - x + 2$ cannot be closed any further. There is no single 'number' which is the answer. As all mathematics teachers know, children will often try to close algebraic expressions inappropriately, by combining terms in any one of a number of incorrect ways. One example of this is to give '$3x$' as the 'answer' to $x + 3$, another is to give '$x$' as the 'answer' to $2x - 1$, though these are not the only wrong attempts at closure which we are likely to encounter in lessons. Perhaps by the age of around fifteen years, after several years of studying algebra, many pupils will have fully accommodated to the notion that such expressions cannot be closed any further. Then, when this accommodation has finally been reached, students have attained a stage of understanding described by Collis as 'acceptance of lack of closure'. Other obstacles in learning algebra have been discussed by Herscovics (1989) under the general description of concatenation, that is, the kind of abbreviated form of combinations of symbols which is such a feature of algebra.

Many incorrect answers result from this obstacle, for example, when substituting $x = 3$ in the term $2x$ pupils will often conclude that the answer is 23.

These examples clearly suggest that pupils have a tendency to fall back on an arithmetic frame of reference when learning algebra. In our teaching, however, we are very likely to use what we perceive to be corresponding arithmetical examples in order to try to help pupils to learn algebra, in other words we often encourage such comparison or analogy. A simple example is when we suggest that the sum $x + y$ is equivalent to $2 + 3$; a more difficult example is when we use $3(2 + 5)$ as equivalent to $a(b + c)$. The expansion of $(x + y)^2$ into $x^2 + 2xy + y^2$ is a more advanced example which has been mentioned in earlier chapters. Students have a tendency to expand $(x + y)^2$ as $x^2 + y^2$, but the use of a numerical equivalent like $(2 + 3)^2$ reveals that $2^2 + 3^2$ cannot be correct. However, difficulties with using this assumed comparability start arising very early in the study of algebra, for example, with the concatenation of the product '$x$ multiplied by $y$' to $xy$, as illustrated above. And $3(2 + 5)$ can be simplified to $3 \times 7$, whilst $a(b + c)$ cannot be simplified in the same way. Basically, the problem is that the operations of arithmetic are often fundamentally different from corresponding operations in algebra, so there is inevitably an obstacle here. In arithmetic, $4 + 7$ is a question to be answered, but in algebra $x + 7$ is both process and answer. In other words, a major cognitive adjustment is required in order to come to terms with the algebra. Piaget's notions of assimilation and accommodation are helpful in understanding what the problem is for learners. Here, the point is that accommodation requires the conflict between the old and new frames of reference to be overcome in order for the algebraic notions to be assimilated.

The task which is usually described as the 'Student-Professor' problem is a well known example of an algebraic cognitive obstacle. The problem is this:

> There are six times as many students (or pupils) as professors (or teachers) at this university (or school). Write an equation to represent this information using S for the number of students and P for the number of professors.

The task has been set to many different groups of university students, yet these talented learners often answer incorrectly, providing a reversal of the correct answer by writing 6S = P. Other similar tasks reveal the same obstacle. Rosnick and Clement (1980) have explored whether tutoring removes the problem, but came to the conclusion the reversal is not easily corrected, and that 'students' misconceptions pertaining to variable are not easily "taught" away'.

One important issue concerns precisely what is meant by a cognitive obstacle – after all, the whole of learning could be considered to be about overcoming obstacles. How should the notion be defined? When is a difficulty encountered in learning just a minor setback and when is it a cognitive obstacle? Herscovics (1989) suggests that cognitive obstacles are learning difficulties whose occurrence is widespread. Even then, this would suggest that there are probably a very large number of such obstacles in learning mathematics. Here, we are not interested in obstacles which could have been avoided by better teaching, we mean those obstacles which are difficult to deal with even under the most ideal circumstances, and which are being experienced year after year by large numbers of pupils. As we have seen, cognitive obstacles may be understood best as problems of accommodation, and pedagogically they are very challenging. Fundamentally, they can only be overcome by the learner succeeding in making alterations to the mental structure in the mind, and presumably effecting a suitable reorganization of the connections in the neural networks.

Constructivism seems to provide us with a way of coping with the issue of cognitive obstacles better than most other theories associated with learning, in that it is a very clear example of learners having to make sense of new notions by their own efforts. As we have seen, Piaget's concept of equilibration is an important one in the understanding of cognitive obstacles, but up to now no attempt has been made to relate them to stages of intellectual development, and at the moment it does not appear likely that such an approach would be helpful. After all, cognitive obstacles can arise at any time, even with students who ought to be firmly at the ultimate stage of formal operations. Neo-behaviourism, with its belief in the efficacy of stimulus-response connections, optimum sequencing, practice and readiness based on the existence of prior knowledge does not seem to provide any way of explaining the problem of cognitive obstacles and how to tackle them. As for Ausubel, it seems possible that his notion of cognitive dissonance could be closely related to, or might even incorporate, the problem of cognitive obstacles, but it is doubtful whether his original explanation did. Naturally, solutions to the problem of cognitive obstacles are not easy to find anyway, and Herscovics (1989) suggests, not surprisingly, that there are no guaranteed recipes. All we can do is to create conditions likely to enable pupils to tackle and ultimately conquer the obstacle through the difficult process of accommodation. Such conditions are precisely those required for the construction of understanding anyway.

There is no doubt that the adoption of methods of teaching which reflect constructivist beliefs present difficulties, but effective teaching has always been, and probably always will be, hard work. It is appropriate to leave the last word to Wood (1988, p. 210):

> The perspective I have adopted on the nature of knowledge and its relation to formal systems of thinking . . . precludes an approach to teaching that is based on universal and invariant 'steps' and 'stages' . . . Rather, it invites interaction, negotiation and the *shared construction* of experiences . . . The only way to avoid the formation of entrenched misconceptions is through discussion and interaction. A trouble shared, in mathematical discourse, may become a problem solved.

## Suggestions for further reading

Baroody, A. J. (1987) *Children's Mathematical Thinking*. New York: Teachers College Press.

Hughes, M. (1986) *Children and Number*. Oxford: Blackwell.

Kamii, C. K. with DeClark, G. (1985) *Young Children Reinvent Arithmetic: Implications of Piaget's Theory*. New York: Teachers College Press.

von Glasersfeld, E. (ed.) (1991) *Radical Constructivism in Mathematics Education*. Dordrecht: Kluwer.

Winston, R. (2003) *The Human Mind*. London: The British Broadcasting Corporation and Bantam Press.

Wood, D. (1988) *How Children Think and Learn*. Oxford: Blackwell.

# Questions for discussion

1. To what extent does constructivism provide a theory of learning which teachers can accept and put into practice?
2. What evidence is there that children today are benefiting from our accumulated knowledge about how mathematics is learned?
3. What cognitive obstacles are you aware of and how do you try to help learners to overcome the difficulties presented by them?
4. In what ways have you changed your views about the most effective ways of promoting the learning of mathematics as a result of reading this book?

# References

Abreu, G., Bishop, A. J. and Pompeu, G. (1997) 'What children and teachers count as mathematics', in T. Nunes and P. Bryant (eds), *Learning and Teaching Mathematics*. Hove, East Sussex: Psychology Press, pp. 233–63.

Anderson, J. R. (1985) *Cognitive Psychology and its Implications*. New York: W. H. Freeman.

Askew, M. and Wiliam, D. (1995) *Recent Research in Mathematics Education 5–16*. London: HMSO.

Assessment of Performance Unit (1980) *Mathematical Development: Primary Survey Report Number 1*. London: HMSO.

Assessment of Performance Unit (1982a) *Mathematical Development: Primary Survey Report Number 3*. London: HMSO.

Assessment of Performance Unit (1982b) *Mathematical Development: Secondary Survey Report Number 3*. London: HMSO.

Assessment of Performance Unit (undated) *Mathematical Development: A Review of Monitoring in Mathematics 1978 to 1982*. Slough: NFER.

Aubrey, C. (1993) 'An investigation of the mathematical knowledge and competencies which young children bring into school', *British Educational Research Journal*, 19(1), 27–41.

Austin, J. L. and Howson, A. G. (1979) 'Language and mathematical education', *Educational Studies in Mathematics*, 10, 161–97.

Ausubel, D. P. (1960) 'The use of advance organizers in the learning and retention of meaningful verbal material', *Journal of Educational Psychology*, 51, 267–72.

Ausubel, D. P. (1963) 'Some psychological and educational limitations of learning by discovery', *New York State Mathematics Teachers Journal*, XIII, 90–108. (Also in *The Arithmetic Teacher*, 11(5), 290–302, 1964.)

Ausubel, D. P. (1968) *Educational Psychology: A Cognitive View*. New York: Holt, Rinehart & Winston.

Balacheff, N. (1991) 'Treatment of refutations: Aspects of the complexity of a constructivist approach to mathematics learning', in E. von Glasersfeld (ed.), *Radical Constructivism in Mathematics Education*. Dordrecht: Kluwer, pp. 89–110.

Barnes, D. (1976) *From Communication to Curriculum*. Harmondsworth: Penguin.

Baroody, A. J. (1987) *Children's Mathematical Thinking*. New York: Teachers College Press.

Bartlett, F. (1958) *Thinking*. London: George Allen & Unwin.

Bell, A. W., Costello, J. and Küchemann, D. (1983) *Research on Learning and Teaching*. Windsor: NFER-Nelson.

Bell, A., Swan, M., Onslow, B., Pratt, K. and Purdy, D. (1989) *Diagnostic Teaching for Long Term Learning*. Nottingham: Shell Centre for Mathematical Education.

Bell, P. (1970) *Basic Teaching for Slow Learners*. London: Muller.

Bereiter, C. (1997) 'Situated cognition and how to overcome it', in D. Kirshner and J. A. Whitson (eds), *Situated Cognition: Social, Semiotic and Psychological Perspectives*. Mahwah, NJ: Lawrence Erlbaum, pp. 281–300.

Berry, J. W. (1985) 'Learning mathematics in a second language: Some cross-cultural issues', *For the Learning of Mathematics*, 5(2), 18–23.

Bigge, M. L. (1976) *Learning Theories for Teachers*, 3rd edn. New York: Harper & Row.

Biggs, E. E. (1972) 'Investigational methods', in L. R. Chapman (ed.), *The Process of Learning Mathematics*. Oxford: Pergamon, pp. 216–40.

Biggs, E. and Shaw, J. (1985) *Maths Alive!* London: Cassell.

Bishop, A. J. (1973) 'The use of structural apparatus and spatial ability – a possible relationship', *Research in Education*, 9, 43–9.

Bishop, A. J. (1980) 'Spatial abilities and mathematics education – a review', *Educational Studies in Mathematics*, 11, 257–69.

Bishop, A. J. (1988a) 'Mathematics education in its cultural context', *Educational Studies in Mathematics*, 19, 179–91.

Bishop, A. J. (1988b) *Mathematical Enculturation: A Cultural Perspective on Mathematics Education*. Dordrecht: Kluwer.

Bishop, A. J. (1991) 'Mathematics education in its cultural context', in M. Harris (ed.), *Schools, Mathematics and Work*. London: The Falmer Press, pp. 29–41.

Bloom, B. S., Engelhart, M. D., Furst, E. J., Hill, W. H. and Krathwohl, D. R. (1956) *Taxonomy of Educational Objectives: Cognitive Domain*. London: Longman.

Boaler, J. (1997) *Experiencing School Mathematics*. Buckingham: Open University Press.

Booth, L. R. (1984) *Algebra: Children's Strategies and Errors*. Windsor: NFER-Nelson.

Branford, B. (1921) *A Study of Mathematical Education*. Oxford: The Clarendon Press.

Brown, G. and Desforges, C. (1977) 'Piagetian psychology and education: Time for revision', *British Journal of Educational Psychology*, 47, 7–17.

Brown, M. (1978) 'Cognitive development and the learning of mathematics', in A. Floyd (ed.), *Cognitive Development in the School Years*. London: Croom Helm, pp. 351–73.

Brown, M. (1981a) 'Number operations', in K. M. Hart (ed.), *Children's Understanding of Mathematics: 11–16*. London: John Murray, pp. 23–47.

Brown, M. (1981b) 'Place value and decimals', in K. M. Hart (ed.), *Children's Understanding of Mathematics: 11–16*. London: John Murray, pp. 48–65.

Brown, S. I. and Walter, M. I. (1983) *The Art of Problem Posing*. Philadelphia: The Franklin Institute Press.

Bruner, J. S. (1960a) 'On learning mathematics', *The Mathematics Teacher*, 53, 610–19.

Bruner, J. S. (1960b) *The Process of Education*. Cambridge, MA: Harvard University Press.

Bruner, J. S. (1966) *Toward a Theory of Instruction*. Cambridge, MA: Harvard University Press.

Bruner, J. S. (1973) *Beyond the Information Given*. London: George Allen & Unwin.

Bruner, J. S. and Kenney, H. J. (1965) 'Representation and mathematics learning', in L. N. Morrisett and J. Vinsonhaler (eds), *Mathematical Learning*. Monograph of the Society for Research in Child Development, 30(1), pp. 50–9.

Bruner, J. S., Goodnow, J. J. and Austin, G. A. (1956) *A Study of Thinking*. New York: Wiley.

Bruner, J. S., Olver, R. R. and Greenfield, P. M. (1966) *Studies in Cognitive Growth*. New York: Wiley.

Bryant, P. (1974) *Perception and Understanding in Young Children*. London: Methuen.

Burger, W. F. and Shaughnessy, M. J. (1986) 'Characterizing the van Hiele levels of development in geometry', *Journal for Research in Mathematics Education*, 17, 31–48.

Burton, L. (1984) *Thinking Things Through*. Oxford: Blackwell.

Buxton, L. (1981) *Do You Panic About Maths?* London: Heinemann.

Byers, V. and Erlwanger, S. (1985) 'Memory in mathematical understanding', *Educational Studies in Mathematics*, 16, 259–81.

Carpenter, T. P. and Moser, J. M. (1982) 'The development of addition and subtraction problem-solving skills', in T. P. Carpenter, J. M. Moser and T. A. Romberg (eds), *Addition and Subtraction: A Cognitive Perspective*. Hillsdale, NJ: Lawrence Erlbaum, pp. 9–24.

Carraher, T. N., Carraher, D. W. and Schliemann, A. D. (1987) 'Written and oral mathematics', *Journal for Research in Mathematics Education*, 18(2), 83–97.

Child, D. (1986) *Psychology and the Teacher*, 4th edn. London: Holt, Rinehart and Winston.

Chipman, S. F. and Mendelson, M. J. (1979) 'Influence of six types of visual structure on complexity judgements in children and adults', *Journal of Experimental Psychology: Human Perception and Performance*, 5(2), 365–78.

Cobb, P. (1987) 'Information-processing psychology and mathematics education – a constructivist perspective', *Journal of Mathematical Behaviour*, 6, 3–40.

Cobb, P., Wood, T. and Yackel, E. (1991) 'A constructivist approach to second grade mathematics', in E. von Glasersfeld (ed.), *Radical Constructivism in Mathematics Education*. Dordrecht: Kluwer, pp. 157–76.

Cockcroft, W. H. (1982) *Mathematics Counts*. London: HMSO.

Collis, K. F. (1975) *A Study of Concrete and Formal Operations in School Mathematics: A Piagetian Viewpoint*. Hawthorn, Victoria: Australian Council for Educational Research.

Copeland, R. W. (1979) *How Children Learn Mathematics*. New York: Macmillan.

Cormier, S. M. and Hagman, J. D. (1987) 'Introduction', in S. M. Cormier and J. D. Hagman (eds), *Transfer of Learning: Contemporary Research and Applications*. San Diego, CA: Academic Press, pp. 1–8.

d'Ambrosio, U. (1985) 'Ethnomathematics and its place in the history and pedagogy of mathematics', *For the Learning of Mathematics*, 5(1), 44–8.

d'Ambrosio, U. (1991) 'Ethnomathematics and its place in the history and pedagogy of mathematics', in M. Harris (ed.), *Schools, Mathematics and Work*. London: The Falmer Press, pp. 15–25.

Dasen, P. R. (1972) 'Cross-cultural Piagetian research: A summary', *Journal of Cross-Cultural Psychology*, 3(1), 23–39.

Dasen, P. R. (1977) 'Introduction', in P. R. Dasen (ed.), *Piagetian Psychology: Cross-Cultural Contributions*. New York: Gardner Press, pp. 1–25.

Davis, R. B. (1966) 'Discovery in the teaching of mathematics', in L. S. Shulman and E. R. Keislar (eds), *Learning by Discovery: A Critical Appraisal*. Chicago: Rand McNally, pp. 115–28.

Davis, R. B. (1984) *Learning Mathematics: The Cognitive Science Approach to Mathematics Education*. London: Croom Helm.

Dearden, R. F. (1967) 'Instruction and learning by discovery', in R. S. Peters (ed.), *The Concept of Education*. London: Routledge and Kegan Paul, pp. 135–55.

Department of Education and Science (1985) *Mathematics from 5 to 16*. London: HMSO.

Department of Education and Science/Welsh Office (1988) *Mathematics for Ages 5 to 16*. London: HMSO.

Dewey, J. (1910) *How We Think*. Boston, MA: Heath.

Dickson, L., Brown, M. and Gibson, O. (1984) *Children Learning Mathematics*. Eastbourne: Holt, Rinehart & Winston (Schools Council).

Dienes, Z. P. (1960) *Building Up Mathematics*. London: Hutchinson.

Dienes, Z. P., translated by P. Seaborne (1973) *The Six Stages in the Process of Learning Mathematics*. Windsor: NFER.

Donaldson, M. (1978) *Children's Minds*. Glasgow: Fontana/Collins.

Durkin, K. and Shire, B. (eds) (1991) *Language in Mathematical Education*. Buckingham: Open University Press.

Eliot, J. and Smith, I. M. (1983) *An International Directory of Spatial Tests*. Windsor: NFER-Nelson.

Entrekin, V. S. (1992) 'Mathematical mind mapping', *The Mathematics Teacher*, 85(6), 444–5.

Esler, W. K. (1982) 'Physiological studies of the brain: Implications for science teaching', *Journal of Research in Science Teaching*, 19, 795–803.

Evans, J. (2000) *Adults' Mathematical Thinking and Emotions*. London: Routledge/Falmer.

Fasheh, M. (1991) 'Mathematics in a social context: math within education as praxis versus math within education as hegemony', in M. Harris (ed.), *Schools, Mathematics and Work*. London: The Falmer Press, pp. 57–61.

Fennema, E. and Tartre, L. A. (1985) 'The use of spatial visualization in mathematics by girls and boys', *Journal for Research in Mathematics Education*, 16, 184–206.

Fitzgerald, A. and Rich, K. M. (1981) *Mathematics in Employment (16–18)*. Bath: University of Bath.

Flanders, N. A. (1970) *Analyzing Teaching Behaviour*. Reading, MA: Addison-Wesley.

Fogelman, K. R. (1970) *Piagetian Tests for the Primary School*. Windsor: NFER.

Freudenthal, H. (1968) 'Why to teach mathematics so as to be useful', *Educational Studies in Mathematics*, 1, 3–8.

Frobisher, L. (1994) 'Problems, investigations and an investigative approach', in A. Orton and G. Wain (eds), *Issues in Teaching Mathematics*. London: Cassell, pp. 150–73.

Frobisher, L. (1999) 'Primary schoolchildren's knowledge of odd and even numbers', in A. Orton (ed.), *Pattern in the Teaching and Learning of Mathematics*. London: Cassell, pp. 31–48.

Frobisher, L., Monaghan, J., Orton, A., Orton, J., Roper, T. and Threlfall, J. (1999) *Learning to Teach Number*. Cheltenham: Stanley Thornes.

Furneaux, W. D. and Rees, R. (1978) 'The structure of mathematical ability', *British Journal of Psychology*, 69, 507–12.

Fuys, D., Geddes, D. and Tischler, R. (1988) *The Van Hiele Model of Thinking in Geometry among Adolescents*. Reston, VA: NCTM.

Gagné, R. M. (1975) *Essentials of Learning for Instruction*. Hinsdale, IL: The Dryden Press.

Gagné, R.M. (1985) *The Conditions of Learning and Theory of Instruction*, 4th edn. New York: Holt, Rinehart & Winston.

Gagné, R. M. and Briggs, L. J. (1974) *Principles of Instructional Design*. New York: Holt, Rinehart & Winston.

Gagné, R. M. and Brown, L. T. (1961) 'Some factors in the programming of conceptual learning', *Journal of Experimental Psychology*, 62, 313–21.

Gagné, R. M. and Smith, E. C. (1962) 'A study of the effects of verbalization on problem-solving', *Journal of Experimental Psychology*, 63, 12–18.

Garrick, R., Threlfall, J. and Orton, A. (1999) 'Pattern in the nursery', in A. Orton (ed.), *Pattern in the Teaching and Learning of Mathematics*. London: Cassell, pp. 1–17.

Gattegno, C. (1960) *Modern Mathematics with Numbers in Colour*. Reading: Educational Explorers.

Gay, J. and Cole, M. (1967) *The new mathematics and an old culture*. New York: Holt, Rinehart & Winston.

Gerdes, P. (1985) 'Conditions and strategies for emancipatory mathematics education in underdeveloped countries', *For the Learning of Mathematics*, 5(1), 15–20.

Gerdes, P. (1988) 'On culture, geometrical thinking and mathematics education', *Educational Studies in Mathematics*, 19, 137–62.

Gerdes, P. (1994) 'Reflections on ethnomathematics', *For the Learning of Mathematics*, 14(2), 19–22.

Getzels, J. W. and Jackson, P. W. (1962) *Creativity and Intelligence*. New York: Wiley.

Ghent, L. (1956) 'Perception of overlapping and embedded figures by children of different ages', *American Journal of Psychology*, 69, 575–86.

Ginsburg, H. (1977) *Children's Arithmetic: The Learning Process*. New York: Van Nostrand.

Ginsburg, H. P., Choi, Y. E., Lopez, L. S., Netley, R. and Chao-Huan, C. (1997) 'Happy birthday to you: early mathematical thinking of Asian, South American, and U.S. children', in T. Nunes and P. Bryant (eds), *Learning and Teaching Mathematics*. Hove, East Sussex: Psychology Press, pp. 163–201.

Goldin, G. A. (1989) 'Constructivist epistemology and discovery learning in mathematics', in G. Vergnaud, J. Rogalski and M. Artigue (eds), *Proceedings of the Thirteenth Annual Conference for the Psychology of Mathematics Education*, Volume 2. Paris, France: G. R. Didactique, CNRS, pp. 15–22.

Gray, E. M. (1991) 'An analysis of diverging approaches to simple arithmetic: Preference and its consequences', *Educational Studies in Mathematics*, 22, 551–74.

Gray, E. M. and Tall, D. O. (1994) 'Duality, ambiguity and flexibility: A "proceptual" view of simple arithmetic', *Journal for Research in Mathematics Education*, 26(2), 116–40.

Grünbaum, B. and Shephard, G. (1986) *Tilings and Patterns: An Introduction*. San Francisco: Freeman.

Guilford, J. P. (1959) 'Three faces of intellect', *The American Psychologist*, 14, 469–79. (Also in Wiseman, S. (ed.) (1967) *Intelligence and Ability*. Harmondsworth: Penguin Books, pp. 218–37.)

Gura, P. (1992) *Exploring Learning: Young Children and Block Play*. London: Paul Chapman.

Hadamard, J. (1945) *The Psychology of Invention in the Mathematical Field*. Princeton, NJ: Princeton University Press.

Harris, M. (1997) *Common Threads: Women, Mathematics and Work*. Stoke on Trent: Trentham Books.

Hart, K. (1980) 'A hierarchy of understanding in mathematics', in W. F. Archenhold, R. H. Driver, A. Orton and C. Wood-Robinson (eds), *Cognitive Development Research In Science and Mathematics*. Leeds: University of Leeds Centre for Studies in Science Education, pp. 39–61.

Hart, K. M. (ed.) (1981) *Children's Understanding of Mathematics: 11–16*. London: John Murray.

Hart, K. M. (1984) *Ratio: Children's Strategies and Errors*. Windsor: NFER-Nelson.

Hart, K. M. (1989) 'There is little connection', in P. Ernest (ed.), *Mathematics Teaching: The State of the Art*. Lewes: The Falmer Press.

Hartley, J. R. (1980) *Using the Computer to Study and Assist the Learning of Mathematics*. Leeds: University of Leeds Computer-Based Learning Unit.

Harvey, R., Kerslake, D., Shuard, H. and Torbe, M. (1982) *Language Teaching and Learning 6: Mathematics*. London: Ward Lock.

Heim, A. W. (1970) *AH4 Group Test of General Intelligence*. Windsor: NFER.

Her Majesty's Inspectorate (1985) *Mathematics from 5 to 16*. London: HMSO.

Her Majesty's Inspectorate (1989) *Aspects of Primary Education: the Teaching and Learning of Mathematics*. London: HMSO.

Herscovics, N. (1989) 'Cognitive obstacles encountered in the learning of algebra', in S. Wagner and C. Kieran (eds), *Research Issues in the Learning and Teaching of Algebra*. Reston, VA: NCTM, pp. 60–86.

Hershkowitz, R. (1990) 'Psychological aspects of learning geometry', in P. Nesher and J. Kilpatrick (eds), *Mathematics and Cognition*. Cambridge: Cambridge University Press, pp. 70–95.

Hill, C. C. (1979) *Problem-solving: Learning and Teaching*. London: Frances Pinter.

Holt, J. (1964) *How Children Fail*. Harmondsworth: Penguin.

Hope, J. A. (1985) 'Unravelling the mysteries of expert mental calculation', *Educational Studies in Mathematics*, 16, 355–74.

Howard, R. W. (1987) *Concepts and Schemata*. London: Cassell.

Hoyles, C. and Sutherland, R. (1989) *Logo Mathematics in the Classroom*. London: Routledge.

Hoyles, C., Küchemann, D. and Foxman, D. (2003) 'Comparing geometry curricula: Insights for policy and practice', *Mathematics in School*, 32(3), 2–6.

Hudson, L. (1966) *Contrary Imaginations*. Harmondsworth: Penguin.

Hughes, E. R. (1980) 'Should we check children?', in W. F. Archenhold, R. H. Driver, A. Orton and C. Wood-Robinson (eds), *Cognitive Development Research in Science and Mathematics*. Leeds: University of Leeds Centre for Studies in Science Education, pp. 87–104.

Hughes, M. (1986) *Children and Number*. Oxford: Blackwell.

Hutt, C. (1972) *Males and Females*. Harmondsworth: Penguin.

Johnson, D. A. and Rising, G. R. (1967) *Guidelines for Teaching Mathematics*. Belmont, CA: Wadsworth.

Johnson-Laird, P. N. (1983) *Mental Models*. Cambridge: Cambridge University Press.

Joint Matriculation Board/Shell Centre for Mathematical Education (1984) *Problems with Patterns and Numbers: An O-level Module*. Manchester: Joint Matriculation Board.

Kamii, C. K. with DeClark, G. (1985) *Young Children Reinvent Arithmetic: Implications of Piaget's Theory*. New York: Teachers College Press.

Kane, R. B., Byrne, M. A. and Hater, M. A. (1974) *Helping Children Read Mathematics*. New York: American Book Co.

Karplus, R. and Peterson, R. W. (1970) 'Intellectual development beyond elementary school II: Ratio, a survey', *School Science and Mathematics*, 70, 813–20.

Katona, G. (1940) *Organizing and Memorizing*. New York: Columbia University Press.

Kirshner, D. and Whitson, J. A. (1997) 'Editors' introduction', in D. Kirshner and J. A. Whitson (eds), *Situated Cognition: Social, Semiotic and Psychological Perspectives*. Mahwah, NJ: Lawrence Erlbaum, pp. 1–16.

Kolinsky, R., Morais, J., Content, A. and Cary, L. (1987) 'Finding parts within figures: A developmental study', *Perception*, 16, 399–407.

Krathwohl, D. R., Bloom, B. S. and Masia, B. B. (1964) *Taxonomy of Educational Objectives: Affective Domain*. London: Longman.

Krutetskii, V. A. (1976) *The Psychology of Mathematical Abilities in Schoolchildren*. Chicago: University of Chicago Press.

Küchemann, D. (1980) 'Children's difficulties with single reflections and rotations', *Mathematics in School*, 9(2), 12–13.

Küchemann, D. (1981) 'Reflections and rotations', in K. M. Hart (ed.), *Children's Understanding of Mathematics: 11–16*. London: John Murray, pp. 137–57.

Laborde C. with Conroy, J., de Corte, E., Lee, L. and Pimm, D. (1990) 'Language and mathematics', in P. Nesher and J. Kilpatrick (eds), *Mathematics and Cognition*. Cambridge: Cambridge University Press, pp. 53–69.

Lancy, D. F. (1983) *Cross-cultural Studies in Cognition and Mathematics*. New York: Academic Press.

Larkin, J. H. (1989) 'Eight reasons for explicit theories in mathematics education', in S. Wagner and C. Kieran (eds), *Research Issues in the Learning and Teaching of Algebra*. Reston, VA: NCTM, pp. 275–7.

Lave, J. (1988) *Cognition in Practice: Mind, Mathematics and Culture in Everyday Life*. Cambridge: Cambridge University Press.

Lave, J. (1997) 'The culture of acquisition and the practice of understanding', in D. Kirshner and J. A. Whitson (eds), *Situated Cognition: Social, Semiotic, and Psychological Perspectives*. Mahwah, NJ: Lawrence Erlbaum, pp. 17–36.

Leder, G. (1985) 'Sex-related differences in mathematics: An overview', *Educational Studies in Mathematics*, 16, 304–9.

Lee, L. and Wheeler, D. (1987) *Algebraic Thinking in High School Students: Their Conceptions of Generalization and Justification*. Montreal: Concordia University.

Lerman, S. (1989) 'Constructivism, mathematics and mathematics education', *Educational Studies in Mathematics*, 20(2), 211–23.

Lester, F. K. Jr. (1977) 'Ideas about problem-solving: A look at some psychological research', *The Arithmetic Teacher*, 25(2), 12–14.

Lester, F. K. Jr. (1989) 'Mathematical problem-solving in and out of school', *The Arithmetic Teacher*, 37(3), 33–5.

Lindsay, P. H. and Norman, D. A. (1977) *Human Information Processing*. New York: Academic Press.

Lochhead J. (1985) 'New horizons in educational development', *Review of Research in Education*, 12, 3–9.

Lochhead, J. (1991) 'Making math mean', in E. von Glasersfeld (ed.), *Radical Constructivism in Mathematics Education*. Dordrecht: Kluwer, pp. 75–87.

Lovell, K. (1971a) 'Proportionality and probability', in M. F. Rosskopf, L. P. Steffé and S. Taback (eds), *Piagetian Cognitive-Development Research and Mathematical Education*. Reston, VA: NCTM, pp. 136–48.

Lovell, K. (1971b) *The Growth of Understanding in Mathematics: Kindergarten Through Grade Three*. New York: Holt, Rinehart & Winston.

Lysaught, J. P. and Williams, C. M. (1963) *A Guide to Programmed Instruction*. New York: Wiley.

MacNamara, E. A. (1990) *Subitizing and addition of number: A study of young children learning mathematics*. Unpublished M.Ed. thesis, University of Leeds.

Magajna, Z. (2001) *Geometric thinking in out-of-school contexts*. Unpublished Ph.D. thesis, University of Leeds.

Mager, R. F. (1975) *Preparing Instructional Objectives* (issued 1962 as *Preparing Objectives for Programmed Instruction*). Belmont, CA: Fearon.

Masingila, J. O., Davidenko, S. and Prus-Wisniowska, E. (1996) 'Mathematics learning and practice in and out of school: A framework for connecting these experiences', *Educational Studies in Mathematics*, 31, 175–200.

Mason, J., Burton, L. and Stacey, K. (1985a) *Thinking Mathematically* (revised). Wokingham: Addison-Wesley.

Mason, J., Graham, A., Pimm, D. and Gowar, N. (1985b) *Routes to/Roots of Algebra*. Milton Keynes: Open University Press.

Mathematical Association (1923) *The Teaching of Geometry in Schools*. London: G. Bell & Sons.

Mathematical Association (1939) *A Second Report on the Teaching of Geometry in Schools*. London: G. Bell & Sons.

Mathematical Association (1970) *Primary Mathematics – A Further Report*. London: Mathematical Association.

Matthews, G. (1964) *Matrices*. London: Edward Arnold.

Midlands Mathematical Experiment (1964) *Report 1962–63*. London: Harrap.

Miller, G. A. (1956) 'The magical number seven, plus or minus two: Some limits on our capacity for processing information', *Psychological Review*, 63, 81–97.

Ministry of Education (1958) *Teaching Mathematics in Secondary Schools*. London: HMSO.

Mitchelmore, M. C. (1980) 'Three-dimensional geometrical drawing in three cultures', *Educational Studies in Mathematics*, 11, 205–16.

Mobley, M. (1987) *Making Ourselves Clearer: Readability in the GCSE*. London: Secondary Examinations Council.

Morgan, C. (1998) *Writing Mathematically*. London: The Falmer Press.

Morris, R. W. (1974) 'Linguistic problems encountered by contemporary curriculum development projects in mathematics', in *Interactions Between Linguistics and Mathematical Education*. Paris: UNESCO/CEDO/ICMI.

Newell, A. and Simon, H. A. (1972) *Human Problem Solving*. Englewood Cliffs, NJ: Prentice-Hall.

Noss, R. and Hoyles, C. (1996) *Windows on Mathematical Meanings: Learning Cultures and Computers*. Dordrecht: Kluwer.

Novak, J. D. (1977) *A Theory of Education*. Ithaca, NY: Cornell University Press.

Novak, J. D. (1980) 'Methodological issues in investigating meaningful learning', in

W. F. Archenhold, R. H. Driver, A. Orton and C. Wood-Robinson (eds), *Cognitive Development Research in Science and Mathematics*. Leeds: University of Leeds Centre for Studies in Science Education, pp. 129–55.

Novak, J. D. and Gowin, D. B. (1984) *Learning How to Learn*. Cambridge: Cambridge University Press.

Nuffield Mathematics Project (1967) *I Do, and I Understand*. Edinburgh, London, New York: Chambers/John Murray/Wiley.

Nuffield Mathematics Project (1969) *Computation and Structure 4*. Edinburgh, London, New York: Chambers/John Murray.

Nuffield Mathematics Project (1970, 1973) *Checking Up I, II, III*. Edinburgh, London, New York: Chambers/John Murray/Wiley.

Nuffield Maths 5–11 (1983) *Nuffield Maths 6 Teacher's Handbook*. Harlow: Longman.

Nunes, T. and Bryant, P. (1996) *Children Doing Mathematics*. Oxford: Blackwell.

Nunes, T., Schliemann, A. D. and Carraher, D. W. (1993) *Street Mathematics and School Mathematics*. Cambridge: Cambridge University Press.

Orton, A. (1971) 'Teaching about functions in the secondary school', *Mathematics Teaching*, 57, 45–9.

Orton, A. (1983) 'Students' understanding of differentiation', *Educational Studies in Mathematics*, 14, 235–50.

Orton, A. (1994) 'Learning mathematics: implications for teaching', in A. Orton and G. Wain (eds), *Issues in Teaching Mathematics*. London: Cassell, pp. 35–57.

Orton, A. (2001) 'Psychology of learning and instruction, overview', in L. S. Grinstein and S. I. Lipsey (eds), *Encyclopedia of Mathematics Education*. New York: RoutledgeFalmer, pp. 594–602.

Orton, A. and Orton, J. (1999) 'Pattern and the approach to algebra', in A. Orton (ed.), *Pattern in the Teaching and Learning of Mathematics*. London: Cassell, pp. 104–20.

Orton, J. (1997) 'Matchsticks, pattern and generalization', *Education 3–13*, 25(1), 61–5.

Orton, J. (1999) 'Children's perception of pattern in relation to shape', in A. Orton (ed.), *Pattern in the Teaching and Learning of Mathematics*. London: Cassell, pp. 149–67.

Orton, J. and Orton, A. (1996) 'Making sense of children's patterning', in L. Puig and A. Guitiérrez (eds), *Proceedings of the Twentieth International Conference for the Psychology of Mathematics Education*, Volume 4. Valencia, Spain: Universitat de València, pp. 83–90.

Orton, J., Orton, A. and Roper, T. (1999) 'Pictorial and practical contexts and the perception of pattern', in A. Orton (ed.), *Pattern in the Teaching and Learning of Mathematics*. London: Cassell, pp. 121–36.

Otterburn, M. K. and Nicholson, A. R. (1976) 'The language of (CSE) mathematics', *Mathematics in School*, 5(5), 18–20.

Papert, S. (1980) *Mindstorms*. Brighton: The Harvester Press.

Pegg, J. and Redden, E. (1990) 'Procedures for, and experiences in, introducing algebra in New South Wales', *Mathematics Teacher*, 83(5), 386–91.

Piaget, J. (1973) *The Child's Conception of the World*. London: Paladin.

Picciotto, H. and Wah, A. (1993) 'A new algebra: Tools, themes, concepts', *Journal of Mathematical Behavior*, 12, 19–42.

Poincaré, H. (1970) 'Mathematical creation', in P. E. Vernon (ed.), *Creativity*. Harmondsworth: Penguin, pp. 77–88.

Polya, G. (1954) *Mathematics and Plausible Reasoning*. Princeton, NJ: Princeton University Press.

Polya, G. (1957) *How to Solve It*. New York: Doubleday Anchor Books. (First published in 1945 by Princeton University Press.)

Polya, G. (1962) *Mathematical Discovery*. New York: Wiley.

Popper, K. R. (1972) *Objective Knowledge: An Evolutionary Approach*. Oxford: The Clarendon Press.

Presmeg, N. (1986) 'Visualization in high school mathematics', *For the Learning of Mathematics* 6(3), 42–6.

Reed, S. K. (1973) *Psychological Processes in Pattern Recognition*. New York: Academic Press.

Rees, R. (1974) 'An investigation of some common mathematical difficulties experienced by students', *Mathematics in School*, 3(1), 25–7.

Rees, R. (1981) 'Mathematically gifted pupils: Some findings from exploratory studies of mathematical abilities', *Mathematics in School*, 10(3), 20–3.

Renwick, E. M. (1935) *The Case Against Arithmetic*. London: Simpkin Marshall.

Resnick, L. B. and Ford, W. W. (1984) *The Psychology of Mathematics for Instruction*. Hillsdale, NJ: Lawrence Erlbaum.

Richards, J. (1991) 'Mathematical discussions', in E. von Glasersfeld (ed.), *Radical Constructivism in Mathematics Education*. Dordrecht: Kluwer, pp. 13–51.

Rosnick, P. and Clement, J. (1980) 'Learning without understanding: The effect of tutoring strategies on algebra misconceptions', *Journal of Mathematical Behavior*, 3(1), 3–27.

Rosskopf, M. F., Steffé, L. P. and Taback, S. (eds) (1971) *Piagetian Cognitive-development Research and Mathematical Education*. Reston, VA: NCTM.

Russell, S. (1983) *Factors Influencing the Choice of Advanced Level Mathematics by Boys and Girls*. Leeds: University of Leeds Centre for Studies in Science and Mathematics Education.

Sawyer, W. W. (1955) *Prelude to Mathematics*. Harmondsworth: Penguin.

Saxe, G. (1991) *Culture and Cognitive Development: Studies in Mathematical Understanding*. Hillsdale, NJ: Lawrence Erlbaum.

Saxe, G. B. and Posner, J. (1983) 'The development of numerical cognition: Cross-cultural perspectives', in H. P. Ginsburg (ed.), *The Development of Mathematical Thinking*. New York: Academic Press, pp. 292–317.

Scandura, J. M. and Wells, J. M. (1967) 'Advance organizers in learning abstract mathematics', *American Educational Research Journal*, 4, 295–301.

Scheerer, M. (1963) 'Problem-solving'. *Scientific American Offprint 476*. (From *Scientific American*, 208(4), 118–28).

Schliemann, A. (1984) 'Mathematics among carpenters and apprentices', in P. Damerow, M. W. Dunckley, B. F. Nebres and B. Werry (eds), *Mathematics for All*. Paris: UNESCO, pp. 92–5.

Schliemann, A. (1995) 'Some concerns about bringing everyday mathematics to mathematics education', in L. Meira, and D. Carraher, (eds), *Proceedings of the 19th International Conference for the Psychology of Mathematics Education*, Volume 1. Recife, Brazil: Universidade Federal de Pernambuco, pp. 45–60.

Schools Council (1965) *Mathematics in Primary Schools*. London: HMSO.

Scribner, S. (1984) 'Studying working intelligence', in B. Rogoff and L. Lave (eds), *Everyday Cognition: Its Development in Social Context*. Cambridge, MA: Harvard University Press, pp. 9–40.

Seaborne, P. L. (1975) *An Introduction to the Dienes Mathematics Programme*. London: University of London Press.

Sewell, B. (1981) *Use of Mathematics by Adults in Everyday Life*. Leicester: ACACE.

Shuard, H. (1982a) 'Differences in mathematical performance between girls and boys', in W. H. Cockcroft, *Mathematics Counts*. London: HMSO, pp. 273–87.

Shuard, H. (1982b) 'Reading and learning in mathematics', in R. Harvey, D. Kerslake, H. Shuard and M. Torbe, *Language Teaching and Learning 6: Mathematics*. London: Ward Lock, pp. 84–121.

Shuard, H. and Rothery, A. (eds) (1984) *Children Reading Mathematics*. London: John Murray.

Shuard, H., Walsh, A., Goodwin, J. and Worcester, V. (1991) *Calculators, Children and Mathematics*. London: Simon and Schuster.

Shulman, L. S. (1970) 'Psychology and mathematics education', in E. G. Begle (ed.), *Mathematics Education*. Chicago: NSSE, pp. 23–71.

Skemp, R. R. (1964) *Understanding Mathematics: Teacher's Notes for Book I*. London: University of London Press.

Skemp, R. R. (1971) *The Psychology of Learning Mathematics*. Harmondsworth: Penguin.

Skemp, R. R. (1976) 'Relational understanding and instrumental understanding', *Mathematics Teaching*, 77, 20–6.

Skemp, R. R. (1982) 'Communicating mathematics: Surface structures and deep structures', *Visible Language*, XVI, 281–8.

Skinner, B. F. (1961) 'Teaching machines'. *Scientific American Offprint 461*. (From *Scientific American*, 205(5), 90–102).

Skinner, B. F. (1974) *About Behaviourism*. London: Jonathan Cape.

Smith, I. M. (1964) *Spatial Ability: Its Educational and Social Significance*. London: University of London Press.

Solomon, Y. (1989) *The Practice of Mathematics*. London: Routledge.

Springer, S. P. and Deutsch, G. (1981) *Left Brain, Right Brain*. San Francisco: Freeman.

Stacey, K. (1989) 'Finding and using patterns in linear generalizing problems', *Educational Studies in Mathematics*, 20, 147–64.

Stern, C. with Stern, M. B. (1953) *Children Discover Arithmetic*. London: Harrap.

Sternberg, R. J. (1989) 'A componential approach to intellectual ability', in R. J. Sternberg (ed.), *Advances in the Psychology of Human Intelligence*, Volume 1. Hillsdale, NJ: Lawrence Erlbaum, pp. 413–57.

Stewart, J. (1985) 'Cognitive science and science education', *European Journal of Science Education*, 7, 1–17.

Stewart, J. and Atkin, J. (1982) 'Information processing psychology', *Journal of Research in Science Teaching*, 19, 321–32.

Sutton, C. (ed.) (1981) *Communicating in the Classroom*. London: Hodder & Stoughton.

Suydam, M. N. and Weaver, J. F. (1977) 'Research on problem-solving: Implications for elementary school classrooms', *The Arithmetic Teacher*, 25(2), 40–2.

Tait, K., Hartley, J. R. and Anderson, R. C. (1973) 'Feedback procedures in computer-assisted arithmetic instruction', *British Journal of Educational Psychology*, 43, 161–71.

Thorndike, E. L. (1922) *The Psychology of Arithmetic*. New York: Macmillan.

Threlfall, J. (1996) 'The role of practical apparatus in the teaching and learning of arithmetic', *Educational Review*, 48(1), 3–12.

Threlfall, J. (1999) 'Repeating patterns in the early primary years', in A. Orton (ed.), *Pattern in the Teaching and Learning of Mathematics*. London: Cassell, pp. 18–30.

Threlfall, J. and Frobisher, L. (1999) 'Patterns in processing and learning addition facts', in A. Orton (ed.), *Pattern in the Teaching and Learning of Mathematics*. London: Cassell, pp. 49–66.

Torbe, M. and Shuard, H. (1982) 'Mathematics and language', in R. Harvey, D. Kerslake, H. Shuard and M. Torbe, *Language Teaching and Learning 6: Mathematics*. London: Ward Lock, pp. 1–21.

Underhill, R. G. (1991) 'Two layers of constructivist curricular interaction', in E. von Glasersfeld (ed.), *Radical Constructivism in Mathematics Education*. Dordrecht: Kluwer, pp. 229–48.

UNESCO (1974) *Interactions Between Linguistics and Mathematical Education*. Paris: UNESCO/CEDO/ICMI.

Ursini, S. (1991) 'First steps in generalization processes in algebra', in F. Furinghetti (ed.), *Proceedings of the Fifteenth International Conference for the Psychology of Mathematics Education*, Volume 3. Assisi, Italy: Università di Genova, pp. 316–23.

Vergnaud, G. (1982) 'A classification of cognitive tasks and operations of thought involved in addition and subtraction problems', in T. P. Carpenter, J. M. Moser and T. A. Romberg (eds), *Addition and Subtraction: A Cognitive Perspective*. Hillsdale, NJ: Lawrence Erlbaum, pp. 39–59.

Vergnaud, G. (1990) 'Epistemology and psychology of mathematics education', in P. Nesher and J. Kilpatrick (eds), *Mathematics and Cognition*. Cambridge: Cambridge University Press, pp. 14–30.

Vernon, P. E. (1950) *The Structure of Human Abilities*. London: Methuen.

Verschaffel, L. and De Corte, E. (1997) 'Word problems: A vehicle for promoting authentic mathematical understanding and problem-solving in the primary school', in T. Nunes and P. Bryant (eds), *Learning and Teaching Mathematics*. Hove, East Sussex: Psychology Press, pp. 69–97.

Vithal, R. and Skovsmose, O. (1997) 'The end of innocence: A critique of "ethno-mathematics" ', *Educational Studies in Mathematics*, 34, 131–57.

von Glasersfeld, E. (1987) 'Learning as a constructive activity', in C. Janvier (ed.), *Problems of Representation in the Teaching and Learning of Mathematics*. Hillsdale, NJ: Lawrence Erlbaum, pp. 3–17.

von Glasersfeld, E. (1991) 'Introduction', in E. von Glasersfeld (ed.), *Radical Constructivism in Mathematics Education*. Dordrecht: Kluwer, pp. xiii–xx.

Vygotsky, L. S. (1962) *Thought and Language*. New York: MIT Press/Wiley.

Walkup, L. E. (1965) 'Creativity in science through visualization', *Perceptual and Motor Skills*, 21(1) 35–41.

Wall, W. D. (1965) 'Learning to think', in W. R. Niblett (ed.), *How and Why Do We Learn?* London: Faber & Faber.

Waring, S., Orton, A. and Roper, T. (1999) 'Pattern and proof', in A. Orton (ed.), *Pattern in the Teaching and Learning of Mathematics*. London: Cassell, pp. 192–206.

Warren, E. (1992) 'Beyond manipulating symbols', in A. Baturo and T. Cooper (eds), *New Directions in Algebra Education*. Red Hill, Australia: Queensland University of Technology, pp. 252–8.

Wertheimer, M. (1961) *Productive Thinking*. London: Tavistock Publications.

Wickelgren, W. A. (1974) *How to Solve Problems*. San Francisco: Freeman.

Williams, E. and Shuard, H. (1982) *Primary Mathematics Today*, 3rd edn. Harlow: Longman.

Williams, J. S. (1985) 'Using equipment in teaching mechanics', in A. Orton (ed.), *Studies in Mechanics Learning*. Leeds: University of Leeds Centre for Studies in Science and Mathematics Education, pp. 55–86.

Wilson, B. (1981) *Cultural Contexts in Science and Mathematics Education*. Leeds: University of Leeds Centre for Studies in Science and Mathematics Education.

Winston, R. (2003) *The Human Mind*. London: British Broadcasting Corporation and Bantam Press.

Witkin, H. A., Moore, C. A., Goodenough, D. R. and Cox, P. W. (1977) 'Field-dependent and field-independent cognitive styles and their educational implications', *Review of Educational Research*, 47(1), 1–64.

Wood, D. (1988) *How Children Think and Learn*. Oxford: Blackwell.

Wood, R. (1977) 'Cable's comparison factor: Is this where girls' troubles start?', *Mathematics in School*, 6(4), 18–21.

Wrigley, J. (1963) 'Some programmes for research', in F. W. Land (ed.), *New Approaches to Mathematics Teaching*. London: Macmillan, pp. 30–9.

Young, R. G. (1966) *Sets: A Programmed Course*. London: Methuen.

Zachos, I. (1994) *Problem-solving in Euclidean geometry in Greek schools*. Unpublished Ph.D. thesis, University of Leeds.

Zaslavsky, C. (1973) *Africa Counts*. Boston, MA: Prindle, Weber & Schmidt.

# Author index

Abreu, G. 123
Anderson, J. R. 84
Askew, M. 11, 15, 24, 25, 194
Assessment of Performance Unit 107, 108, 116, 150, 152–4
Atkin, J. 192
Aubrey, C. 101
Austin, J. L. 157, 174
Ausubel, D. P. 24, 26, 68, 70, 75, 76, 139, 176, 185–91, 201, 206, 211

Balacheff, N. 198, 199
Barnes, D. 157, 166, 167
Baroody, A. J. 211
Bartlett, F. 141, 177, 180
Bell, A. W. 63, 112, 116, 117, 145, 183, 201
Bell, P. 158
Bereiter, C. 133, 134
Berry, J. W. 68, 168, 170
Bigge, M. L. 28, 37
Biggs, E. E. 37, 73, 75, 76, 98, 99
Bishop, A. J. 127, 130, 131, 149, 171
Bloom, B. S. 11, 13, 31
Boaler, J. 135
Booth, L. R. 68
Branford, B. 3, 7, 12
Briggs, L. J. 33
Brown, G. 66, 75
Brown, M. 7, 13, 146
Brown, S. I. 90, 91, 98
Bruner, J. S. 58, 60, 73–6, 149, 154, 166, 176–80, 186, 191
Bryant, P. 26, 64, 65, 70
Burger, W. F. 182
Burton, L. 93
Buxton, L. 11, 155
Byers, V. 26

Carpenter, T. P. 172, 173, 194

Carraher, D. W. 133, 135
Carraher, T. N. 133
Child, D. 22
Chipman, S. F. 115
Clement, J. 210
Cobb, P. 192, 197, 198, 203
Cockcroft, W. H. 7, 10, 14, 23, 29, 54, 62, 63, 72, 76, 81–5, 106, 121–24, 151, 166, 198
Cole, M. 69, 170, 171
Collis, K. F. 209
Copeland, R. W. 70
Cormier, S. M. 127

d'Ambrosio, U. 129, 170, 171
Dasen, P. R. 69, 70
Davis, R. B. 4, 47, 76
Dearden, R. F. 82, 83
DeClark, G. 211
De Corte, E. 172, 173
Department of Education and Science 106, 198
Desforges, C. 66
Deutsch, G. 150, 155
Dewey, J. 88
Dickson, L. 7, 83, 115
Dienes, Z. P. 21, 36, 58, 68, 80, 81, 164, 175–81, 188, 193, 196
Donaldson, M. 65, 70, 134, 165, 172
Durkin, K. 174

Eliot, J. 149
Entrekin, V. S. 208
Erlwanger, S. 26
Esler, W. K. 192
Evans, J. 132–35

Fasheh, M. 125
Fennema, E. 153
Fitzgerald, A. 124

Flanders, N. A. 166
Fogelman, K. R. 7
Ford, W. W. 26, 80, 195, 196
Freudenthal, H. 119
Frobisher, L. 85, 100, 104, 105, 118
Furneaux, W. D. 147
Fuys, D. 182, 183, 193

Gagné, R. M. 13, 23, 25–30, 33, 42–8, 70, 75, 84, 167, 186
Garrick, R. 101
Gattegno, C. 46
Gay, J. 69, 170, 171
Gerdes, P. 129, 130, 171
Getzels, J. W. 141
Ghent, L. 117
Ginsburg, H. P. 12, 131, 132
Goldin, G. A. 197
Gowar, N. 118
Gowin, D. B. 187
Graham, A. 118
Gray, E. M. 103, 105
Grünbaum, B. 114
Guilford, J. P. 140, 146, 147
Gura, P. 101

Hadamard, J. 5, 87, 88, 144, 147, 148, 155
Hagman, J. D. 127
Harris, M. 131, 135
Hart, K. M. 10, 20, 51, 63, 67, 68, 83, 84, 201
Hartley, J. R. 36, 47
Harvey, R. 174
Heim, A. W. 140
Her Majesty's Inspectorate 8, 13, 85
Herscovics, N. 209–11
Hershkowitz, R. 183
Hill, C. C. 84
Holt, J. 12, 82, 155, 166

Hope, J. A. 145
Howard, R. W. 24, 26
Howson, A. G. 157, 174
Hoyles, C. 98, 132, 133
Hudson, L. 141, 154, 155
Hughes, E. R. 67
Hughes, M. 172, 194, 211
Hutt, C. 152

Jackson, P. W. 141
Johnson, D. A. 84
Johnson-Laird, P. N. 199

Kamii, C. K. 200, 201, 206, 211
Kane, R. B. 160
Karplus, R. 9
Katona, G. 78, 96
Kenney, H. J. 60
Kerslake, D. 174
Kirshner, D. 128
Kolinsky, R. 117
Krathwohl, D. R. 11, 31
Krutetskii, V. A. 142–44, 148, 150, 155, 192
Küchemann, D. 116–18

Laborde, C. 173
Lancy, D. F. 171
Larkin, J. H. 2
Lave, J. 122, 128, 129, 132, 133, 135
Leder, G. 150, 152
Lee, L. 109, 110
Lerman, S. 197
Lester, F. K., Jr. 84, 120
Lindsay, P. H. 192, 193
Lochhead, J. 196–98, 203
Lovell, K. 51, 61, 63, 166
Lysaught, J. P. 28, 35, 37, 39

MacNamara, E. A. 194
Magajna, Z. 126, 130
Mager, R. F. 30, 31, 34, 47
Masingila, J. O. 125
Mason, J. 91, 118
Mathematical Association 61, 181, 182
Matthews, G. 186
Mendelson, M. J. 115
Midlands Mathematical Experiment 76
Miller, G. A. 87, 145
Ministry of Education 181
Mitchelmore, M. C. 149
Mobley, M. 163
Monaghan, J. 118
Morgan, C. 91
Morris, R. W. 168–70
Moser, J. M. 172, 173, 194

Newell, A. 84, 96, 192, 199
Nicholson, A. R. 159
Norman, D. A. 192, 193
Noss, R. 98, 133

Novak, J. D. 21, 179, 186–93
Nuffield Mathematics Project 22, 23, 57, 62, 67, 76
Nunes, T. 26, 122, 123, 133, 135, 195

Orton, A. 21, 48, 108, 118, 159, 164, 209
Orton, J. 108–11, 114, 116–18
Otterburn, M. K. 159

Papert, S. 97, 98
Pegg, J. 111
Peterson, R. W. 9
Piaget, J. 10, 11, 44, 49–70, 73, 80, 97, 115, 128, 142, 165–7, 171, 176–82, 186, 191, 192, 196, 198, 205, 210, 211
Picciotto, H. 208
Pimm, D. 118
Poincaré, H. 88, 144
Polya, G. 13, 25, 26, 86–92, 98, 113
Popper, K. R. 134
Posner, J. 69, 169
Presmeg, N. 109

Redden, E. 111
Reed, S. K. 117
Rees, R. 147, 174
Renwick, E. M. 7, 8, 10, 12
Resnick, L. B. 26, 80, 195, 196
Rich, K. M. 124
Richards, J. 204
Rising, G. R. 84
Roper, T. 118
Rosnick, P. 210
Rosskopf, M. F. 70
Rothery, A. 160–64, 174
Russell, S. 142, 151, 154

Sawyer, W. W. 99, 114
Saxe, G. B. 69, 128, 129, 133, 135, 169
Scandura, J. M. 187
Scheerer, M. 77, 95, 155
Schliemann, A. 133, 135, 195
Schools Council 23, 60, 67, 73
Scribner, S. 125
Seaborne, P. L. 177
Sewell, B. 121
Shaughnessy, M. J. 182
Shaw, J. 99
Shephard, G. 114
Shire, B. 174
Shuard, H. 99, 151, 160–64, 168, 174, 201, 202
Shulman, L. S. 4, 68, 72, 73, 175
Simon, H. A. 84, 96, 192, 199
Skemp, R. R. 8, 13, 18, 21–3, 26, 45, 46, 57, 157, 164, 179, 187
Skinner, B. F. 27, 28, 36, 37, 47

Skovsmose, O. 131
Smith, E. C. 167
Smith, I. M. 148, 149
Solomon, Y. 69, 198, 199
Springer, S. P. 150, 155
Stacey, K. 108
Steffé, L. P. 70
Stern, C. and M. B. 2, 79–81, 98
Sternberg, R. J. 192
Stewart, J. 176, 192
Sutherland, R. 98
Sutton, C. 167
Suydam, M. N. 143, 150

Taback, S. 70
Tait, K. 39
Tall, D. O. 103
Tartre, L. A. 153
Thorndike, E. L. 28
Threlfall, J. 81, 83, 102–5, 118
Torbe, M. 168,174

Underhill, R. G. 201, 209
UNESCO 174
Ursini, S. 110

Vergnaud, G. 173, 193
Vernon, P. E. 145
Verschaffel, L. 172, 173
Vithal, R. 131
von Glasersfeld, E. 196–99, 204, 211
Vygotsky, L. S. 128, 166, 167, 198

Wah, A. 208
Walkup, L. E. 148
Wall, W. D. 167
Walter, M. I. 90, 91, 98
Waring, S. 112
Warren, E. 110
Weaver, J. F. 143, 150
Wells, J. M. 187
Wertheimer, M. 77–9, 180
Wheeler, D. 109, 110
Whitson, J. A. 128
Wickelgren, W. A. 13, 26, 86, 91–3
Wiliam, D. 11, 15, 24, 25, 194
Williams, C. M. 28, 35, 37, 39, 99
Williams, J. S. 58, 204
Wilson, B. 171
Winston, R. 4, 11, 14, 54, 88, 150, 153, 206, 211
Witkin, H. A. 148
Wood, D. 103, 211
Wood, R. 152, 153
Wrigley, J. 145

Young, R. G. 35

Zachos, I. 182, 183
Zaslavsky, C. 130

# Subject index

ability 5, 35, 53, 55, 66, 86, 91, 114–17, 121, 131, 139–55, 175, 194, 198, 206

abstract 6, 21, 22, 53–5, 62, 73, 83, 84, 134, 176–9, 183, 187, 188, 205

accelerating learning 5, 56–9, 179, 180

accommodation 56, 57, 76, 184–6, 189–92, 206, 209–11

activity 3, 6, 23, 37, 39, 52, 55, 58, 61, 62, 68, 70–6, 80–6, 97, 98, 102, 119–22, 127, 133, 161–3, 177, 178, 200, 204–6

addition 8, 18, 19, 27, 29, 44, 45, 48, 101, 105, 119, 163, 170–3, 187, 188, 192–5, 204

affective 11, 12, 73, 141

algebra 5, 6, 9–12, 53, 80, 99, 102, 103, 106–14, 118, 124, 126, 139, 177, 179, 186, 190–2, 208–10

algorithm 13, 18–20, 26, 29, 83, 124, 129, 172, 184, 195, 200, 202

anxiety 1, 11, 39, 40, 143, 151, 155, 156

apparatus 1–3, 6, 53, 72, 73, 79–84, 98, 164, 176–8, 181, 204, 205

assimilation 56, 57, 76, 164, 184–6, 190, 192, 210

attitude 12, 77, 106, 132, 133, 139, 151–5, 202

behaviourist 2, 3, 27–48, 56, 60, 70, 73, 175, 176, 192, 193, 205, 206, 211

brain 4, 14, 55, 144, 176, 206

calculator 1, 8, 9, 34, 74, 201, 202

calculus 1, 9, 28, 46, 60, 99, 159, 188

capability 25, 42, 55, 73, 119, 200

cognitive 2, 3, 6, 11, 13, 29, 37, 60, 70, 73, 77, 101, 134, 139, 149, 176, 180, 189, 193, 201, 209–11

cognitive conflict 56–8, 117, 189, 201, 205

computer 34, 37–40, 47, 97, 98, 125, 126, 192, 193

concept 3, 6–9, 12, 13, 15, 20–4, 26, 44–6, 49, 61–3, 67–9, 83, 84, 98, 103, 125–7, 159, 164, 172, 176–9, 185, 187, 190, 193, 199, 203, 208

concept map 16, 17, 187–9, 191, 207, 208

conservation 43, 44, 49–52, 61, 64–9, 165

construction 17, 18, 46, 56–8, 69, 80, 97, 127, 129, 134, 153, 176–80, 192, 194–212

convergent thinking 139–42, 146, 167

creativity 25, 75, 76, 84, 85, 90, 102, 130, 141, 148, 195, 204

culture 66–70, 112, 113, 129–32, 135, 152, 155, 168–71, 199, 201

curriculum 7, 10, 60–3, 67, 75, 76, 85, 89, 97–103, 106, 109–14, 119, 120, 124–127, 130–2, 141, 149, 170, 181, 188, 189, 199, 202–5, 208

daily life mathematics 5, 26, 69, 119–23, 126, 127, 133

definition 21, 22, 27, 46, 112, 159, 183

development 49, 54, 66–70, 77, 116, 178

discovery 25, 26, 34, 37, 71–80, 84, 92, 97, 98, 176, 185, 195–7, 205

discrimination 15, 44, 45, 163

discussion 1, 33, 57–60, 67, 83, 91, 112, 117, 154, 157, 159, 162, 166–8, 184, 198–211

divergent thinking 139–42, 146, 147, 152, 167,

division 1, 8, 12, 18, 19, 128, 163, 172, 173, 184, 187, 192

environment 3, 5, 6, 11, 24, 37, 49, 56, 60, 62, 66, 68, 70, 73, 80, 83, 97, 98, 101, 130, 134, 145, 151, 166, 176, 195, 197, 199, 203, 204

equation 19, 34, 42, 46, 57, 58, 74, 140, 206

errors 33, 105, 116, 154, 168, 174, 192

ethnomathematics 129–32, 135, 170, 171

exposition 6, 29, 71, 72, 75, 79, 85, 86, 154, 166, 185, 191

facts 13, 21, 172, 179, 194

formula 13, 14, 26, 32, 33, 78, 91, 92, 108, 111–14, 124, 180

fractions 1, 8, 9, 18–22, 29, 33, 40–2, 46, 48, 56, 70, 74, 81, 119, 124, 125, 153, 162, 184, 187

gender 66, 91, 98, 131, 136, 150–3, 171

generalization 23, 44, 53, 59, 86, 91, 92, 98, 100, 102, 106–13, 135, 138, 143, 180, 182

geometry 4, 9, 22, 90, 97, 99, 100, 112–20, 126, 147–9, 153, 179, 181–3, 186, 193
Gestalt 2, 77–9, 96, 117, 150, 182

individual differences 4, 5, 74, 136–55, 179, 180
information processing 4, 86, 96, 192, 193
insight 25, 73, 77, 79, 84, 95, 99, 108, 111, 190, 196
instrumental understanding 18–20, 26, 124, 147
integer 22, 56, 90, 173, 184
interaction 3, 39, 49, 68, 80, 98, 152–4, 161, 162, 168, 177, 194, 199
investigation 25, 27, 34, 46, 53, 60, 71–4, 85–91, 98, 99, 141, 176, 182, 201, 203, 209

knowledge network 14–16, 25, 206, 211

language 5, 6, 11, 63–5, 69, 72, 129, 130, 150, 156–74, 193, 196, 198

mastery 7, 8, 44, 45, 119, 120, 126, 130, 134, 145
maturation 49, 55, 66, 68, 70, 182, 183
meaningful learning 14, 184–91, 206
mechanics 57, 58, 158, 204
memory 13–15, 18, 24, 26, 65, 96, 97, 104, 106, 120, 145, 192, 193
misconception 3, 98, 116, 117, 201, 210, 211
motivation 11, 26, 30, 31, 36, 40, 47, 55, 57, 60, 63, 75, 96, 102, 113, 120, 123, 130–3, 136, 139, 145, 155, 184, 186, 196, 200, 201
multiplication 1, 8, 13, 15, 18, 27, 29, 40–6, 48, 100, 105, 106, 124, 125, 128, 163, 170–3, 186–8, 192, 195, 200, 206

natural numbers 22, 46, 56, 71, 72, 81, 82, 86–9, 92, 99–101, 104–9, 158, 184
notation 3, 59, 86, 164, 194
number sets 9, 22, 23, 27, 40–2, 45, 48, 56–9, 62, 70–2, 78, 80, 89, 92, 100, 104–9, 111, 114, 128, 169, 184, 194

objectives 3, 6, 13, 30–4, 40–2, 47, 81, 111, 167
obstacles 5, 12, 92–8, 157, 209–12
operation 48, 52, 66, 68, 100, 103, 168, 171–3, 187, 188, 210

pattern 15, 27, 59, 71, 89–92, 99–118, 159
place value 2, 3, 5, 7, 8, 10, 12, 46, 54, 56, 80, 81, 100, 164, 176–9, 209
practice 3, 13, 14, 24, 29, 72, 85, 86, 154, 176, 178, 202, 206, 209, 211
preferences 5, 41, 139, 141, 153–5
prerequisites 41–6, 70, 180, 186
problem-posing 39, 89–91, 98
problem-solving 9, 13, 24–6, 45, 47, 69, 72, 77, 84–99, 122, 123, 127, 128, 133, 143, 154, 171, 172, 192, 195, 199, 203
programmed learning 30, 31, 35–40, 73, 161
progression 9, 10, 16, 19, 23, 68, 83, 84, 91, 127, 181, 200, 202
proof 4, 92, 112–14, 118, 143, 168, 181–3, 209
proportion 9, 10, 46, 48, 51, 53, 57, 59, 60, 63, 125, 153

ratio 5, 8–10, 12, 15, 19, 46, 48, 51, 60, 63, 70, 100, 152, 184, 209
rational numbers 1, 8, 9, 18–22, 29, 33, 40–2, 46, 48, 56, 70, 74, 81, 119, 124, 125, 153, 162, 184, 187
readability 157, 160–3, 174
readiness 43–9, 51, 60–2, 70, 180, 186, 190, 211
real numbers 22, 48, 56, 188, 189
recall 13–18, 27, 97, 191
reinforcement 28, 30, 36, 37, 105
relational understanding 18–20, 23, 26, 147, 167
repetition 14, 15, 27, 40, 176, 190, 206
retention 14–18, 24, 163
revision 15, 17, 40, 161, 166, 190
rote learning 3, 14, 15, 18, 47, 75, 78, 96, 105, 152, 170, 184, 185, 190, 200, 206, 207

rule 25, 26, 44–6, 56, 75, 86, 90, 91, 102, 109, 110, 117, 121, 172

sequencing 24, 28, 30–3, 36–40, 47, 102, 163, 167, 176, 200, 211
situation 15, 29, 64, 85–7, 99, 119–122, 126–8, 132–5, 155, 165, 201, 202
skill 4, 11–14, 43, 48, 53, 61, 69, 72, 85, 86, 102, 119, 126, 127, 141, 172, 176, 205, 206
social 68–70, 129, 131–3, 152, 153, 198, 201, 205
spatial ability 61, 66, 143, 147–50, 152, 153
stages 44, 46, 51–70, 86, 89, 90, 97, 103, 116, 165, 171, 178, 181, 182, 186, 200, 209, 211
stimulus-response 27–30, 35–9, 44–7, 161, 175–7, 192, 211
structural apparatus 1–3, 79–83, 98, 176–81, 185, 204, 205
structure 3, 5, 15, 16, 20, 51, 66, 77–83, 97–102, 111, 113, 125, 135, 149, 150, 163, 164, 170, 172, 176–87, 190, 193, 204
subtraction 18, 119, 163, 172, 173, 184, 187, 188, 192, 194
symbol 6, 13–15, 21, 44, 45, 53, 56, 59, 72, 73, 80, 86, 100, 106, 113, 121, 125, 143, 147, 157–64, 169, 174, 178, 183, 193, 194, 209
symmetry 99–102, 114–17, 168, 188

thinking 25, 26, 47, 51, 53, 66, 102, 110, 131–4, 140, 141, 166, 168, 178, 181, 184, 198–202, 204, 211
transfer 4, 5, 26, 84, 98, 114, 119, 126, 129, 133–5, 180, 196
transmission 195, 196, 199, 203, 209
trialling 19, 20, 78, 88, 96, 97, 109, 190

vocabulary 157–60, 169, 170–4, 190

word problems 84, 133, 150, 171–4
work mathematics 123–6, 135

zero 48, 104, 169, 189, 194